D0928136

A
COMPASSIONATE
PEACE

A Report Prepared for the
American Friends Service Committee

REVISED EDITION

HILL AND WANG / NEW YORK

A
COMPASSIONATE
PEACE

A Future for Israel, Palestine, and the Middle East

Everett Mendelsohn

A division of Farrar, Straus & Giroux

Copyright © 1982, 1989 by American Friends Service Committee
All rights reserved
Printed in the United States of America
Published simultaneously in Canada by Collins Publishers, Toronto
Revised edition, 1989

Library of Congress Cataloging-in-Publication Data
Mendelsohn, Everett.
A compassionate peace: a future for Israel, Palestine, and the Middle East
Everett Mendelsohn.—Rev. ed.
p. cm.
"A Report prepared for the American Friends Service Committee."
Bibliography p.
1. Jewish-Arab relations—1973-   2. West Bank—International status.
3. Gaza Strip—International status.
4. Middle East—Politics and government—1945-
I. American Friends Service Committee.   II. Title.
DS119.7.M443   1989   956.04—dc20   89-2125

Maps by Joan Forbes, from *The Christian Science Monitor*,
Copyright © 1986, 1988 the Christian Science Publishing Society

Acknowledgments

The first edition of this report was prepared under the direction of a Working Party appointed by the Board of Directors of the American Friends Service Committee. The members included:

Arthur Day, former Consul General, United States Consulate in Jerusalem, former Deputy Assistant Secretary of State for Near Eastern and South Asian Affairs

Joseph Elder, Professor of Sociology and South Asian Studies, University of Wisconsin

Marcia Sfeir-Cormie, former AFSC Middle East Staff person in AFSC Chicago office

Gail Pressberg, former Director of Middle East Programs, AFSC, and currently Executive Director of the Foundation for Middle East Peace, Washington, D.C.

Ann Mosely Lesch, former AFSC Staff person in Jerusalem and Professor of International Relations, Villanova University

Everett Mendelsohn, Professor of the History of Science, Harvard University, Middle East Panel, AFSC, chaired the Working Party and served as principal author of the report.

The revised edition of this report benefited significantly from comments made on the draft by Arthur Day, Joseph Elder, Gail Pressberg, and Ann Mosely Lesch. In addition, Catherine Essoyan and Denis Doyon of the AFSC Middle East staff in Philadelphia read and commented on the report in its several drafts. The text for the revised edition was prepared by Everett Mendelsohn.

Contents

Maps

Preface

Two years ago the American Friends Service Committee began considering the usefulness of preparing a new edition of its 1982 study, *A Compassionate Peace*, which offered an analysis of the deeply troubled scene in the Middle East and suggested steps that might lead to a brighter future for the region. Widespread changes had occurred that we believed required an updated version of the earlier text.

Little did we anticipate the magnitude of the changes that took place during the course of the rewriting process. These events had substantially altered the political landscape of the Middle East by early 1989. The Palestinian uprising and Israeli efforts to suppress it, the declaration of an independent Palestinian state, the PLO statements of recognition of the State of Israel and rejection of terrorism, the ending of hostilities in the Iran–Iraq war, Jordan's withdrawal from West Bank affairs, the Soviet withdrawal from Afghanistan, and the warming of U.S.–Soviet relations all have served to reshape issues and relationships in the Middle East. The foreign policies of the United States and other nations with interests in the region have had to be recast in the face of these dramatic events.

This breathtaking pace of change within the Middle East has provided an occasion for exploration of alternative courses for the region's future. Israelis and Palestinians are challenging themselves with visions of mutual recognition and respect. Other parties, within and outside of the Middle East—including those that historically have been closed to the concept of a shared future of Israeli Jews and Palestinian Arabs—are now engaged in consideration and debate of alternatives that until recently have been limited to the margins of mainline policy considerations. The views and recommendations the American Friends Service Committee espoused in the 1969 *Search for Peace* and the 1982 edition of *A Compassionate Peace* served as lightning rods for widespread anger and dismay among critics. We believe that this updating and restatement of our long-standing perspectives may have new currency in 1989. We hope it will advance the new thinking which may support needed steps toward peace for Israelis and Palestinians and others in the Middle East region.

We recognize, however, that while the outline of solutions to the conflicts that have plagued the region for decades may now be more discernible, deep divisions remain. The human toll arising from the conflicting claims of Israelis and Palestinians continues to spiral upward.

We are grateful to Everett Mendelsohn for his role as primary researcher and as author of this new edition. He is Chairperson of the AFSC's Middle East Panel and Professor of the History of Science at Harvard University. During the course of his work on this new edition he visited widely throughout the Middle East on three occasions. As in the preparation of the earlier edition, he undertook fresh consultation and dialogue with journalists, government leaders, activists, scholars, and religious leaders throughout that region. He drew again on insights available to the AFSC through our continuing work based in the area.

This revised edition of *A Compassionate Peace* carries the same endorsement by the American Friends Service Committee Board of Directors as did its predecessor.

On behalf of the Board of Directors
American Friends Service Committee

Stephen G. Cary, Chairperson
February 1989

Preface to the 1982 Edition

> Force may subdue, but love gains.
> And he that forgives first wins the
> laurel . . . Let us then try what love
> can do.

These words, written by William Penn nearly three centuries ago, express the political philosophy that he brought with him to the new world to establish the Quaker colony of Pennsylvania.

Trying what love can do has been a Quaker mission ever since. John Woolman labored in the eighteenth century to persuade his fellow Friends to renounce slavery; in the 1820s Elizabeth Fry ministered to the wretched in Newgate Prison; in the 1850s English Friends cared for the wounded in the Crimea; and in the 1890s Joseph Sturge and Joseph Elkinton heeded Tolstoy's plea and brought 6,000 persecuted Russian Doukhobors to Canada for re-settlement. Wherever suffering and injustice have been acute, Friends have wanted to help.

In our own violent century, part of the Quaker experiment to try what love can do has been carried into the world by the American Friends Service Committee, beginning with the rebuilding of French villages, and the feeding of millions of German children in the wake of World War I, and continuing with humanitarian service among the homeless and the suffering in the years since, working as far as we've been permitted, on every side. Indeed, it is a commentary—and an indictment—of our age that there have been only two years since the committee was founded in 1917 that we have not been called upon to minister to the needs of refugees driven from their homes by the ebb and flow of human warfare. More recently, the committee has gone beyond only providing immediate aid in the wake of war to try to deal with the roots of violence, which lie in injustice and the denial of human rights and the terrible poverty that afflict so many millions at home and around the world. To change these conditions is to build the foundations of peace, which must be the concern of all men and women of goodwill.

In these difficult enterprises, we have often known disappointment. Our workers have provided food, comforted the homeless, marched for justice, and stood beside the outcast, but they have failed to reach to the hatreds and the despair that corrode the soul and alienate the human family across neighborhoods and across nations.

But we have also seen miracles, where humanity and caring were reborn and compassion returned, where hatred has given way to forgiveness and where community has been rebuilt. These miracles happened because special individuals dared to live as if change was possible, and it became possible. They were competent people; able to understand difficult problems, able to find places to take hold, and able to discover what tasks needed to be done. But competency wasn't enough; it had to be undergirded with the certain faith that human beings can rise above their baser natures and respond to stimuli other than fear and threat and naked power.

These pioneers, the known and the unknown, have shown us how to challenge the harsh evils and animosities that divide mankind. The problem does not lie in the inadequacy of the messages in the great world religions, but in the timidity and the lack of imagination of men and women in applying them. We need to be as wise as serpents and as gentle as doves, as the Scriptures advise us, but neither will avail without the courage to dare.

It is in this context that the American Friends Service Committee has undertaken this fresh exploration of the tangled web that is the Middle East, twelve years after our first such study, *Search for Peace in the Middle East*, appeared. As in that earlier effort, we have drawn on our own long experience in the area, buttressed by the judgments of scholars and diplomats and tested against the viewpoints of moderates on all sides of the conflict, to suggest approaches to peace that flow from our Quaker religious faith.

We know the dangers of entering this arena. Emotions run deep on the Middle East. The passion of centuries inflames every issue to make rational analysis difficult and to obscure the road to settlement. These problems are intractable enough in isolation, but they are more and more being compounded by the politics of oil and the rivalry of great powers, which make even more volatile an already explosive scene.

Under these melancholy circumstances, whoever offers suggestions for a way out will likely be seen by all sides as partial to its enemies, and by those obsessed with the instrument of power as naïve. We assume that risk, acknowledging that our recommendations don't represent final answers, since human wisdom is finite and human judgment fallible. What we do claim, and affirm to the world, is that the approach here undertaken represents the best hope for an end to violence in the Middle East. There will never be peace for either Israeli or Arab without the effort to understand the measure of legitimacy in the enemy's views and a willingness to seek accommodation with him. The alternative of continued belligerence and intransigence and the mindless accumulation of ever more terrible weapons on every side may be the way of today's realist, but it is also the way of madness. We see nothing but disaster lying down that road.

Therefore, we call on our own nation and all men and women everywhere to turn away from the politics of violence and dare to explore the politics of reconciliation. This study attempts to do this by approaching the problems of the Middle East in the spirit of reason and compassion.

The Board of Directors of the American Friends Service Committee, mindful that they do not speak for all Friends, endorses this report. It approves the publication of this study as a contribution to the dialogue now underway about the Middle East.

On behalf of the Board of Directors
American Friends Service Committee

Stephen G. Cary, Chairperson
December 1981

A
COMPASSIONATE
PEACE

1

Introduction

THE POLITICS AND STRUCTURE OF MIDDLE EAST PEACE

In 1988 almost every element in the Middle East conflict underwent marked change, leaving a situation in which new pressures and new dynamics replaced the old. Although the underlying confrontation between Israel, the Palestinians, and the Arab states has not been resolved, the dimensions of a resolution have become strikingly clearer and the necessary political choices have become explicit. The missing element remains the political will to undertake the historic compromise necessary to resolve the four-decades-long conflict. The irony today is that as the Palestinians, and with them most Arab states, have reached the point at which they are ready to enter meaningful negotiations with Israel to achieve a just and durable peace, Israeli politics have moved the nation further away from territorial compromise toward a harder line rejecting Palestinian legitimacy.

Four events, separate but linked, force a reevaluation of the situation. First, the uprising, or *intifadah* as the Palestinians call it, that broke out on December 9, 1987, demonstrated the extent to which the Israeli occupation of the West Bank and Gaza was untenable as a continuing option. The depth of rejection of the occupation was shown by the broad participation in continuing acts

3

of civil disobedience and highly visible protest. The uprising returned the confrontation between Israelis and Palestinians to the soil of Palestine, putting the population under occupation at the center of the conflict. The Palestinianization of the conflict, which has increased in recent years, became dramatically clear as the Palestinians, largely led by a new generation, took their future into their own hands; neither the Jordanians nor the Arab League nor the Soviets nor the Americans would lead; the struggle for self-determination would be carried on by the Palestinians themselves. The mode of opposition was civil resistance, largely devoid of lethal violence (few guns or bombs, some Molotov cocktails), not the work of guerrilla bands or terrorists but a civilian population in rebellion. What was also striking was the pragmatic and clear goal of the uprising, an independent Palestinian state in the West Bank and Gaza living side by side and in peace with Israel. On November 15, 1988, the day the Palestine National Council declared independence for the occupied territories, the Israelis, in order to forestall any demonstrations, put the Palestinian population under curfew and sealed off the whole of the West Bank and Gaza; the Green Line, which had separated Israel from the territories prior to June 1967, was reconstructed; unintentionally, Israel "recognized" the Palestinian state it continued to occupy. The *intifadah* was forcing Israel's hand; to suppress it Israel would have to take violent action, almost certainly not acceptable to the international community. The prospect for Israel was a sustained, costly, and repressive confrontation; the status quo would not be easily maintained.

When on July 31, 1988, Jordan severed legal and administrative ties with the West Bank, the second precipitating event had occurred. In actuality King Hussein was only giving recognition to a trend that had been some years in the making. The Palestinians did not want Jordan to be their representative, nor did they seek the return of the territories to the Hashemite Kingdom. King Hussein acknowledged publicly that he would not, indeed could not, speak for the Palestinians. He turned that task over to the Palestine Liberation Organization. The "Jordanian option," whereby Israel would negotiate an agreement on the Palestine question with Jordan, conceivable in the decade after 1967 but politically infeasible for Hussein since then, was now explicitly foreclosed. Israel, fearful of undermining its own legitimacy if it were to negotiate directly with the Palestinian national movement, was now faced with no other alternative if it wished a negotiated settlement of the conflict.

The third critical event occurred at the mid-November 1988 meeting, in Algiers, of the Palestine National Council (the "Parliament-in-Exile"). Taking its cues from the *intifadah* and King Hussein's withdrawal, the PNC culminated a decade-long internal political debate when it declared Palestine an independent state, which the accompanying resolutions indicated would be established in the territories of the West Bank and Gaza. With the resolutions explicitly renouncing terrorism, accepting the legitimacy of the 1947 UN partition of Palestine, and adopting UN Security Council Resolution 242 as the basis for international negotiations, the Palestinian nationalist movement took a major step forward in seeking a diplomatic and political resolution of the Palestine question. For long-term observers of Palestinian politics, the manner of the adoption of the PNC resolutions was almost as important as their texts; an open vote was taken (a large majority, 253–46, favored the new political steps) and the minority who had urged a "harder" line indicated they would accept the majority decision and stay with the organization. The previous rules that required consensus had often bound the PNC to the less flexible politics of the left. The steps taken at the PNC meeting presaged an intense diplomatic and political effort on the international scene. Within weeks of the declaration of independence, over seventy countries (largely non-aligned, Arab, and socialist) had granted recognition to the new state and many others had given positive appraisals. In giving up maximalist claims and adopting the politics of compromise, the PLO had taken a major step to meet the conditions set for its legitimacy by Israel and the United States. The question left unanswered (and in doubt) by initial responses was whether Israel and its superpower patron, the United States, would take "yes" for an answer. The Palestinian state, proclaimed politically, remained occupied by the Israelis militarily.

There followed several dizzying weeks of diplomatic maneuvering which included Washington's rejection of a visa for Yasir Arafat's proposed visit to the UN General Assembly, overwhelming votes in the UN condemning the American action and moving the whole General Assembly Palestine debate to Geneva, a Swedish-arranged meeting between Arafat and several prominent American Jews at which Arafat tried further to clarify the PNC declarations, Arafat's UN speech on December 13, 1988, widely judged his most conciliatory to date, and a subsequent press conference at which Arafat read a three-point statement aimed at meeting Washington's "requirements" for a U.S.–PLO dialogue. Finally, Secretary of State George Shultz reversed fifteen years of American rejection of direct talks with the PLO and announced an immediate beginning of joint U.S.–PLO discussions. This last decision added another crucial dimension to Middle East peace efforts. Explicit Palestinian moderation was matched by Washington's recognition of the PLO as a legitimate participant in the next stages of peacemaking.

These four events, as important as they were, could not by themselves reshape the politics of the Arab–Israeli conflict. Several other factors, involving the Soviet Union, Iraq, Egypt, Europe, Israel, and Syria, created an important change in the political climate of the region. Probably the most important of these was the marked shift in Soviet policy toward regional conflicts, entailing explicit new moves in the Middle East. At the core was the Soviet decision to forgo a zero-sum-game attitude toward local confrontations and no longer to assume that any loss for American interests was necessarily a gain for the Soviets. In addition, the Soviet Union has worked hard to avoid direct confrontations with the United States and instead has sought diplomatic and political resolutions to regional conflicts; specifically, withdrawal from Afghanistan and support of the UN-mediated end to the Iran–Iraq war were indications of new policies. The Soviets have indicated their intention to be part of any Israeli–Arab settlement and to have a strong and legitimate role in the Middle East. They have undertaken a series of initiatives to better relations with Israel, including an exchange of consular missions, a series of high-level diplomatic meetings with Israelis and international leaders of the Jewish community, and direct action both to ease the life of Jews in the Soviet Union and to simplify the process of Jewish emigration (moves strongly urged by Israel). In addition, the Soviets have worked closely with the PLO—some have interpreted it as putting on pressure—to heal the rifts in the Palestinian nationalist movement and to offer viable political and diplomatic moves for a settlement with Israel. They have publicly derided the rhetoric of confrontation, and when Syrian President Hafez al-Assad visited Moscow in 1987, Soviet leader Mikhail Gorbachev noted in his welcoming speech that it was "unnatural" for the Soviet Union not to have active diplomatic relations with Israel. Two key members of the socialist bloc, Poland and Hungary, have reopened middle-level formal relations with Israel, and other Soviet allies will probably soon follow suit. The Soviets have long supported the calling of an international peace conference to resolve the Arab–Israeli conflict, but their terms for such a conference were unacceptable to the United States; there is every indication that they have been moderating their ideas to a point where they might be acceptable to the United States. In this they stand in some contrast to their Syrian allies. However, the Soviets are believed to have put some pressure on Syria.

Another important change in the Middle East was the July 1988 cease-fire between Iran and Iraq, achieved through tireless UN mediation. While Iran and Iraq are only slowly inching toward a real peace (some observers even expect some episodes of renewed local battles), the war seems to have given the Middle East a firm lesson that the battlefield is not the way to achieve political ends; the costs to both societies were staggering. But the end of the fighting sharply decreased the fear that had gripped the oil-rich Arab Gulf states and removed the Gulf war from center stage in the region. Indeed Iran and the Gulf states have taken the initial steps to reestablish equilibrium in their relations. A second consequence of the cease-fire was to reduce the sense of threat posed to the region by a politically militant Islam.

During the course of its war with Iran, Iraq came to rely very heavily on the support of the "moderate" Arab states, including Egypt. A new relationship has emerged bringing Iraq into the circle of regional nations ready to engage in some form of negotiated settlement with Israel. This marks a significant shift from the late 1970s, when Iraq was among the leaders of the so-called rejectionist front. Iraq has become a supporter of Palestinian diplomatic and political initiatives and welcomed the steps taken at the November 1988 PNC meeting in Algiers.

Egypt, after a decade of isolation which followed its signing of a separate peace with Israel, has once again become involved in the Middle East peace maneuvers. The decision taken at the Arab summit in Amman in November 1987 allowing each country to reestablish its own relations with Egypt gave new legitimacy to the Cairo government. Together with Jordan, Iraq, Saudi Arabia, and the PLO, it has created an informal bloc of major Middle East powers seemingly committed to resolving the Israeli–Palestinian conflict through diplomatic efforts. This emerging alignment has the effect of further blunting any Syrian efforts to block the PLO's attempts at political initiatives in peacemaking. With the Iran–Iraq war reduced to political sparring and the *intifadah* giving clear voice to Palestinian demands for resolution, this new Middle East grouping is in a position both to focus attention on the need to end the Israeli–Palestinian conflict and to support the politics of realistic and just compromise. One hope, of course, was that Egypt, which enjoys close relations with the United States and has diplomatic relations with Israel, might serve as an "interpreter" and "honest broker" between the Arab group and these two parties. The realities of the politics of both Israel and the United States do not make this an easy task, and there is fear that the current period of fairly broad consensus on peacemaking among the Arabs will be dissipated and that an important opportunity for a negotiated settlement will be missed.

Ariel Sharon's vision for Israel's invasion of Lebanon in June 1982 was that a Christian-led Lebanon would emerge from the war which would sign a peace treaty with Israel and replace the haven for the PLO with a government friendly to Israel and united with the West against perceived Arab radicals. The physical, political, and social shambles that Israel left when forced to withdraw from Lebanon in 1985 is sad testimony to the failure of Israel's war aims. Instead, Lebanon today offers a grim lesson to Israel and the international community of the costs of unresolved conflict and an indication of what might happen to Israel if it fails to reach a peace with the Palestinians. The possibility of unending civil confrontation is a sobering one for many Israeli analysts.

When Margaret Thatcher came to pay a farewell call on Ronald Reagan in mid-November 1988, she gave a clear reminder that Europe's views on Middle East peacemaking are at odds with those of the United States. Even this most faithful friend of the United States publicly announced that Britain reacted quite favorably to the steps taken by the Palestine National Council even while she encouraged further change. The American response, on the contrary, ranged from tepid to critical, including the denial of a visa for PLO chairman Yasir Arafat, who had been invited to address the UN General Assembly in early December; Britain was joined by most other NATO members in sharply criticizing the U.S. refusal. In the spring of 1988, the European Economic Community, when turning down Israel's request for better trading terms, remarked on Israel's harsh repression of the *intifadah* and the socialist members of the European Parliament invited Yasir Arafat to address them in September. (The EEC reinstated Israel's request later in the fall but included special agreements to protect Palestinian rights to direct exports to Europe.) All this was seen as reviving an independent European position on Middle East peacemaking that was first enunciated in the Venice statement of June 1980. With the United States seemingly locked into tight relations with Israel, the potential for a useful European role has become even more important. A number of observers have suggested that the traditional roles of leader and follower on Middle East issues may be in the course of being reversed and a more economically confident and politically independent European community, working together with the Soviets and the socialist bloc in Europe, may be able to take important initiatives in the Middle East which will pave the way for the United States to follow.

THE SITUATION IN ISRAEL

But if there were important positive signs in many quarters, that was not the case in Israel. As the new year of 1989 began and a new government took the reins, Israeli leaders searched for some initiatives that would lessen Israeli isolation and soften the judgment that Israeli policy had slipped further into a rejectionist mode. Not that there were no supporters of the proposal to exchange land for peace, but they had lost their political power; the government had moved to the right in the 1988 elections. Although many observers saw the election as having been fought over the peace issue, post-election analysts largely agreed that Israel had decided not to decide—no strong mandate was given—and therefore the status quo of occupation, uprising, and repression remained. In fact, it turned out that the most pressing issue to emerge when the votes were counted was how influential would the ultra-Orthodox be in shaping Israel's social, religious, and political life. While still only a minority (15 percent of the Knesset), the religious parties were the big winners in the election (a 50 percent increase) and were potentially kingmakers in forming a new coalition government. Israelis and Jews in the diaspora found themselves thoroughly involved with demands from the religious parties to enforce stricter observance of religious laws within Israel and to amend the Law of Return and rely on Orthodoxy to answer the question "Who is a Jew?" These concerns pushed aside the pressing question of the election debate: "What kind of Israel?"

In forming another "national unity" government as a means of avoiding the demands of the religious parties, Israel chose an additional period of paralysis on the core political issues. With the new team of Yitzhak Shamir as Prime Minister, Moshe Arens as Foreign Minister, and Yitzhak Rabin as Defense Minister (Shimon Peres moved to the domestically important post of Finance Minister), policy on the Palestinian issue was firmly in the hands of hard-liners. The coalition partners agreed not to negotiate with the PLO, to reject an independent Palestinian state, and to build eight new settlements in the occupied territories.

Israel's options, shaped by the conquest of the West Bank and Gaza in the 1967 war, are not many. They are framed by the tension between democracy and demography on one hand and religious nationalism and territorial compromise on the other. The population figures are straightforward. Not long after the turn of the millennium (in about 2010) the numbers of Jews and Palestinians living within the post-1967 boundaries, including the West Bank and Gaza (as well as the Golan Heights with its much smaller Arab population), will be equal. If democracy is to exist within these expanded borders, Palestinians must be full citizens and the numerous laws and privileges favoring Israeli Jews will be subject to marked change—a democratic Jewish state cannot exist with a non-Jewish majority (or even large minority). If an exclusively Jewish state is to be maintained, many of the fundamental terms of democracy will have to be abandoned. It was largely this dilemma which was behind the Labor Party's program of exchanging land (and Palestinian population) for peace. But on the other side were the Israeli maximalists, who claimed that Israel had conquered the territories and should hold them, either because of the security argument (their strategic depth was necessary) or on the grounds of the religious-nationalist claim (God gave Eretz Yisrael to the Jews). Thus Israel has several options:

1. Annex the territories either de facto or de jure, suppress the uprising, and convince the Palestinians to accept some form of limited autonomy—self-rule and a second-class citizenship in Greater Israel, the position taken by Prime Minister Yitzhak Shamir.
2. Annex the territories and expel the Palestinians, by force if necessary, in large numbers, thus giving Israel a completely free hand in the territories. This is the position of the far-right faction (Moledet) in the Knesset and it is given tacit support by others on the right (and is surprisingly acceptable to a large segment of the population).
3. The "Jordanian option," the traditional Labor Party choice. Negotiate the Palestine question with Jordan, ceding some territory and sharing in a Jordan–Israel condominium of the West Bank and Gaza. Any Palestinian component would be represented in a joint Jordanian–Palestinian negotiating team. Israel would avoid the necessity of direct negotiations with the Palestinians and foreclose the opportunity for an independent Palestinian state. This option lost most of whatever potential it had when King Hussein relinquished Jordan's claim to the territories and severed administrative and legal ties on July 31, 1988.
4. The two-state solution, reactivating the principles of the 1947 UN partition plan, with an independent Palestinian state being created within pre-June 1967 boundaries of the West Bank and Gaza, alongside Israel, which would return to its pre-1967 borders. The option of confederation with Jordan is often raised in this context. This is the solution of choice of the dovish Israeli political parties and nonparliamentary groups as well as the group of retired Israeli generals and colonels in the Council for Peace and Security; it is the consensus position of the Palestinians in the West Bank and Gaza and of the PLO.

The status quo that Israel has slipped into is, of course, a form of de facto annexation with all its negative consequences. In the face of the Palestinian uprising, it has involved Israel in a campaign of massive repression, utilizing what Defense Minister Rabin referred to as a policy of "force, might, and beatings," a variety of forms of collective punishment, large-scale arrests, imprisonment without trial, and other assaults on basic human rights. Israel can contemplate postponing its critical decisions only because it has been able to count on the United States to help pay the bills of the costly occupation and shield it politically and economically from an increasingly critical international community. But time is not on Israel's side. The erosion of confidence internationally, the increase in the pressure of Palestinian nationalism (internally and externally), the inexorable progress of demographic change, and the escalating and cumulative costs of the occupation are beginning to be felt and will become greater in time.

If reasonableness prevailed, the United States would be firmly involved in efforts to achieve a just and durable peace. But U.S. policy has been confused and, when not confused, hostile to a solution that is just for both the Israelis and the Palestinians. During the eight years of the Reagan presidency American Middle East policy became fixated on the need to build an anti-Soviet "strategic consensus" in the region and focused on Israel as the only reliable ally in this effort. Regional problems were pushed aside, and the pretense of American evenhandedness in the Israeli–Palestinian conflict was generally abandoned. While several U.S. peace efforts were undertaken, they were marked by one-sidedness and an effort to delegitimize any Palestinian claims for independence. Israel, supported by the United States, rejected the concept of a Palestinian state alongside Israel and instead focused on achieving a Jordanian solution. The United States rejected direct contact with the leadership of the Palestinian nationalist movement—the PLO—and sought negotiations with Jordan and, if necessary, some Palestinians linked to a Jordanian delegation and acceptable to both Israel and the United States. The *intifadah* caught the United States by surprise, as did Jordan's withdrawal from West Bank ties. The initiative by Secretary of State Shultz, taken late in the Reagan administration, seemed designed more to show that the United States was "doing something" than to try to find a real solution. No new concepts were advanced, and the firm "no" from Israeli Prime Minister Shamir ended that round of American efforts. Unlike the relatively positive response the United States' European allies gave to the new PLO initiatives taken at the November 1988 meeting of the Palestine National Council, the U.S. response was tepid if not negative. No U.S. moves were made to support or encourage the Palestinian program of reaching accommodation with Israel. In fact, when Yasir Arafat tried to come to New York to address the UN General Assembly and explain the new Palestinian moves, he was rebuffed by Secretary of State Shultz. Interpreted by many as arising out of personal pique, Shultz's move was deplored by America's friends in Europe and the Middle East and applauded only by Israel. U.S. policy at the end of the 1980s came largely to mirror that of Israel's right wing, seemingly rejecting Palestinian moves toward compromise and leaving itself tacitly supporting the Israeli maximalist policies—continued occupation and rejection of Palestinian independence. The last-minute acceptance of Arafat's public statements as meeting American requirements and opening direct dialogue with the PLO added an important new element to the Middle East equation and partially reversed Washington's largely one-sided approach; it left the new Bush administration room for political and diplomatic maneuvering.

One relatively unknown element in the Arab–Israeli equation is the role that Syria will play. There is no doubt that Syria must be seriously involved in peacemaking efforts, although to date Syria has shown reluctance to become directly included. In the past Syria could rely on Soviet backing of its efforts to slow down or derail U.S.-sponsored peace initiatives. This is probably no longer the case. Syria has also resisted diplomatic initiatives undertaken by the Arafat-led PLO; and while it supported the Palestinians' declaration of independence, it rejected their recognition of Israel and their renunciation of violence and acceptance of UN Security Council Resolution 242 that came out of the November 1988 PNC meeting. Because of its support of Iran in the war with Iraq, Syria is largely isolated in the Arab world. The Syrians have traditionally held the position that they can enter negotiations with Israel only when they have achieved military parity, for which they have depended on Soviet help. But it is clear that Syria has legitimate interests in any agreement with Israel. The Golan Heights remain occupied (annexed) by Israel and there is a constant and palpable military tension between the two countries. While Syria has not put forward any real peace initiatives or proposals and has dragged its feet on those offered by others, it is absolutely essential that, earlier rather than later, it becomes a party to peacemaking efforts. Skillful international diplomacy, probably involving American–Soviet cooperation, is certainly required.

PRINCIPLES OF A SETTLEMENT

A look at the current state of the Israeli–Palestinian conflict clarifies the dimensions of a settlement, even if the politics of agreement are very difficult. Reality, however, can be a powerful force. Three basic principles guide our judgment:

- Self-determination for both the Israelis and the Palestinians. Self-determination was a leading principle in creating independent countries after World War II and in the breakup of the colonial empires. In many instances it was achieved through compromise of competing claims.
- Mutual recognition, a means of creating parity between two conflicting national groups, enabling each to emerge with dignity and respect.
- Mutual security, ensuring that both parties construct the appropriate forms of security so that neither feels threatened by the other. It involves not only military arrangements but border agreements and attention to other threats, physical, economic, and political.

In the current context of the Israeli–Palestinian conflict we believe these principles are best met through two states—Israeli and Palestinian—side by side. This was the solution embodied in the UN partition resolution (181) of 1947. Initially accepted by Israel (their act of self-determination), but rejected at the time by the leaders of the Arab world, it has now been accepted by the Palestine National Council as the basis for its declaration of independence (a move toward fulfillment of Palestinian self-determination). Israel has a forty-year history, and its internationally recognized boundaries are those of pre-June 1967. In recognizing Israel and accepting UN Security Council Resolution 242, the PLO indicated that the new state of Palestine would be established in the West

Bank and Gaza Strip, currently occupied by Israel. Any minor modifications of the borders for economic, social, or security reasons would be arrived at through mutual agreement. The framework for negotiating the establishment of Palestine would be UN Security Council Resolution 242, which envisaged Israeli withdrawal and peaceful and secure relations among all states in the region. How an undivided Jerusalem might be shared as the capital of two sovereign states will require imaginative planning and negotiation.

It seems self-evident that a stable, strong, and peaceful Palestinian government would make both Israelis and Palestinians feel more secure. A weak government or one impeded by excessive claims arising from the asymmetrical situation of negotiations will be prey to fears and threats and more vulnerable to extremist claims.

A link between Palestine and Jordan through confederation or other arrangements negotiated by two sovereign powers seems both natural and beneficial. Family, social, religious, economic ties bind these two states and make confederation a viable arrangement. While it is too early to talk seriously about the economic and social links that will grow between Palestine and Israel, some of the same factors that suggest the link with Jordan are also operative.

Carefully planned and executed security arrangements for both Israel and Palestine can provide the added confidence that will be needed to make the two-state proposal viable. The explicit military elements of security will have to be supplemented by agreements on other critical issues, some physical (such as water and boundaries), others social (such as movement of people across borders) and political (such as control over potential extremist or rejectionist elements in either society). A role for the United Nations or other multinational agencies in initiating and maintaining security is important.

The problem of refugees is an old one for the Israelis. The history of ingathering from the diaspora, especially of those living in difficult situations, should evoke deep understanding among both Israelis and Palestinians. There is a potential for actual physical movement to Palestine for many, but also a renewed sense of identity and hope for those who remain living in the diaspora.

It has been apparent from an early period in Arab–Israeli relations that piecemeal or partial solutions may have an immediate limited advantage but in the long run they may hinder fuller resolution. An international peace conference of all the involved parties seems by far the best means to ensure that problems are truly met rather than marginalized and that none of the parties is excluded or forced into opposition. The challenges of Middle East peacemaking have never been easy. But recent events make a peace effort imperative. Of course, peace should always be sought rather than war, but the current situation both magnifies the need and demonstrates the means.

Edu.

THE AFSC AND THE SEARCH FOR PEACE

Our report is frankly biased and unashamedly visionary. It is biased toward people and against arms, toward peace and against strife and suffering, toward justice and against fear and insecurity. It is visionary because we believe, in spite of all the difficulties and setbacks, that peace, justice, and security can be achieved in the Middle East.

Our bias is based on realism. The many and long-term experiences of the American Friends Service Committee (AFSC) in the Middle East keep us aware of the intense, multilayered conflicts that have flared into open warfare and may do so again. We also know that strong traditions in the Middle East are undergoing rapid change. It is a region where nationalism has been closely linked to religion and where religious beliefs continue to influence government policies.

Our concern is for all the people of the Middle East. The years of AFSC work with refugees, from the Holocaust in Europe and the wars and oppression in the Middle East, have given us firsthand knowledge of the human costs of conflict. We are, however, also aware that the people of the region live within a political matrix of contending states and movements and that suffering cannot be lessened until the nations and movements of the region take seriously the process of peacemaking. While outside influences and interference have often fed the conflicts and while external aid may well be helpful in seeking resolutions, the fundamental responsibility for achieving a just peace lies with the people of the Middle East.

The AFSC involvement in the region dates back to its work during and after World War II with Jewish and non-Jewish refugees. The intimate engagement in programs of feeding and relocation gave us a personal understanding of the plight of European Jewry. On the basis of that experience and previous efforts to aid refugees, the AFSC was called upon by the United Nations in 1948 to work with the 200,000 Arab refugees who had fled to the Gaza Strip during the first Arab–Israeli war. In the wake of the third Arab–Israeli war (1967) the AFSC in 1969 returned to Gaza to establish and run a series of preschool/kindergarten centers in the refugee camps. This program continues today in cooperation with the United Nations Relief and Works Agency (UNRWA).

Believing that an important element in dealing with suffering is to prevent it, the AFSC assigned a Quaker International Affairs Representative to the Middle East in 1967 and has had Middle East Representatives in the region ever since. This Representative developed channels through which even differing perceptions of the conflicts could be shared. Through personal visits, conferences, and meetings, the AFSC gained many insights and helped many people in the Middle East cross long-standing barriers to communication and exchange of views.

Other service projects were established by the AFSC, one in Jerusalem to give legal-aid assistance to Arabs of East Jerusalem and the West Bank, another in Beersheba to provide a variety of services to mentally retarded individuals and their families in the Israeli community (since devolved to a local agency), and more recently involvement with a school-based educational program directed at countering stereotypes and creating better relations between Jewish and Arabic citizens of Israel.

The day-to-day experiences of AFSC workers among Israelis and Palestinian Arabs have led to personal friendships and relations of deep trust. We have heard fears and concerns behind political expressions and seen justice and right on all sides of the conflict. We also have seen error, prejudice, mistrust, and mistakes on all sides. The knowledge we have gained and the responsibility we feel to help relieve and prevent suffering have led us to this book.

The same spirit of seeking to bring an end to conflict prompted the AFSC to publish *Search for Peace in the Middle East*[1] in 1970 and a second report, *A Compassionate Peace*, in 1982. *Search for Peace* dealt with the problems generated by the 1967 Arab–Israeli war, and it outlined steps that could lead to stability, justice, and peace in the Middle East. It recognized the depths of division and the seriousness of the situation. "Time," the authors wrote, "is working against everyone." Indeed, within three years of publication the fourth Arab–Israeli war broke out in 1973. We expressed the deep commitment of the AFSC and of humane people everywhere to the safety and security of Israel and its people, and the book endorsed UN Security Council Resolution 242 as the most practical and acceptable basis for achieving peace. But *Search for Peace in the Middle East* also recognized and identified an important new factor in the Arab–Israeli equation: the explicit role to be played by the Palestinians, who sought to have their voices heard in the search for a solution. Indeed, the 1970 book was significant in focusing attention on the pivotal position of the Palestinians in the Middle East. The importance of this realization has been borne out. It is now even more apparent that solving the Palestinian question is critical to solving the Arab–Israeli conflict.

There is one important shift in emphasis that emerges in this revised edition of *A Compassionate Peace*. In 1970 it seemed obvious that the contending parties—Israel, the Arab nations, and the Palestinians—could not reach a meaningful settlement on their own and therefore vigorous and sustained outside initiatives were needed. After a decade and a half of efforts at peacemaking and a decade and a half of changes in the Middle East, it now seems clear that no one from the outside can make peace in the area. No one from the outside can save the nations of the Middle East from themselves. But it is equally true that there are critical, helpful efforts that can be undertaken by outside parties—the United Nations, the United States, and the Soviet Union, among others. Outsiders, especially the United States and the Soviet Union, must not thwart the peace process by further arming the nations of the region and thus making conflict more likely. Instead, they should work vigorously with Israel, the Arab states, and the Palestinians to take the hard steps now necessary to assure a realistic and just peace.

But we are led by our conclusions to demand that the Middle Eastern parties assume greater initiative in taking steps toward peace. We are led to demand of our own government that it not use that part of the world as a surrogate battlefield, that it not assert claims to special interests in the Middle East, and that it stop serving as an arsenal for Middle Eastern wars.

Our interest leads us to restate the urgent necessity of rejecting violence and terror. Certainly we are aware that even the most ardent peacemaking efforts will not easily erase decades of distrust and conflict. Political agreements, as important to peace as they are, will not fully resolve all conflicts and differences. But a just peace can dramatically reduce and finally eliminate the killing and destruction that have disrupted Middle Eastern life for too long.

We are aware that even as we write, the situation is rapidly changing. No report can be fully current or predict events with certainty. But even rapid change has left fundamental issues unresolved. It is to these that we turn.

2

Israel

An Israeli author was overheard in 1978, at the time of a West Bank protest, to comment that Israel had to decide whether it wanted to live in the West Bank or the Middle East. Conflict over the first, he said, would preclude peace in the second.

The stunning Israeli military victory in the Six Day War of June 1967 left Israel in control of all the land from the Jordan River and the Golan Heights in the east to the Mediterranean Sea in the west, from the Lebanese border in the north to Sharm-el-Sheikh at the southern tip of the Sinai peninsula. Israeli control extended across the Sinai desert to the eastern shore of the Suez Canal and the Red Sea. There was more than territory involved. Over a million human beings lived in the occupied areas and were largely clustered in the West Bank, the Gaza Strip, and the Mediterranean northern shore of the Sinai peninsula.

Some Israelis saw in the conquered territory a chance to achieve militarily important strategic depth. Some saw the fulfillment of a religious ideal—Jewish rule over all of the territory of biblical Eretz Yisrael. For others concerned with the implications of including more than a million Arabs in Israel's population or presiding over a hostile, occupied population, the victory raised new problems. The ensuing years have been marked with conflict—a war of attrition with Egypt, another full-scale Arab–Israeli war in 1973, a costly invasion of Lebanon in 1982, and continued hostilities with the Palestinians, erupting finally in the full-scale *intifidah* which began in December 1987. Today Israel faces the fundamental issue of how to deal with a people in rebellion in the occupied territories. The Egyptian–Israeli peace treaty of 1979 has served only to underscore the problem of how to deal with the West Bank and the Gaza Strip, how to come to terms with a more articulate Palestinian nationalism and with the Palestinian people.

In 1970 the American Friends Service Committee wrote in *Search for Peace in the Middle East*:

> It is the judgment of the authors of this paper that the long-held Israeli policy of maintaining indefinitely the military occupation of Arab territories and of disclaiming responsibility for the plight of the Arab refugees . . . must be abandoned if an Arab–Israeli settlement is to be made. It is our further judgment that by using flexibility Israel can bring an end to the conflict and the change needed to build a firm national security upon the basis of slowly emerging trust between the Arabs and the Israelis.[1]

The book declared that UN Security Council Resolution 242 is "the most practical and acceptable basis for achieving a peaceful settlement . . ." and called on Israel to undertake a firm commitment to withdraw from Arab lands contingent upon Arab commitments to accept the existence of Israel. It asked that the Arabs accept an Israeli state within mutually agreed and recognized borders as part of a total peace settlement. These aims, spelled out with hope tempered with realism, remain critically important nearly two decades later.

The report of 1970, the first edition of *A Compassionate Peace* (1982), and this revision strongly affirm the AFSC's belief in Israel's right to live in peace, with secure borders, among her Arab neighbors but couple this with recognition that this peace will only be achievable when the Palestinians attain self-determination and statehood.

Modern Israel has several roots, each with its own history. Each has a different influence on the state today and each projects a different image in the community of nations. One tradition connects modern Israel with the ancient Jewish kingdom of biblical times; it has meaning not only for those who live in Israel but for those around the world for whom the Scriptures are a religious

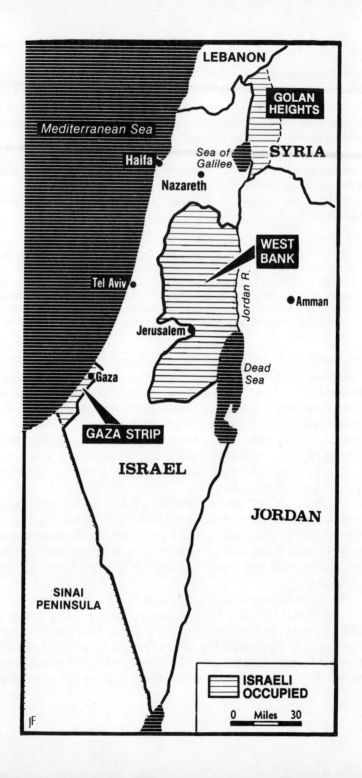

and moral guide. While a remnant of the ancient Jewish community remained in the Holy Land through the centuries, active Jewish settlement began in the late nineteenth century, guided by a new social movement. This movement, Zionism, was in part a response to the pogroms carried out against the Jews of Europe. The attempt to bring Jews to the Holy Land after centuries of living in the diaspora was very much a political event, reaffirming the land of Palestine as the Jewish homeland. Migration, increasing into the 1930s, exploded when World War II and the Holocaust made the homeland a haven vital for Jewish survival. What did not enter deeply enough into the consciousness of the early-twentieth-century settlers was the extent to which their national aspirations conflicted with legitimate Arab claims to the same land. The need to resettle the hundreds of thousands of Jewish refugees from Europe pushed such awareness even further into the background. Few thought to ask the other residents in the land, the Arabs, how to resolve the desperate need of the refugees. To ask today whether the Jewish refugees could have been settled differently is to engage in nonproductive discussion. To ask now how to reconcile the needs of two peoples within the same area can lead to innovative solutions.

The experience, anguish, and commitment of many Israelis can be understood through reading their autobiograhical writings. Arie "Lova" Eliav, Knesset member and former General Secretary of the Labor Party, wrote of himself:

> A Jew born in Russia to refugees from violence in the midst of a bloody civil war; a man whose Zionist parents brought him to the Land of Israel as an infant and planted him in the golden sands of Tel Aviv; . . . a Jew who, after fighting as a youth in the battlefields of the Western Desert and Europe in World War II, was among those who opened up the Nazi death camps and helped to save the survivors; a man who went on to fight in the War of Independence and the wars of Israel that followed, until he was sent back to the rear; a father whose son continued to fight in the Yom Kippur War, while he himself was called to serve in the most terrible unit he had ever known, whose task it was to tell the parents about the deaths of their sons . . .[2]

If the experiences of history have produced anguish and commitment, recent developments have intensified them. Israelis remain aware of the depth of Arab hostility, and the recurrent wars and continued conflicts have led to a profound preoccupation with security in all segments of the population. The actuality, the fear, the propaganda about terrorist actions—a bomb in a bus or marketplace, a settlement attacked—have assumed large proportions in the lives and perspectives of Israelis. They have fueled their distrust of the very idea of a negotiated settlement with those who directly or indirectly have been terrorists. They have deeply marked Israeli attitudes toward their Arab neighbors. They have become a tool in the hands of some Israeli political leaders to discredit the very idea of an agreement with Arab states or the Palestinians.

Israel in the past several decades has witnessed economic and social growth coupled with significant political change. Three major groups of immigrants have made their special mark on its society and consciousness. The first came from communities across North Africa, the Arab countries, and Iran in the wake of the wars of 1948 and 1956. They fled from countries in which hostility toward Israel was frequently vented upon the indigenous Jewish populations. Restrictions of varying severity on human and civil liberties, expropriation of property, and various forms of religious persecution became more and more common. Jews from these countries accordingly either elected to leave their homeland or were forced to go.

At least 550,000 Jews have left Arab lands to come to Israel since the establishment of the state; others have migrated elsewhere. Flourishing Jewish communities have been decimated. Yemen today has between 1,000 and 2,000 Jews living in scattered groups; there are approximately 175 Jews in Egypt; fewer than 4,000 in Syria; 250 in Iraq.[3] A substantial Jewish population remains in Morocco (10,000), but there has been a significant emigration to France and Israel. Today, Jews who remain in Arab countries, with the exception of Egypt and Morocco, live in uncertainty. Since the revolution, intense pressures on the Jewish community in Iran threaten its existence, although it still numbers over 22,000. In a meeting with a Syrian Jewish leader of Damascus in 1979, an AFSC delegation was told when it asked to visit a synagogue that it would not be possible. "It would not be a good idea for you to be asking around for Jewish institutions." As the delegation was leaving, he told an AFSC representative, "Please do not forget us if trouble should develop."[4] Persecution (including murder) of the small Jewish community remaining in Lebanon has been one consequence of the prolonged civil turmoil that has marked that unhappy country since 1975.

Jews from Arab countries, North Africa, Iran, and Turkey brought their traditions with them—traditions at variance with the outlook of European refugees from the Holocaust or earlier Zionist immigrants from Europe. The Sephardic and Oriental Jews tend to be traditional in their religious practices and even more traditional in their social behavior. Their families are often larger and their growth rate is more rapid than that of their Ashkenazi, or European, fellow citizens. Their communities often remain separate and their integration into the mainstream of Israeli life is slower. By the mid-1970s Oriental and Sephardic Jews were a majority of the Israeli population, but in jobs, education, income, and social status they were clustered at the lower end of Israeli society. By 1977 their disaffection from the Labor Party leadership of Israel resulted in a striking shift of political power as they provided the margin of victory for the Likud conservative coalition to come to power. Sephardic votes contributed to Likud's victory in 1981 and continued to supply political strength, albeit in diminished proportion, to the Israeli right in the 1984 and 1988 elections. This support probably stems as much from continued disaffection from the Labor Party as from an acceptance of Likud's domestic or international policies. The Sephardic community also has a small but explicitly progressive wing that takes pride in its Oriental traditions. East for Peace, a Sephardic group, is among the more progressive elements in the Israeli peace movement.

Another important group of immigrants was comprised of those fleeing religious persecution in the Soviet Union. Many who had not been practicing Jews in their youth discovered their heritage while still in the Soviet Union, through awareness of the experiences of the Jews of Israel. More highly educated and trained than the Sephardic immigrants, they made their way into the mainstream of Israeli society. They brought with them a greater awareness of anti-Semitism in the outer world and often, through their experiences in the Soviet Union, developed an anticommunist and antisocialist outlook.

A third group of immigrants—the ultra-Orthodox Jews—were

a very visible Jewish remnant who brought the customs and law of the Eastern European Jewish ghettos to the neighborhoods of Israel. They are largely non-Zionist or even anti-Zionist, believing that a "Jewish state" could be achieved only with the coming of the Messiah. Their aim was to live in the promised land and study the Scriptures. They push for greater adherence to religious law and strict Sabbath observance; they oppose abortion and autopsy, and demand increased financial support for religious education and draft deferment for yeshiva students. Demographically, they have been the fastest-growing segment of Israeli society—Jew or Arab—and most recently they have overcome their reluctance to engage in the politics of Israel and have become a well-organized (if segmented) and forceful voting minority.

SOCIETAL STRAINS

The decade of the 1970s witnessed severe economic problems in Israel as the burdens of military defense and the cost of occupying the West Bank and the Gaza Strip created inflation of over 100 percent a year. Because wages and social services are indexed to the rate of inflation, individuals do not suffer from these rates as might be expected. The national economy, however, falls deeper into debt, and the balance of payments suffers. Without subtantial external aid, the Israeli economy would have difficulty surviving.[5] Despite social and economic problems that would tear most societies apart, Israel maintains a high degree of cohesion, due, in part, to the continuing sense of external threat that Israelis across the political spectrum share. While the economy remained chaotic through the early 1980s, inflation was brought under control after a "unity" government representing Labor and Likud was formed following the indecisive elections of 1984. Shimon Peres of Labor, as Prime Minister for the first two years of a rotating leadership, was able to take the necessary strong steps to rein in galloping inflation and return the economy to relative normality.

During the 1970s Israel experienced, for the first time, the loss of a significant number of its Jewish population through emigration. For some years during the decade this trend outward was probably greater than immigration. This pattern continued during the 1980s, and it is estimated that for the decade so far there has been a net loss each year, with emigration exceeding immigration. This was particularly true after the 1982 Israeli invasion of Lebanon and during the intense strife of the *intifadah* of 1987–88. Howard Sachar, in his major popular history of Israel, blames the trend on economic pressures and a decline in spirit and values in the society:

> At the least, an insight into what was happening should have been provided by the hemorrhage of emigration. Few spoke of the phenomenon openly. The statistics of departure rarely were published by the newspapers, and least of all by the government . . . Yet in the very midst of the post-1967 prosperity, with the nation's tastes whetted for a less arduous existence, with its tolerance fading for drudgery and danger of endless military reserve service, Israelis were leaving the country by the thousands . . .[6]

Sachar estimates that by 1975 at least 300,000 Israelis had settled in the United States alone; by the mid-1980s over 500,000 Israeli citizens out of a total of 3.5 million Israeli Jews were living outside Israel.[7]

The Yom Kippur War of October 1973 shocked Israel. In a maneuver carefully planned by Egyptian President Anwar Sadat, Egyptian troops defeated the Israelis at the Suez Canal and crossed into the Sinai peninsula. Although the war was fought to a stalemate and much territory was recaptured by the Israelis, the Egyptians and Syrians who fought acquitted themselves extremely well in the eyes of the Arab world. The image of defeat that the Arab nations found humiliating in 1967 was reversed in Arab eyes by their ability to fight the superior Israeli forces to a draw. One school of analysis links Sadat's "victory" in 1973 to his surprising and important trip to Jerusalem in 1977. As early as 1975, when Egypt entered a second disengagement agreement with Israel in the Sinai under U.S. auspices, there were signs that Sadat was charting an independent course from the other Arab countries and had already begun to rupture the close Egyptian ties to the Soviet Union. For Israel this represented a lessening of military tensions and threats to the south and west and ultimately led to the first break in Israel's isolation from her Arab neighbors since 1948.

A second event of 1973 indirectly affected Israel quite deeply. This was the decision of the Arab oil-producing states sharply to increase oil prices and to impose a partial embargo on oil shipments to the United States and Europe in reprisal for the aid they gave Israel before and during the war. The resulting shift in wealth and political power to the Arab states led many European governments to reassess their Middle East policies and to enter a series of new relationships with the Arab states, often at the expense of their relationships with Israel.

The wars of 1967, 1973, and 1982 demonstrated that Israel remained the preeminent military power in the region. With its technically superior weapons, higher troop morale, and better-trained army, Israel offset the numerical superiority that favored the Arab states.[8] But the 1973 war, in which Israel was caught off guard, began raising for some Israeli analysts questions about long-term security and the extent to which military power alone can guarantee security. This issue became particularly acute after 1973 as the Arab states accelerated their weapons-acquisitions programs, especially highly sophisticated weapons in which Israel had previously enjoyed a clear advantage. To Israel's real concern, Western-oriented Arab states found the United States a willing supplier of the newest high-technology armaments.[9] Paradoxically, even the Israeli peace with Egypt resulted in substantial new arms shipments from the United States to Egypt. Indeed, securing modern arms and economic aid from the United States was a high priority for Sadat. European countries, eager to sell their own advanced weapons systems, also have weapons contracts with many Arab states.

A real jolt to Israel's military self-confidence came in the course of another very costly "victory"—Israel's June 1982 invasion of Lebanon. General Ariel ("Arik") Sharon succeeded to the post of Minister of Defense in the second Begin government of 1981. Known for his daring, if often dangerous, military exploits during previous wars, Sharon convinced the Cabinet to allow a full-scale invasion of Lebanon. While it is still unclear whether Sharon was given permission for only a limited military incursion into southern Lebanon and subsequently misled the Cabinet, what is clear is that Israeli forces fought their way to the hills surrounding Beirut, laid siege to the city for more than a month, and, after Palestinian and Syrian forces withdrew, entered the city. While Israel was in control of the city a massacre of hundreds of Palestinian civilians in the refugee camps of Sabra and Shatila was carried out by Lebanese

Christian forces allied with Israel. The ensuing shock in Israel (including massive public demonstrations) and condemnation by the international community led to severe doubts about the new roles being assumed by the Israeli Defense Forces. In addition, this first "offensive" war by Israel, and the occupation of southern Lebanon which ensued, led to major clashes with Shiite militia in the south involving continuing and substantial Israeli casualties. By the time Israeli troops withdrew to the "security zone" (a narrow band reaching five or more miles into Lebanese territory above the entire border with Israel) in June 1985, many Israelis interpreted the series of battles as an Israeli "defeat." Sharon had undertaken the war to drive the PLO from Lebanon (partially successful) and to destroy the credibility of the PLO, demoralize Palestinian nationalist sentiment in the occupied territories, and establish a friendly Christian-led government in Lebanon. Subsequent history shows Israel's failure to achieve the latter goals.[10]

Security has particular meaning for the Israelis that is hard for those who have not been part of the society to understand. For people who have been hated, persecuted, and killed in lands where they have lived, the security of their land is essential. It is impossible not to appreciate this perception. However, for Israel, the certainty of maintaining continued military superiority over the Arabs is thoroughly in question as the Arab states gain access to more advanced weapons; this overcommitment to military security has made it clear that a reappraisal of the issue is necessary. On what, Israelis now must ask, is true security based?

One Israeli who asked this question and proposed a visionary answer was the well-known historian Jacob Talmon. In an open letter to Prime Minister Begin published in the Hebrew daily *Ha'aretz* shortly before he died, Talmon made the case for Israel's giving up the occupied territories as part of a solution involving security considerations. His argument is political, responsible, and moral. He wrote:

> There are those who say, "But our vital security interests make it imperative that we hold on to our sovereignty over all of the present territories of the Land of Israel and settlements in the territories are crucially needed for our defense." . . . Such claims . . . are mere rationalizations for the pursuit of other goals. On the contrary, these

settlements are at present destructive to our vital interests and our Zionist goals—and especially of peace with our neighbors, which is the precondition for achieving all other goals.[11]

Referring to the settlers moving into the West Bank, Talmon compares them unfavorably with the original pioneers who established the Jewish homeland. These new settlements, he claims, are a "political act" having as their primary purpose to determine who will rule, "or as the settlers put it, 'to show the Arabs who is boss here . . . to put the Arabs in their place.' " He is fearful of this attitude: "[S]uch settling, it seems to me, is tantamount to conducting a kind of war."

For Talmon the basic moral issue was his greatest concern:

> For all the shame and pain we feel over the harm done to us by our neighbors because of anachronistic perverse policies, our fear should be greater over what these acts will do to us, to the Jewish people and to our dream of social and moral justice and renaissance. For this dream was one of the vital and beautiful aspects of Zionism . . .

Like a number of other thoughtful Israelis, Talmon was concerned that Israel's leaders had become blinded to any changes occurring in the minds of the potential enemies and had become so convinced of the implacable resolve of the Arabs to annihilate Israel that the Israelis were forced to act accordingly, despairing of any possibility of peace, of international guarantees of borders, or of demilitarization or other solutions. "I am afraid, Mr. Prime Minister, that this attitude is likely to become a self-fulfilling prophecy," he wrote. When he turned to the question of peace talks or negotiations, Professor Talmon was unafraid. "We should talk with anyone who is prepared to talk with us . . . and by talking with Israel engages in recognizing its existence and right to continue."[12] More recently a group of more than two hundred retired senior officers (generals and colonels) of the Israeli Defense Forces, acting through their newly formed Council for Peace and Security, have made explicit their view that Israel's security does not depend on continued occupation of the West Bank and Gaza and, indeed, that holding these territories with their 1.7 million hostile inhabitants may itself be detrimental to security.

THE BEGIN GOVERNMENT AND
THE PEACE WITH EGYPT

Since November 1977, when Egyptian President Anwar Sadat broke decades of Arab–Israeli hostility and visited Jerusalem to launch a new peace effort, the issue of peacemaking has been a recurrent and often divisive political theme. Several shifts in Israeli political life have influenced deeply Israel's policy and role in the peace efforts.

The government in office at the time of Sadat's visit was Menachem Begin's six-month-old Likud-led coalition. Likud had come into office after thirty years of unbroken leadership by the Labor Party. The election of the politically more right-wing Likud government was seen as a repudiation of Labor's lackluster performance on domestic issues, of its vacillation in foreign affairs, and of its inconclusive policy on the Palestinian question. It also represented the emerging political influence of the Sephardic Jewish communities, comprised of immigrants from North African and Arab countries. By 1977, although a majority of the Israeli population, the Sephardim felt pushed aside by the dominant European-descended Ashkenazi Jews who had led the country since its founding in 1948 and who had dominated the activities of successive Labor governments. The Sephardim felt separated, by class and ethnic background, from the Israeli mainstream. As outsiders, largely unconnected to the kibbutz ethic and the implicit socialism of the Israeli center, they were drawn to the political and social conservatism of Menachem Begin, the charismatic leader of Israeli right-wing politics.[13] The Sephardic vote gave Begin his new strength. Also, fifteen Labor seats were lost in the election to a new middle-of-the-road coalition led by the well-known archaeologist and former general Yigal Yadin. Yadin's Democratic Movement for Change (DASH) was comprised of a split from the Labor Party by those of its traditional constituency who resented what they viewed as drift in government and laxness on matters of corruption. DASH, together with the National Religious Party (which had brought its members into coalition in every government since 1948) and Agudat Yisrael (a small ultra-Orthodox party), gave Begin his political majority in the 9th Knesset.

There is irony in the fact that it was Menachem Begin, from the hawkish end of the Israeli political spectrum, who was the Prime Minister when President Sadat chose to make his dramatic visit. Begin's politics have marked Israeli participation in the peace process that developed and, in large measure, complicated the Palestinian issue. The events that led from Sadat's visit to Jerusalem to the faltering exchanges between the Egyptian and Israeli leadership that finally brought direct U.S. participation and the intense meetings involving President Jimmy Carter, Begin, and Sadat at the presidential retreat at Camp David, Maryland, have been well chronicled.

The accords that emerged from Camp David were split into two distinct sections—one focused on Egyptian–Israeli issues and the other on the Palestinian question. The first involved a phased withdrawal of Israeli military forces and civilian settlements from the Sinai peninsula, which Israel had occupied since 1967. A small sector along the eastern shore of the Suez Canal had been returned to Egypt as part of the Sinai II agreement negotiated by Henry Kissinger in 1975 in the aftermath of the 1973 Arab–Israeli war. What is notable about the Camp David accords is that Israel agreed to a total withdrawal from all Egyptian territory in return for a formal peace treaty (signed in March 1979), demilitarized zones in the Sinai, and the normalization of relations between Egypt and Israel. Ambassadors have been exchanged, limited tourism and trade have been arranged, and the final sector of the Sinai (with the exception of disputed Taba) was returned to Egypt in April 1982. While the formal peace has been maintained and the military threat eliminated, the hope for cordial political and profitable economic relations has not yet materialized. The Egyptian leadership was frustrated by the failure of the autonomy talks, and both the leadership and the public were dismayed by Israel's invasion of Lebanon. Egypt's ambassador to Israel was withdrawn in 1982, following the Sabra and Shatila massacres, and returned only in 1986. In addition, the failure to achieve any positive approach to resolving the Palestinian question has left Egypt far from satisfied with the outcome of the peace treaty.

Some members of Begin's own party and coalition, including Yitzhak Shamir, then Foreign Minister and subsequently Prime Minister, opposed the treaty. Geula Cohen, a longtime Begin ally in the Knesset, was so strongly opposed that she withdrew from the coalition, formed another political faction, and ran for reelection in June 1981 with the Tehiya Party. Opposition centered on the treaty's requirement that Israel give up the productive oil field in the Sinai peninsula, and agree to close down its settlements in the northern Sinai and move several major air bases it had earlier constructed in the eastern Sinai. Nevertheless, Israel stood to gain much from the treaty. Peace with the most populous Arab country, security along its western borders, and assurance that another full-scale Arab–Israeli war could not be fought since Egypt was no longer in military opposition were major achievements. Egypt, of course, regained significant territory and, like Israel, became a recipient of large-scale U.S. military and economic assistance.

But there were important failures in the Camp David process. Egypt and Israel remain alone as Middle East participants in the Camp David peace process, and the hoped-for inclusion of other key Middle East nations—Jordan and Saudi Arabia—never materialized. Nor did the Palestinians join the process. The second part of the Camp David accords, dealing with the Palestinian question, has had no success and has been almost totally shelved. The accords established a framework for achieving "full autonomy" and a "five-year transition period" for the inhabitants of the West Bank and Gaza, but the meaning of autonomy, the powers to be granted to the administrative council set up to administer it, and the goal after the transition were all left so vague in the initial agreements that widely divergent interpretations have emerged. The Begin government adopted a restrictive interpretation of autonomy and, from the beginning, rejected giving up Israeli sovereignty over the occupied territories.[14] Indeed, on assuming office in June 1977, Begin gave an indication of his position when he changed the designation of the West Bank to the biblical names Judea and Samaria. When he went before the Knesset for approval of the Camp David accords, he promised its members that the West Bank and Gaza would never fall under foreign sovereignty, that Jerusalem would never again be divided and would remain the eternal capital of Israel, and that a Palestinian state would never be established. The "legitimate rights of the Palestinian people" which he recognized at Camp David became the rights of the "Arabs of Judea and Samaria and the Gaza district" to cultural and religious freedoms within a very restrictive administrative autonomy. Jordan and the Palestinians felt there was nothing in Begin's formulation to encourage their involvement in the Camp David process or the subsequent treaty.[15]

Though Begin's government has given the sharpest expression to the idea of an expanded Israel, including the West Bank and the Gaza Strip, elements of this position can be found in earlier Labor governments. There has been growth in the Labor Party of those who envision a Greater Israel. This represents a serious departure from the policy of Prime Minister Levi Eshkol, who in the early days of the occupation expressed a willingness to return almost all of the West Bank to Jordanian rule. By 1969, when Golda Meir became Prime Minister, her coalition partner, the National Religious Party, had developed a strong interest in retaining the territories. Israel, then, began to retreat from the widely held interpretation of UN Security Council Resolution 242, which included Israeli withdrawal from occupied territories in return for peace and secure borders. On several occasions in 1987 and 1988, Prime Minister Yitzhak Shamir indicated his belief that Israel had fulfilled all its requirements for return of territory when it relinquished the Sinai.

By October 1973 and the outbreak of a new Arab–Israeli war, tens of thousands of Israelis had settled in previously Arab territories, many within the greatly expanded borders of the city of Jerusalem, already governed by Israeli law. Israel claims that this was in response to rising Palestinian nationalism and Arab states' designation of the PLO as the legitimate representative of the Palestinians; at the time, neither the PLO nor the Arab states fully accepted Resolution 242 as a basis for negotiations. (Although laws had been passed in the wake of the 1967 war bringing all of Jerusalem under Israeli "law, jurisdiction, and administration," it was formally annexed by the Knesset after the Camp David agreements.)[16] In addition, Jewish settlements had been established before 1973 in the Jordan Valley, in Hebron, and in the Gaza Strip. While some of these settlements represented an emerging government policy of securing borders through placing settlements in strategic areas, others were independent efforts of ultranationalist Israeli groups. The Labor Party asserted what it believed was national sentiment, that a Palestinian state would never be acceptable on the West Bank, largely because of security considerations, but it also claimed in these years that the settlements were negotiable and that those considered nonstrategic would be withdrawn in return for peace agreements. Labor throughout the years since 1967 has indicated its belief in the formula of Resolution 242—giving up territory in return for peace. But just which territory would be ceded and which kept has remained ambiguous. Most recently Labor became impressed by the implications of the demographic "time bomb": that Palestinian population growth was outstripping Israeli and that in the foreseeable future Palestinians would outnumber Israelis in Greater Israel.

The settlement policy of the Labor government left broad ambiguity and, in the final analysis, permitted the establishment of a large number of settlements, many in places that had no clear relation to security. Strong annexationist commitments became part of the Israeli political pattern. Movements like Gush Emunim (Bloc of the Faithful) and others committed to an expanded Israel gained a government commitment to make no decision on return of the West Bank and Gaza without going to the country in a referendum or elections. In addition, they created the "facts"— numerous settlements in the West Bank.

By the time that Begin won election in May 1977, Labor had permitted construction of 24 settlements housing 3,200 settlers in the West Bank. When Begin won his second election in June 1981, there were approximately 75 settlements with 18,000 settlers in the West Bank. Between 1977 and 1984 Likud-led governments established 90 new settlements. These settlements occupy over 40 percent of the total area of the West Bank, with approximately 65,000 regular inhabitants, 80 percent of whom are clustered near metropolitan Tel Aviv and Jerusalem. In Gaza there are 2,700 Israelis in 19 settlements occupying approximately 120 square kilometers, or one-third of the total territory that Israel has taken or purchased.[17] In addition, about 90,000 Israelis now live in apartment blocks constructed in the former Arab lands to the north, east, and south of Jerusalem and are now incorporated within the expanded metropolitan boundaries. Up until 1984 the government pursued an accelerated program of appropriating occupied lands and settling them. After 1984 and the establishment of the joint Labor–Likud unity government, the establishment of new settlements was sharply restricted, although enlargement was permitted.

While much of the land was identified as public land belonging previously to the Jordanian government (but lived on by Palestinians), or absentee-owned land, some has been taken directly from Palestinian residents. In the latter case some compensation has been offered but in many instances the total procedure has been rejected. Combining lands expropriated for settlers and that taken for Israeli military purposes, over 52 percent of the West Bank is designated for the use of Israelis only.

This land acquisition and settlement policy has transformed the issue of eventual disposition of the settlement areas from an issue of government policy and diplomatic strategy to a question of deep national significance. Settlers are armed and organized into paramilitary units, and, together with their ultranationalist political supporters within Israel, they promise vigorously to resist any return of the land. A strong response by the Israeli peace movement has also been stimulated by this policy.

The policy became one of de facto annexation. The Begin-led coalition had defined the occupied regions as part of the biblically promised land of Israel; it would not accept any plan that would allow withdrawal. Instead the coalition set about building the infrastructure for permanent control and invested significant amounts of government money in a network of roads, settlements, and other facilities.

This policy of unyielding commitment to the maintenance of Israeli sovereignty over the West Bank brought the Begin government into conflict with Egypt and the United States, both of whom realized that there was little chance of resolving the Palestinian question without significant Israeli compromise on the issue of sovereignty over the territories. This policy was also responsible for the resignation from the first Begin Cabinet of its two senior ministers, Foreign Minister Moshe Dayan and Defense Minister Ezer Weizman. Begin's new Cabinet, appointed in August 1981, elevated ultranationalists to key ministries. Retired general Ariel Sharon, who in his former position as Agriculture Minister coordinated the government's settlement policy, became the new Defense Minister, directly responsible for the military government of the occupied territories. Yitzhak Shamir, who became Foreign Minister after Dayan's resignation, was among the handful in Begin's own party who refused to support the Camp David accords when Begin presented them to the Knesset. Yosef Burg, head of the National Religious Party and Minister of the Interior, was given the post of chief negotiator on autonomy. The appointment of Burg, an advocate of permanent Israeli sovereignty in the territories, to replace the then Foreign Minister, Moshe Dayan, as autonomy negotiator prompted Dayan's resignation. This switch from Foreign to Interior Minister underlined the Begin position that issues concerning the West Bank and Gaza were more internal matters than foreign policy issues. Begin apparently believed that if he negotiated the return of the Sinai to Egypt he would receive at least tacit acceptance from his negotiating partners of his plan for continued Israeli sovereignty in the West Bank and Gaza. This interpretation has been kept by Shamir during his terms as Foreign Minister and as Prime Minister.

The annexationist policy runs head-on into even the most moderate Arab's views and, of course, clashes directly with even limited Palestinian nationalist aspirations. Many Jews also object. The official Israeli position on the territories has markedly hardened during the same period when there has been a perceptible moderating of Palestinian views.

The June 1981 Israeli elections made clear that Begin's policies were not rejected by the Israeli public, but the closeness of the election (48 seats for the Likud and 47 for Labor in a 120-member Knesset) by no means gave Begin an unequivocal mandate. In order to form a government, Begin had to enter into coalition with three religious or ethnically oriented parties (National Religious Party, 6 seats; Agudat Yisrael, 4 seats; Tami, 3 seats). The coalition gave him a slim two-vote majority; the nature of this coalition had the effect of forcing the Begin government to adopt even more rigid positions and was in some measure responsible for approving the Lebanon invasion. New levels of theocratic influence were introduced into the governing process. During the campaign, the Labor Party muted its criticisms of Begin's foreign policies, and several of the small progressive and peace parties were either severely reduced in number or eliminated from the Knesset by the election. Politically, Israel slipped further to the right, a shift that may not be transitory since it seems to reflect demographic changes in the society. In assessing the internal implications of the elections, and thus the political forces to which an Israeli government will have to respond, one thoughtful analyst, Bernard Avishai, lamented: "The mean-spirited campaign that preceded the June 30 election has, in fact, revealed a country passionately divided by ideology, class, age, attitudes toward Orthodox faith and law—and crucially, ethnic origin."[18] Much the same can be said about the implications of the 1984 and 1988 elections.

Israel's relations with Syria, which had never been good, further deteriorated during the Begin years. With the breakdown of efforts to achieve a comprehensive peace and the focus on negotiating a bilateral treaty between Egypt and Israel, Syria's attitudes hardened as it saw its bargaining position for the occupied Golan Heights weakened. In addition, the Syrian role in Lebanon, which involved approximately 30,000 troops, first in ending the Lebanese civil war (1976) and then in remaining as a strong military presence, increased Israeli fears of Syria's intentions. This problem came to a head in the spring and summer of 1981. Israel increased its military activities inside Lebanon, attacking suspected Palestinian targets and giving direct military support to the Lebanese Phalangist militia when it was under attack by Syrian forces in the strategic mid-Lebanese city of Zahle. Syria countered the latter Israeli action by moving sophisticated surface-to-air missiles into Lebanon near Zahle, thus denying Israel supremacy in the air. This confrontation remained unresolved in spite of the efforts of special U.S. negotiator Philip Habib, although a cease-fire was achieved and was in effect for almost a year.

In December 1981, Israel made the surprise move of annexing (extending Israeli law, jurisdiction, and administration) the Golan Heights, which had come under Israeli occupation in 1967. The move, explained by Israel in terms of the strategic nature of the Heights and the continuous threat that Syrian forces had posed in the pre-1967 years, had the broader effect of directly abrogating the terms of UN Security Council Resolution 242. Except for the annexation of Jerusalem and some surrounding West Bank land, it was the most serious move taken by Israel to make explicit its intention to maintain sovereignty over territories occupied in the 1967 war. It further strained the already frail peace process, and again brought Israel into sharp conflict with international opinion and the U.S. government. The move deeply embarrassed the new government of Egypt and presented it with a dilemma. If it responded sharply, it would put at risk the fulfillment of the Egyptian–Israeli Treaty and the return to Egypt of the final portion of the Sinai. If Egypt did not respond, it would be even more isolated from the Arab world. Egypt stuck with its treaty.

The results of the Israeli elections of 1984 reflected the deeply divided society at that time. The invasion of Lebanon in June 1982 had kindled as strong a reaction as the state had seen since its foundation.[19] A series of new antiwar organizations sprang up alongside Peace Now, which had been established in response to President Sadat's initiatives. In turn, the right wing itself organized, and a series of acrimonious political confrontations developed, culminating in a bomb attack on a Peace Now public meeting in February 1983, which resulted in the death of an activist. The Kahan Commission report of February 1983 assigning blame for the massacre of Palestinians at the Sabra and Shatila camps not only forced the resignation of Defense Minister Ariel Sharon and Chief of Staff Rafael Eytan but left many Israelis with a deep sense of moral uncertainty. Prime Minister Begin's abrupt and not fully explained resignation in September 1983 further undermined any sense of political rootedness.[20]

The 1984 elections yielded no clear political mandate. Both Likud and Labor lost seats to smaller parties with whom they were, or could be, allied and neither bloc commanded enough seats in the Knesset to form a government. Six places were held by two political lists of largely Arab votes, denying both blocs the 61 seats (of the 120-member parliament) needed to form a government. The result: a national "unity" government with a rotating Prime Minister and a series of agreements calculated to ensure stalemate. Although measures to deal with the economy and withdrawal from Lebanon could be agreed upon, almost no action was possible on procedures for peacemaking or how to deal with the occupation and, ultimately, the Palestinian uprising. Since it was necessary to maintain "unity," all real opposition was confined to the marginal parties in the Knesset (both right and left) and to the nonparliamentary groups which came into being over such issues as support for West Bank settlements, opposition to the occupation, or concern for civil and human rights. But the political influence of these groups was severely limited by the nature of the parliamentary system and the "unity" agreement, which left both major parties unwilling to risk the government's fall.

In Israel there was a growing religious fundamentalism and intolerance; bus kiosks with advertisements showing women in bathing suits were burned; cars driving near religious communities on the Sabbath were stoned; a major dispute blocked the building of a new sports stadium in Jerusalem since games were often played on the Sabbath; and a major campaign to ban showing movies on the Sabbath eve brought opposing groups into physical confrontation. Jewish defenders of secular rights retaliated, and on at least one occasion set fire to a synagogue.[21] Israeli Arabs (about 17 percent of the population), responding to their sense of social injustice and second-class citizenship in Israel and showing their sympathy with the Palestinian *intifadah* in the occupied territories, further distanced themselves from the Jewish majority. Two widely observed general strikes were called, and an Arab Labor member of the Knesset resigned from the party to establish an alternative Arab party. This new activism by the customarily compliant Arab population in Israel deeply worried many political leaders, both because it showed a deep fissure in Israeli social and political life and because it suggested that internal Arab political unity, with a potential for up to 17 seats in the Knesset, could have significant effects on Israeli politics. Already during the spring 1987 Knesset session four Arab votes made the difference in a closely contested battle over legislation determining "who is a Jew."

As Israel prepared for its 1988 elections, the already divided society was confronted with the most serious challenge to its twenty-one years of occupation of the West Bank and Gaza—the *intifadah*. In addition, the peace maneuverings of Shimon Peres, the Foreign Minister and leader of the Labor Party, represented a direct challenge to the largely rejectionist position of Yitzhak Shamir, Prime Minister and Likud leader. For the first time an Israeli election campaign was fought largely over foreign/peace policy and how to deal with Palestinians and the occupation. This situation was put forcefully by Naomi Chazan, a prominent Israeli political analyst:

In 1988 Israel was at a paradigmatic conjecture. Minor adjustments were no longer adequate to the challenge of facing some of the basic tenets of the Zionist ethos. The issue of the preservation of the democratic foundations of the state and its Jewish character could not be neatly divorced from the question of the occupation. The protracted retention of the West Bank had already altered the human composition of the state and its political structures. Adherence to democratic principles and Jewish considerations could hardly be preserved without an adjustment in the post-1967 boundaries.[22]

But Israel decided not to decide. When Israelis awoke on November 2, the morning after the elections, they found that the electorate had slipped further to the right. But even more challenging for the society, the Orthodox parties increased their Knesset representation by 50 percent, giving them 18 seats and denying a majority to the blocs led by Labor and Likud. In the new Knesset, Likud and its allies gained one seat, but the three small right-wing parties all favored annexation of the territories and one party, the new Moledet (Homeland), openly campaigned for mass expulsion of the Palestinians. Labor and its partners lost three seats and the old Arab bloc dropped one. Although assessing the full impact of the elections will take months, several key points emerged with clarity. Without a major shift in outlook no active search for resolution of the Palestine question will be undertaken by a government led by Yitzhak Shamir, albeit that the Shamir government will almost certainly have to undertake "political" initiatives. Rejection of the new Palestinian peace initiatives was coupled with more forceful attempts to assert full control over the rebellious Palestinians in the West Bank and Gaza. The government still believes that it can indefinitely postpone dealing with the deep contradictions of the occupation.

Indeed, the unpredicted electoral achievements of the non-Zionist ultrareligious parties have focused the attention of Israelis inward and forced them to face the full implications of the augmented strength of Jewish fundamentalism. The religious parties do not, however, represent a solid bloc against territorial compromise. Although the old-line National Religious Party is led by ultranationalists, two of the other three parties (Degel Hatorah and Shas) contain elements which have publicly supported relinquishing occupied lands in return for peace. The basis in religious law is straightforward: if withdrawal would save more lives than continued occupation, support would be warranted.

Israel has not been well served by its political leaders. They have postponed dealing with the growing consequences of continued occupation. During the first year of the Palestinian uprising they brought forward no new political programs, ignored the "demands" of the local Palestinian leadership, and offered no ideas for compromise. The leadership was caught unprepared by both Arafat's peace initiatives and Washington's decision to open substantive dialogue with the PLO. Israel began 1989 with a new unity government that was just as divided as the previous one on the fundamental questions of dealing with the occupation and making peace with the Palestinians. But the situation has changed, the political dynamics of the Middle East have been thoroughly altered, and Israel seems more isolated than ever before. The problems of governmental paralysis, difficult in normal circumstances, were magnified. But it is clear that if peace is to come Israel must be involved and must be reassured and encouraged just as the Palestinians and the PLO had to be brought to accept the politics of compromise. While Israeli policy has been rigid and often unrealistic, there exists within the society a sizable constituency for peacemaking. Close to half the electorate voted for parties explicitly supporting the exchange of territory for peace, and polls have continually shown that even among Likud voters a substantial portion (about one-third) could conceive of situations in which such an exchange would be acceptable if Israeli security is guaranteed. In these circumstances Palestinian leaders must increasingly and openly address Israeli fears and misunderstandings. Similar reassurances should come from the Soviet Union, which has already helped by supporting moderation in the PLO; Moscow should reestablish normal diplomatic relations with Israel and strengthen its political dialogue with the Jewish state. For the United States, Israel's strongest advocate and supporter, there is a special responsibility. In this time of testing and hard decisions, true friendship would involve American support for real efforts to achieve lasting security and peace.

3

The Occupation

When Israeli troops overran the West Bank and Gaza in the Six Day War of June 1967, they took over territories with more than one million Palestinian residents. The Gazans, living largely in refugee camps established in the aftermath of the 1948 war, had been under Egyptian administration and lived at the margins of Egyptian society. Those on the West Bank, by contrast, were somewhat more fully integrated into Jordanian political culture. Although not as involved as it had been during the 1930s and 1940s, Palestinian nationalism remained active and often clashed with Jordanian authority.

The Israeli occupation of the West Bank and the Gaza Strip has deepened the extent to which other countries are affected by the Palestinian question. In addition to refugees who left during the 1948 and 1967 wars, over 200,000 Palestinians have left the occupied territories since 1967, with most currently living in other parts of the Arab world.[1] The occupation dramatically affects the lives of the occupiers, including the men and women of the military government. Some Israelis have asked the difficult question: Where in the dreams of the Zionist founders of Israel was there a vision of Israel as an army of occupation?

Israel, in response to complaints, has often argued that its treatment of the Palestinian population and overall handling of the occupation affairs is not severe in comparison with military occupations elsewhere. While this claim may have had some truth to it, it is a distinction made by the occupiers and not the occupied and loses importance when we consider that Palestinian resistance to the occupation is greater after twenty-one years than it ever was. The emergence of the policy of the "Iron Fist" after 1984 and the use of large-scale military force in 1987 and 1988 to contain and put down the Palestinian uprising overshadow any prior judgments. The occupation has, of course, had a dramatic impact on the day-to-day lives of Palestinian residents. In addition, the acts of the occupation and the policy it represents have seriously complicated any search for a just, negotiated solution. General Ariel Sharon, Minister of Defense in the second Begin government, has articulated the position of many Israelis:

> It is impossible any more to talk about Jordanian option or territorial compromise. We are going to leave an entirely different map of the country that it will be impossible to ignore. I don't see any way any government will be able to dismantle the settlements of Judea and Samaria.[2]

The attempts made by two successive Likud governments, 1977–84, to fix in place this new map involved encouragement of new settlements (some 90 were built during those years), subsidies for housing and rents for those willing to live in the territories, accelerated seizure of Arab lands, construction of basic infrastructure—roads, communication, utilities, and water—directly linked across the Green Line to Israel, and continued disenfranchisement of the Palestinian population through new restrictive laws and military orders. Meron Benvenisti, one of Israel's best-informed observers of the occupation, has asked whether the steps taken might have succeeded in creating an irreversible transformation of the geographic, economic, and social structures of the occupied territories, linking them inextricably with Israel.[3]

THE RULE OF LAW

As the result of several wars and acts of hostile terrorism, Israel views virtually all the activities in the daily life of citizens of the occupied territory through the lens of security. All actions of the occupation forces are undertaken in the name of security. Israel argues that the provisions of the Fourth Geneva Convention (1949) covering the protection of civilian persons in time of war do not apply to the West Bank and Gaza. The Israelis claim that these areas are not enemy territory because in its view Jordan's prior annexation of the West Bank was illegal. International legal opinion, however, has supported the view that the Geneva Convention rules should apply to the residents of the West Bank and the Gaza Strip because the peoples of these territories are, in fact, "in the hands of an occupying power of which they are not nationals" (from the Convention commentary). Israel has announced that in spite of the Geneva Convention's inapplicability, it would abide by its humanitarian provisions.[4]

The Convention charges the occupying power with protecting persons under occupation. Forbidden under all circumstances are, among other actions: forcible transfers or deportations (article 49); any measures of brutality, whether applied by civilian or military agents (article 32); collective punishments, reprisals against protected persons or their property, and all measures of intimidation (article 33); unlawful confinement or deprivation of rights of fair and regular trial (article 147).[5]

In the judgment of many observers, including Amnesty International, Israel has often violated each of these provisions of international law. Amnesty International's *Report 1988* and the special report of August 1988, *Israel and the Occupied Territories, Excessive Force: Beatings to Maintain Law and Order*, detail their contentions of human rights abuses, prisoner mistreatment, possible torture, lack of legal due process, deportations, and excessive use of force by the police and the military.

In place of full adherence to the Geneva Convention, Israel has chosen to rely on the Defense Emergency Regulations originally promulgated by the British in 1937 and codified in 1945. They consist of 120 sweeping orders meant to cope with the tense situation that existed in the closing years of the mandate when British authority was being challenged by advocates of the nascent State of Israel. Far-reaching powers are given to security authorities to act without due process of law. These regulations, which were vigorously opposed in 1946 by the Federation of Hebrew Lawyers in Palestine, were adopted by the new state in 1948 and applied to the Arab population of Israel until 1966. Beginning in 1967, they were applied to the Arab population in the occupied territories. Ironically, Great Britain itself revoked these regulations as of May 14, 1948, when it relinquished its mandate in favor of the United Nations partition of Palestine.[6]

Israel announced in June 1967 that all laws in force in the occupied territories would be continued if they did not contradict the military governor's proclamations and did not conflict with changes brought by the occupation. Nonetheless, many basic laws and the system of administering justice have been broadly altered since 1967. By declaring in February 1968 that the occupied territories were no longer enemy territory, Israel relieved itself of many constraints widely accepted in international law. The area was from that time referred to as territory administered by Israel.

Since 1967 the Israeli military government has issued over 1,200 military orders claiming to amend the existing Jordanian law in the West Bank that, in fact, replace it in many categories. Since there is no existing legislative authority in the territories, the military government has assumed that role. Powers under law previously given to Jordanian authorities and officials have been taken over by Israelis, and powers and privileges previously held by civilian authority have been shifted to military administration. Thus, for example, the Israeli officer in charge of the judiciary holds and exercises a very wide range of what were previously civil positions and powers, including Minister of Justice, Minister of Commerce, and registrar of lands, companies, trademarks, trade names, and patents. He also holds powers formerly held by the bar association to allow lawyers to train and law schools to be recognized.[7]

One of the most important changes effected by Israel in the West Bank legal system was an alteration of the judiciary, including abolition of the highest court, the Court of Cassation. This court had had responsibility for overseeing proper functioning of the judicial system and for being the arbiter in novel issues of law. It also operated as a special board to hear requests from government departments for interpretation of the law and its ramifications. Of these functions only that of the High Court of Justice has been retained; its functions have been passed on to the West Bank Court of Appeals.

The most controversial element of the legal system is the Military Court. Judges are appointed by the military area commander and all must be military officers or civilian lawyers on reserve duty. Court sessions are held where and when the judge determines, and the judge generally makes the only record of what occurs. Convictions are by either a three-member court or a single judge. The decisions may be accepted, altered, or annulled by the area commander, who, in the case of a single-judge court, may accept written representations for sentence variance but not normal appeal. There is no regular system of judicial appeal from the decision of either of these courts. The lack of a regular appeal mechanism is viewed as one of the most serious breaches of orderly rule of law, since judicial errors cannot be corrected and proper procedures and standards of evidence cannot be guaranteed. Confessions obtained from individuals detained by the military pending trial cannot be challenged during the period when the confession is being obtained, albeit questions may be raised during subsequent trials. In an investigation of the General Security Service (known as Shin Bet) in 1987, it became apparent that there was widespread use of coercion and torture to gain confessions and that on numerous occasions police agents had knowingly lied about this to judges to gain convictions. While condemning torture, the Israeli High Court of Justice did countenance "moderate use of coercion" in cases involving security.[8] In principle, a procedural violation could be brought to the Israeli High Court of Justice, but, in practice, that court has taken an extremely restricted view of its ability to challenge military government decisions taken on security grounds. In a limited number of cases, the Israeli Supreme Court, sitting as a High Court of Justice, has been willing to consider appeal petitions from the occupied territories. These have largely been related to concerns with personal and property matters (on several occasions deportation orders and house demolitions), and have generally excluded security-related cases.[9] The court is limited to challenges to administrative procedure and not issues of substance.

Between 1967 and 1988, over 250,000 individuals in the occupied territories have been arrested and taken to Israeli prisons, detention centers, and police stations. These arrests have occurred under the Security Provisions Orders and the Defense Emergency Reg-

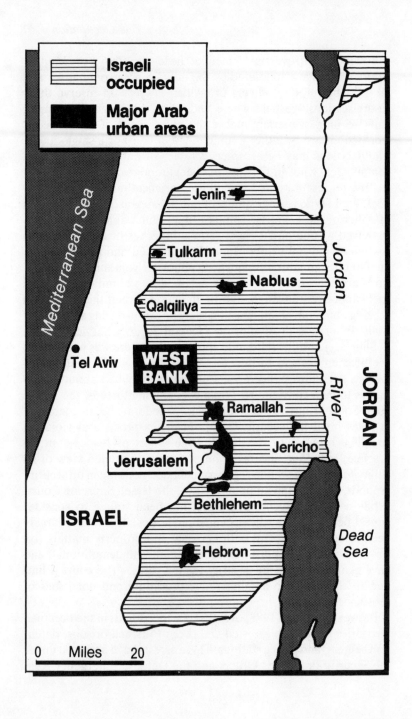

ulations. The pace of arrests remained quite high from 1979 to 1988. Of those arrested, 70 percent were between sixteen and twenty-three years old, and there is agreement by both the International Committee of the Red Cross and the military authorities that until the uprising began in December 1987 up to 90 percent of these arrests were for the sole purpose of eliciting information about political or potential security concerns. While most of those arrested were released after several days, some, with judicial approval but without having faced trial, were detained for extended periods.[10] During the *intifadah* the Israeli military authorities have relaxed the rules; they have given even greater discretion to those making arrests and removed the requirement for review of cases of administrative detention; prisoners could be held for renewable six-month terms without charges being made or without trial.[11]

Any Israeli soldier has the authority to arrest without a warrant any person who commits or is suspected of committing an offense under the security provisions. No detaining order is needed; there is no law of habeas corpus allowing application to a judge for explanation, and although an arrest warrant normally has to be obtained within four days (ninety-six hours), the warrant need not specify any charges. The detention may be extended to eighteen days before the individual must be brought before a judicial authority, who may extend confinement up to six months.

Most Israelis are not familiar with the workings of the Military Courts or, for that matter, with the administration of the law in the occupied territories. Their own experience within Israel leads them to trust the military and the justice it provides. (This trust was shaken, however, by the Shin Bet revelations and the forced resignation of its head and several senior officers.) There also is widespread sentiment that security offenders really don't deserve trials and the niceties of legal protection, since they threaten the existence of the State of Israel. For the residents of the occupied territories, however, the opposite perception prevails. Some of the bitterness, outrage, and sense of injustice are natural, given their conviction that the occupation itself is unjust. Independent observers, including Amnesty International, have corroborated irregularities and injustices within the military justice system.[12] International law has been distorted and violated; rules of evidence, argument, and due process have been lax or altered in ways detrimental to defendants; and the role of the defense counsel has been deeply compromised. In many cases lawyers defending Palestinian prisoners have had difficulty in gaining access to their clients in order to review the charges and evidence brought against them.

In the context of the broad changes in the legal systems of the occupied territories, one important progressive legal reform should be noted—the abolition of the death penalty. It should also be noted, however, that on several occasions, including the Ashkelon bus seizure which precipitated the Shin Bet affair, Palestinian prisoners have died during interrogation. Recent attention has been given to restoring the death penalty in some cases. Though the amendments and reforms of Jordanian law made by the military government have Israel's security as their justification, in the eyes of local residents they seem capricious, oppressive, and unfounded.

ECONOMIC LIFE

The occupation, through conscious policy and by default, has created a situation in which residents of the West Bank and the Gaza Strip have become heavily dependent on Israel for trade and employment. The territories in recent years received 90 percent of their imports from Israel, and every day 100,000 laborers, or approximately one-third of the total Arab work force, commute to Israel. Palestinians make up as much as 60 percent of the work force of unskilled labor, being common in building trades, agriculture, textiles, food processing, and the service sector.[13] Their wages are not covered by Israeli trade union agreements. They are ineligible for most of the basic social welfare and health benefits given Israeli workers, and for the most part the Israeli National Insurance system does not include West Bank and Gaza residents. Some Israeli critics point out that Arab laborers fill jobs that are difficult to mechanize and equally difficult to convince Israeli workers to perform. It is true, on the other hand, that the wage scale of Palestinians employed in Israel is advantageous; their earnings have been of great importance to the occupied territories. Employment in Israel accounts for 30 percent of the total income of West Bank and Gaza Strip Palestinians. But the importance of the territories as an outlet for Israeli goods has also increased. In 1986

Israel sold $730 million in goods in the occupied territories, representing 10 percent of total Israeli exports (and 89 percent of the territories' imports), making the territories Israel's second-largest export market after the United States. The large number of workers who commute into Israel to work also affects the local Palestinian economy. Because most of these workers come from the agricultural sector, the area under cultivation in the West Bank and the Gaza Strip has been reduced by 35 percent, while Israeli rules interfering with industrial development have actually reduced the total industrial productivity to below that of the 1948–67 period. Israeli taxes, collected from the West Bank and Gaza, have been greater than the amount spent by Israel in the territories for social services, education, and the construction of civilian infrastructure. (See the series of detailed reports issued by the West Bank Data Project under the general editorship of Meron Benvenisti.)[14]

Israeli seizure of West Bank and Gaza land has been significant, and it is now estimated that over half of the total area of the occupied territories has been expropriated, "closed," or otherwise seized for Israeli civilian and military purposes. In recent years, with a greatly increased number of Israeli settlements, a system of government has been established consistent with Likud's concept of autonomy (see Chapter 5). In the West Bank, the Jewish settlements are organized into ten regional and ten local councils which operate under Israeli law, with the power to purchase land, levy municipal taxes, and negotiate with Israeli ministries for grants and aid. The settlers have also organized armed paramilitary units linked to the Israeli Defense Forces. There has been a striking shift in land control in the West Bank. At present the municipal areas included in the Israeli West Bank settlements and subject to Israeli law are greater in size than the municipal areas of the Palestinian towns. The current approved master plan for Jewish settlement in the West Bank encompasses an area greater than the approved master plan for Palestinian towns and villages.[15] The current population figures for the territories (excluding East Jerusalem) are approximately 62,000 Israeli settlers and 850,000 Palestinian residents.

In the arid conditions of much of the Middle East, few issues are more sensitive than control of water—its sources and its use.

The drilling of wells is a matter of some concern, since adjacent wells often compete for the same limited supplies. Israel, in assuming occupation powers, has taken control of well-drilling permits. Conflict increases as established Palestinians have difficulty obtaining permits while the new settlements drill for and use West Bank water. By 1979 Israeli settlers had already drilled twenty-four artesian wells, seventeen for use by Jordan Valley settlements. Meters have been placed on Arab wells, limits set for the use of water, and penalties imposed for violations. Israel proper has diverted water from the West Bank for use within the pre-1967 borders. A lesser amount is piped from Israel to the West Bank. The 1979 water-use deficit in Israel was 265 million cubic meters, and rose to 500 million cubic meters by 1985.[16] This has led to increased Israeli seizure of West Bank water.

Israel has for some years been linking the electricity system of the occupied territories into the Israeli grid. An attempt by the Israel Power Corporation to merge the old Jordanian Jerusalem Electric Company into Israel's grid was opposed by the Arab directors. The Israeli High Court supported the Arab opposition. But additional steps have been taken to accomplish this end.[17] Israel's desire to merge West Bank electric systems is based on an overall plan to control West Bank economic activity and its infrastructure and to make electricity available to Israeli settlements.

From surveying Israeli proposals and achievements since 1967, it can be argued that the occupied territories have become de facto colonies; land was appropriated for use by Israeli settlers; the economy of the territories was made largely dependent on Israel, with a cheap labor force available for use within Israel and a captive market created for Israeli products. It should be noted, however, that this dependence has created substantial strains on Israel during the *intifadah*. Strikes by Palestinians have interrupted labor availability, and boycotts of Israeli goods have hurt Israel's economy.

ISRAELI SETTLERS

Yehuda Litani, the well-known correspondent for the Hebrew daily *Ha'aretz*, opened his news story of May 11, 1979, about settlements in the West Bank with the following observation:

If one adds up all the recent events in which West Bank settlers have taken the law into their own hands, the description given them by the American media—"vigilantes," with all the negative connotations of the term—would appear to fit pretty well.[18]

He reported on the settlers' aim to foil any efforts by the Israeli government to implement even a very restricted autonomy plan in the area. Their efforts, he concluded, were coordinated among settlements and would be carried out even at severe disadvantage to the Palestinian residents. From past experience with the military government, the police, and other Israeli agencies, the settlers knew that the government would, according to Litani, "not dare mete out the full severity of the law against the Jewish settlers, while their treatment of the Arab residents is often quite severe." Litani illustrated his claim with a story about the settlers from Kiryat Araba near Hebron who, feeling that the military government was not being tough enough, took the law into their own hands in March 1976 and decided to "impose order." The settlers smashed windows in Arab homes, terrorized the people, and destroyed their vineyards. The incident became widely known, but no police action was taken, although the names of the suspected perpetrators were well known and named by Litani. Litani's accounts, and those of others, have been a regular feature in the Israeli press, yet the incidents continue. The reason, pointed out by Litani, is that the government, with some few exceptions, failed to enforce the law when illegal settlements were established, thereby letting the settlers know that they will be forgiven and that for them the law will be flexible, ignored, or changed.

A Jewish underground was formed, largely from West Bank settlements, which resorted to violence to achieve its ends. Some of the most notorious acts took place in 1980, when the mayors of Ramallah and El Bireh plus the mayor of Nablus were the object of bombing attacks by individuals linked to the Israeli terrorist group.[19] Two of the three were severely injured. An Israeli soldier sent to defuse a bomb intended to harm the third man was blinded when it exploded.

DEPORTATION

The nationalist political consciousness that has developed among many West Bank and Gaza civic and political leaders has prompted a variety of official and unofficial Israeli actions that have had the cumulative effect of attempting to break up any unified or organized Palestinian political organization. Numerous Palestinian leaders have been deported, others have been severely injured by bombs in automobiles and homes, while still others face harassment by the military government and by organized groups of ultranationalist Jewish settlers. A detailed study by Ann Lesch of deportations, listing each name, showed that in the first decade of occupation 1,156 individuals had been deported from the West Bank and Gaza. In December 1977 the *Financial Times* of London received confirmation from the Israeli government that 1,180 Palestinians had been deported. The total number is now estimated to exceed 2,000.[20] Lesch identified many moderate political figures among the deported. Israel claimed that only terrorists and their supporters had been forced to leave.[21]

Among those deported were Hanna Nasir, president of Bir Zeit University, and the mayors Fahd Qawasmi of Hebron and Mohammed Milhem of Halhul. The mayors, deported in May 1980, were widely regarded as political moderates and had regularly met with Israeli doves. They limited their aspirations to support of a Palestinian state side by side with Israel.[22] Milhem and Qawasmi were charged (but never brought to trial) with inciting Palestinians who were involved in a terrorist attack on Jewish settlers in Hebron. The men who committed the crime and were subsequently caught, convicted, and punished were shown to have had no connections whatever with the mayors. The latter repeatedly tried to return to their homes, but in spite of an Israeli High Court recommendation that they be permitted to do so, the military government has refused permission. In 1985, shortly after having been elected to the executive committee of the PLO, Fahd Qawasmi was gunned down outside his house in Amman, Jordan, probably by agents of one of the breakaway Palestinian rejectionist groups. In 1973 the mayors of Ramallah and El Bireh were deported. All the mayors but one (Elias Freij of Bethlehem) elected in the 1976 mayoral election and most of the town councils have been dismissed from office by the Israelis. Many of the cities are currently run by Israeli military officers.

During the first twelve months of the *intifadah* Israel deported 32 Palestinians and served expulsion orders against 27 others, according to Al-Haq (Law in the Service of Man) in its December 1988 report, *Punishing a Nation*. The UN Security Council, with the United States included, unanimously condemned the deportations as a violation of international law (Security Council Resolution 607, January 5, 1988). Numerous commentators have pointedly noted that while Israeli government leaders claim that there is no one to negotiate with on the Arab/Palestinian side, they have deported or jailed many legitimate nationalist leaders who would be among the obvious spokespeople for the Palestinians in both interim and long-term negotiations.

EXPULSION

A new form of deportation—mass expulsion of Palestinians—has for the first time become a subject of open political discourse in Israel. Previously only the extreme right, notably Rabbi Meir Kahane of the Kach Party, openly advocated this course. In the 1988 elections one party, Moledet, campaigned on this issue and other senior figures on the political right, such as retired Chief of Staff Rafael Eytan, and some leaders in parties such as Tehiya call for what is described as population transfer. A poll, reported in the *Jerusalem Post* in August 1988, conducted by the Israel Institute of Applied Social Research and the Communications Institute of the Hebrew University, Jerusalem, found that 49 percent of Jewish Israelis favored population transfer. The poll further revealed that two-thirds of those intending to vote for Likud in the November elections supported expulsions as compared with one-third of the prospective Labor voters. Two other options were presented in the poll: give the Arabs equal right (20 percent) and "relinquish the territories" (30 percent).[23] Writing in the *Jerusalem Post*, Elihu Katz, director of the Israel Institute of Applied Social Research, commented: "Virtually unmentionable (and unaskable) until a few months ago . . . the subject of transfer is no longer taboo; it has gained legitimacy, become a focus of public discussion and swept through the Right." The reasoning that lies behind support for expulsion is the mirror image of that proposed by supporters of trading territory for peace—maintaining the Jewish character of Israel. The center-left is willing to relinquish the territories in order to ensure that large numbers of Palestinians do not become a permanent part of Israel; the right, which is committed to holding the territories at almost any cost, would like to keep the land without the people. Both groups are aware of the population trends. Even within Israel (including Arab East Jerusalem, but excluding the West Bank and Gaza) the Arab population growth rate was twice that of Israeli Jews: 2.4 percent to 1.2 percent.[24] In the occupied territories the Arab rate of increase is even higher: well over 3 percent in the Gaza Strip and just under 3 percent in the West Bank.[25]

In August 1988 a newly established nonpartisan Committee on the Demographic Problem (which includes in its leadership individuals prominent in both Labor and Likud) released figures aimed at bringing out implications for the future. They noted that there were currently 630,000 Palestinian youth under the age of eight in both Israel and the occupied territories, as compared with 590,000 Israeli Jewish children. By the turn of the century, they estimated, there will be 1.4 million Palestinians under eighteen years of age, as compared with 1.3 million Israeli Jews. A committee member pointed to a percentage decline in the number of Jews in Israel and the territories since 1977—65.4 percent to 62 percent—adding that by the end of the century there will be 4.2 million Jews and 3.4 million Palestinians.[26] The authoritative *West Bank Data Project 1987 Report*, basing its population predictions on Central Bureau of Statistics numbers, is even more striking: "All other things being equal by the year 2010, Jewish and Arab populations will attain parity." The link between recognition of emerging demographic realities and policy for dealing with the occupation is being forcefully forged in the Israeli political consciousness, with dramatic implications for choices to be made in the near future. This link serves as a clear reminder of the structural problems built into any attempt to maintain the status quo. Labor Party leader Shimon Peres used the demographic challenge as a major issue in the 1988 election campaign.

EDUCATION

The educational system in the West Bank was developed during the British mandate and expanded by the Jordanians during the two decades (1948–67) of their rule, although the colleges and universities largely date to the post-1967 period when travel to the Arab world for higher education became increasingly difficult. The Israeli occupation government has enacted a series of orders bringing the different parts of the educational system under the direct control of the military governor. Order No. 91 deals with the public schools and Order No. 854 focuses on institutions of higher learning. A controversy has arisen over the nature of these controls and the fairness of their administration. A report by West Bank Palestinian jurists claims that there has been a steady decline in quality in the public schools and a lack of new facilities in the face of considerable population increases. There have been reductions in staff, a decline in the value of salaries (now paid in Israeli currency and not indexed to inflation as they are in Israel), and deterioration of morale. Strict control is exercised over all school activities: meetings, clubs, cultural events, extracurricular activities, and even sports.

Two 1981 reports published in the United States, one in the magazine *Science* and the other in the professional journal *Chronicle of Higher Education*, cite some of the difficulties in higher education. For example, the military government refused to allow the Bir Zeit University library to acquire some 2,000 books and magazines written in Arabic and published in Arab countries. The military government also claims the right to ban anti-Israeli and anti-Zionist publications that it feels might encourage violence. Ironically, many of the banned periodicals are on the shelves of the Hebrew University in Jerusalem. The banned books range widely from Palestinian folklore to Islamic thought and include such titles as *The Islamic Dictionary* and *Arab Society and the Palestine Question*.[27] A committee of Israeli professors at the Hebrew University has, on a number of occasions, protested such book banning. The harassment of the Palestinian universities continues and is chronicled periodically in special reports in the *Journal of Palestine Studies*.

Although there were challenges to the autonomy of these Palestinian institutions throughout the occupation, in 1977, in the wake of Menachem Begin's election when a new wave of Israeli settlement construction brought heightened protest, much of it from students, severe new challenges emerged. In the summer of 1980, the Israeli military government issued Order No. 854, which denied the autonomy of all the colleges and placed them under direct military control. Since then the schools have been required to obtain annual licenses, revocable at will by the Israelis, and they have had to live with new rules giving the army the power to pass on the hiring and firing of instructors, the admission and expulsion of students, and the nature of the academic curriculum, including the subjects taught and the textbooks used. Since 1980 no academic year was completed without incident. On several occasions Israeli intellectuals joined the protest, urging that "the Palestinian Arabs receive the same rights as we demand for ourselves, including the right to a higher education."[28]

In early November 1980, Israeli authorities closed Bir Zeit University on the grounds that the "Palestine Week" it was planning would provoke violence. Planned were nationalistic plays, poetry readings, and songs. Several Israeli professors connected with Arabic studies had expected to participate. On November 18, a few days after the closing, Israeli troops broke up a student protest and shot eleven Arab students in the legs. After reopening for the new term, the university was closed once again in November 1981. University closings have become a regular feature of the continuing clash between nationalist sentiment among Palestinian students and Israeli attempts to contain or eradicate it.[29]

Bir Zeit, with over 1,000 students, is the best known of the five Palestinian universities in the West Bank. In addition to its educational responsibilities, it sees its mission among Palestinians in much the same way as early Jewish settlers saw the role of the Hebrew University—to create a national identity. The other schools, An-Najah University in Nablus, Bethlehem University, Hebron University, Hebron Polytechnic, and the Islamic University in Gaza, perceive similar roles for their staffs and students. Nationalist commitment is high in each center and the universities have come to play an increasingly important role in the intellectual and political life of the Palestinian community.

The Bir Zeit administration reports that the military government withheld permission or refused to reply to requests for residence permits for teachers coming from other countries to work at the university. This has caused inconvenience and scheduling difficulties, since teachers, if they come anyway on shorter-term visas issued at the border, must apply for extensions, and if these extensions are not granted, the teachers are forced to leave the country.

Universities on the West Bank need permits to develop any new programs. For example, approval has been refused for establishing agricultural and engineering schools at An-Najah University in Nablus. Bethlehem University, a Vatican-sponsored institution, was denied permission to open a program to train tour guides in its school of hotel management.

While for the most part not harsh in the sense of being violent (however, a number of university students have been shot and several killed), the Israeli control of West Bank education has been arbitrary and at times punitive. It has interfered with the building of institutions to serve the long-run educational and intellectual needs of the Palestinian residents. Sahar Khalifah, a Bir Zeit instructor and talented novelist, expressed the problem this way in a seminar sponsored by the International Writers' Program at the University of Iowa in 1978:

> Tension inside, tension outside . . . you feel you are in a whirlpool, a whirlwind, a pressure cooker . . . Occupation, demonstrations, news, trials, prisons, demolished houses, demolished souls. Taxes . . . a new devaluation, a new settlement there; tomorrow they'll build a new one here. Where shall I go then? To whom shall I protest?[30]

Almost as soon as the *intifadah* began in December 1987, Israeli authorities started closing schools—elementary, secondary, and college level—both state schools and private institutions. Through much of the spring and fall terms of 1988 *all* schools were closed in the West Bank with only brief periods when elementary schools were opened. Schools in Gaza, however, had many fewer interruptions. The universities remained shut into the winter of 1988, although the lower schools had a brief period of being open late in the new term. Israeli authorities claimed, probably with some justification, that the schools and colleges had become rallying points for resistance activities and that young people had become particularly active in the uprising. Whether, from the Israeli perspective, students out of school and on the streets were safer is debatable. But it became clear that closing the schools was not only a preventive measure but a punitive one as well. Israeli authorities banned the informal gathering of students in homes or community institutions where teachers and parents had organized an impressive program of supplementary or alternative educational activities. The military forcibly broke up nonclassroom elementary, high school, and college sessions, even those organized for students in the final year of degree programs. On a number of occasions both teachers and students were arrested when found in makeshift schools.

For Palestinians, who are among the most highly educated people in the Arab world, education has special meaning; interference with schooling is an important deprivation. But there is another side to the educational success of the Palestinian community in the occupied territories; students are overeducated for the few jobs that exist under the occupation. With restrictions on the development of industry and the professions, many graduates who remain in the occupied territories cannot obtain jobs commensurate with their educational achievement.

THE *INTIFADAH*

The incident that is credited with triggering the uprising—an Israeli military truck ramming a Palestinian van and killing four of its occupants—occurred December 8, 1987, near the northern edge of the Gaza Strip. The rebellion against Israeli occupation erupted the following day in demonstrations and stone throwing in Gaza and spread rapidly into the West Bank on December 10 and 11. Israel at first responded as though this was no more than another in the steady stream of minor demonstrations against occupation— the Defense Minister remained out of the country, claiming all would be well in several days. As weeks and then months of Palestinian revolt and Israeli attempts to quell it went by, it became clear that a new stage in Israeli–Palestinian confrontation had been reached and that the status quo of the occupation was untenable.

The very magnitude of the revolt and the intensity of the suppression of it have all the marks of a broad movement for national liberation. The *Boston Globe* in December 1988 reported that 350 Palestinians had been killed since the uprising began twelve months earlier. Al-Haq estimated that more than 20,000 Palestinians were wounded during the first year. It is conservatively estimated that by the end of December 1988 more than 6,000 prisoners remained in Israeli prisons and detention centers (Al-Haq believes the number is closer to 10,000), that since the *intifadah* began a total of over 19,000 Palestinians have been arrested and held for anywhere from several days to several months.

If the uprising came as a surprise, at another level it seemed long delayed. The basic cause was the occupation itself. While there had been continuing resistance since 1967 (it is estimated that more than 200,000 Palestinians had passed through Israeli prisons in the twenty-one years of occupation), the older generation had come to terms with Israeli occupation without accepting it. But these many years had created deep frustrations. There was a continuing pattern of land confiscation; the military-run system of law was widely considered to be unjust; basic political freedoms were denied; political leaders were harassed, arrested, and deported; all political organizations were banned; collective punishment was common, including the demolition of houses, uprooting of trees and orchards, curfews; severe travel restrictions often brought about long separation of families; and, finally, the economy was managed in an exploitive manner: taxation was unequal and there was no representation in the collecting and spending of tax money; wage inequities, restrictions on economic and industrial development were prevalent; and there were severe limitations on exports and imports that created a privileged market for Israeli products.

The *intifadah* marked a significant turn in the Israeli–Arab conflict; it brought the confrontation back to the territory of Palestine/Israel itself and marked a strong shift to Palestinianization of the conflict.[31] Partial Arab disengagement occurred at the Arab summit in Amman, Jordan, in November 1987, just before the *intifadah*, when the Palestinian issue was relegated to a clear second place behind the Iran–Iraq war and the Palestinian leadership was visibly snubbed by several Arab leaders. These events, watched from across the border on Jordanian TV in many West Bank Palestinian homes, strengthened the hand of those who had given up

believing that Arab diplomacy would bring an end to Israeli occupation and were convinced that Palestinian initiatives were
needed.

A new generation of Palestinians in the occupied territories,
having given up on outside help and not having much faith in the
efforts of local "notables" to change the situation, had begun in
the late 1970s to build local organizations in the towns, villages,
and refugee camps to meet daily needs. They encouraged broad
participation and were decentralized in organization, decision making, and leadership in order to remain less vulnerable to Israeli
harassment or arrests.[32]

The women's groups and the Medical Relief Committee have
nearly a decade of organizational experience and have been especially effective at the local level. The Medical Relief Committee,
for example, involves some 800 health professionals, including 315
physicians, mobile clinics, and local centers in villages and refugee
camps. The group cared for 2,000 patients in 1982, 50,000 in 1987,
and 28,000 during the first five months of the uprising.[33] There are
also active youth organizations, community centers, labor unions,
and agricultural groups. In all these groups, leadership is elected
(and there is turnover) on the basis of merit and skill. The various
Palestinian nationalist factions, primarily Fatah, the Popular Front
for the Liberation of Palestine (PFLP), the Democratic Front for
the Liberation of Palestine (DFLP), and the Palestine Communist
Party, have all been involved in organizing some of these grassroots groups, but in other cases professional organizations have
had primary responsibility. All this indicates that there was a community structure and organizational network capable of responding
to the spontaneous uprising. It is also the reason the military authorities in the occupied territories have now banned all community
organizations and unions and harassed or arrested many of their
leaders.

The leadership of the uprising is much harder to characterize,
primarily because it is out of sight. Responding to Israel's policy
of arresting and/or deporting identifiable Palestinian political leaders, the new generation of younger political activists has maintained a much lower profile and the Unified National Leadership,
which emerged during the *intifadah*, is invisible and known only
by the leaflets, or *bayanaa*, it produces, which include calls for

strikes, boycotts, demonstrations, resignations from councils and police forces, opposition to tax collecting, and pressure on known collaborators. They have explicitly banned some forms of opposition, such as the use of firearms, and have encouraged others, such as throwing stones at army patrols and acts of civil disobedience. What is known is that each of the four major factions is represented by one delegate, probably rotating often, thereby thwarting the efforts of the occupation authorities to seize the leadership.

One of the continuing imperatives has been to recognize the limits of popular response. As one member of the leadership put it early in the uprising, "We don't make demands that people won't follow. We know the pulse of the street."[34] Support for the uprising appears to be quite broad. Few would have dared predict at the beginning that it could sustain itself for so many months; the Israelis on several occasions pronounced it over, especially after large-scale arrests, only to face another upsurge. The impressive unity of the merchants in observing the leadership-mandated opening and closing hours and the response to the various and frequent calls for strike days indicate that the uprising is not an effort on the part of the young stone throwers alone. The declaration by rural villages that they are liberated zones, and their flying the Palestinian flag until the next army patrol ripped it down, showed that the uprising was not limited to urban areas, traditional sites of political engagement. Judging from the large numbers of wounded, killed, and imprisoned, it is probable that no Palestinian family has been uninvolved or unaffected by the uprising.

The main achievement of the uprising in its first year, and quite clearly the main target of the Israeli military government, has been the establishment in the occupied territories of a "condition of dual power," precariously maintained but nonetheless in place.[35] The strikes, boycotts, tax resistance, discipline, are all signs of an alternate source of authority. A second achievement, which many Israelis allude to, is the reestablishment of the Green Line—the pre-June 1967 boundary—as a functional (and symbolic?) dividing line. Few Israelis venture into Arab East Jerusalem or the Arab sector of the Old City; virtually none except the settlers travel to West Bank or Gaza cities and historic sites. On any given day large sectors of the territories are declared "closed military zones" and off-limits even to journalists. Meron Benvenisti, former administrator of the Old City of Jerusalem (1970–74) and deputy mayor of Jerusalem (1967–78), related a personal experience that suggests the impact of these changes:

> Late one afternoon in March I was driving to the Hebrew University campus on Mount Scopus. Suddenly, as I was waiting near Damascus Gate for the traffic light to change, I made a decision: Instead of driving directly as usual, through the Arab section, I turned left, taking "the Jewish way"—through safe Jewish neighborhoods.
> It was at this moment, I realized with astonishment, that I had succumbed to the Geography of Fear.[36]

While Palestinian workers continued to come to jobs in Israel, their attendance was uncertain. Further, by interfering with Israel's large network of Palestinian informers in the occupied territories the *intifadah* has greatly weakened Israel's ability to control the population. By the end of October 1988, nine reputed informers were killed and many others had either publicly repented or fled their villages.[37]

The major immediate goal of the *intifadah* was to demonstrate to Israel that continued occupation was untenable. The political meaning of the action in the streets was spelled out in a document presented at a press conference on January 14, 1988, at the National Palace Hotel in East Jerusalem, by a group of "visible" Palestinian spokespersons.[38] "The conclusion to be drawn from this uprising," the document read in its preamble, "is that the present state of affairs in the Palestinian-occupied territories is unnatural and that Israeli occupation cannot continue forever. Real peace cannot be achieved except through recognition of Palestinian national rights, including the right of self-determination and the establishment of an independent Palestinian state on Palestinian national soil." A UN-supervised international peace conference that would include PLO participation was given direct support. Beyond these broad policies, fourteen specific demands were advanced to "prepare the atmosphere" for negotiations to resolve, in a just and lasting manner, the Palestinian question. They called for release of prisoners, an end to the "iron fist" of occupation, withdrawal of troops from populated areas, adherence to the Fourth Geneva Convention, a cessation of expulsions, lifting restrictions on political freedoms, and allowing neutrally supervised municipal elections; they further demanded the end of restrictions on building permits, industrial licenses, and agricultural development programs; contacts between residents of the occupied territories and the PLO must be permitted and participation in the Palestine National Council should be allowed. In part these demands concern immediate local problems, but they also suggest the explicit connection between the Palestinians of the territories and the PLO. The initial text, prepared by those inside, was first shared with the PLO executive committee before it was made public.[39] Elements of this list of fairly pragmatic points were repeated on several occasions, indicating broad support on the Palestinian side. The Israelis, throughout the first year of the *intifadah*, either ignored or rejected them. No attempts were made to enter into local or limited negotiations. As one American official, based in Jerusalem, commented, the Israelis' response to the uprising was "all stick and no carrot."

In regard to long-range goals, most analysts found Palestinian unanimity for a peace based on two states, Israeli and Palestinian, living side by side. While a few PLO elements, particularly those from the Popular Front (PFLP), have been quoted both inside the territories and from their Damascus headquarters as endorsing the two-state formula only as an interim measure, others responded, "Interim to what?"[40] In the occupied territories a pragmatic realism has taken hold. The residents "know" the Israelis; they deal with them regularly and recognize their military strength. They accept that Israel as a state is there to stay and see that their task is to negotiate a peace settlement that also allows for the realization of Palestinian national aspirations.

One note of uncertainty, however, must be added. Islamic groups, particularly strong in the Gaza Strip, on several occasions during the summer and fall of 1988 issued independent statements sounding much more rejectionist in tone. The Islamic Resistance Movement, operating under the name Hamas (an acronym for their name in Arabic: Harakat al-Muqawama al-Islamiyya), has called for an Islamic state in all of Palestine, objected to any compromise with Israel, and on several occasions issued leaflets of its own announcing different strike days from those of the Unified National Leadership. The cooperation between the Islamic and the more secular leadership that existed during the early months of the *intifadah*, but faltered during the summer, seemed to have been restored by early fall. For a short time it appeared that some Israeli leaders tolerated, or even approved of, the rejectionist tone of Hamas as a way of undermining the much more pragmatic tone of the central leadership, and perhaps splitting an otherwise remarkably unified movement. In any case, the press noted that the Islamic leaders, who were visible and known, had not been arrested during the summer. This changed in early fall, when many of those same leaders were imprisoned.[41]

Response to the uprising has been mixed. In Israel the major operational reaction has been to resort to military steps to put down any public manifestations and to reestablish full control over the territories. The policy announced by Defense Minister Yitzhak Rabin in mid-January 1988 of "force, might, and beatings" has gone through several variants, but has remained largely intact. While international criticism had the effect, from time to time, of altering the form of force used—e.g., from tear gas and beatings to lead bullets, to rubber bullets, to plastic bullets—the intent, as Rabin put it in September, was to wound as many as possible (while keeping the death toll low) in order to dissuade demonstrators and rock throwers. A variety of civil measures were also taken to thwart the various forms of Palestinian civil disobedience and noncooperation. For example, during the harvest season the residents of Beit Omar, a village south of Jerusalem, were denied their usual permits to market their plums and were instead forced to leave them to rot. This cost the village an estimated 90 percent of its annual income.[42]

At the political level in Israel no visible steps were taken by the "unity" government. The Prime Minister, Yitzhak Shamir, of the Likud Party, favored strong methods; the Defense Minister, Yitzhak Rabin, of Labor, carried out strong punitive measures, and the Foreign Minister, Shimon Peres of Labor, unable to criticize the actions of his fellow party leader Rabin, remained largely silent. They all presumably were focused on the November 1988 elections. Political parties on the left, such as Ratz (Citizens Rights Movement), put forward a steady barrage of criticism and exposed some of the most flagrant violations of human and civil rights. But Israeli public opinion as a whole supported the harsh policies.

A *Newsweek* poll, January 18, 1988, found 46 percent of the

Israeli public in full support of the tough means used to suppress the demonstrations; another 40 percent thought the government too soft; only 7 percent considered the policies too harsh. This "hard line" response has continued. Indeed, subsequent polls indicated that the political right had gained. But a contradictory and more hopeful side to Israeli opinion was demonstrated in another poll, conducted by the Israel-based Continuing Survey. Even while it found an "inclination to continue the policy of Jewish colonisation" of the territories there was a marked increase through the months of the *intifadah* of a willingness "to relinquish some part of the West Bank in return for peace": March 1987—54 percent; February 1988—57 percent; June 1988—62 percent; October 1988—65 percent.[43] This same contradiction is found among a number of the senior military officers in charge of suppressing the rebellion. They do their job, but readily admit that there is no military solution to the uprising, only a political one.[44]

Israeli protest activity escalated during the months of the uprising. At least seventy-five peace groups (albeit some quite small and others with overlapping membership) have been identified. They fall into four major categories: (1) those which were active or had roots prior to the *intifadah*: Peace Now, the largest group, organized to support the Camp David initiative in 1978; Year 21, an activist breakaway from Peace Now willing to engage in civil disobedience; Association for Civil Rights in Israel (ACRI), which supports legal efforts to assist Palestinians; Yesh G'vul (There Is a Boundary), which came into being to protest Israel's invasion of Lebanon, many of whose members refuse military or reserve duty beyond the Green Line; Dai Lakibush (Enough of the Occupation), which grew out of the early 1980s Committee for Solidarity with Bir Zeit; Hala Hakibush (Away! with the Occupation), made up largely of young people and high school students; a series of women's groups—Israeli Women Against the Occupation and Women in Black (who conduct a weekly public demonstration); (2) new professionally oriented groups, an Inter-University Committee for a Political Solution (some 1,200 faculty members); Council for Peace and Security (some 130 retired generals and colonels of the Israeli Defense Forces); organizations of psychologists and social workers, lawyers, writers and artists, and psychiatrists; (3) a series of new ad hoc groups focusing on specific incidents or needs: Committee for the People of Beita (the village where an Israeli youth was accidentally killed by an Israeli guard, leading to military demolition of fourteen houses, destruction of crops, and other punitive measures); Committee Against Administrative Detention; a Legal Aid Committee (all these groups work cooperatively with Palestinian groups and individuals); (4) grassroots groups which are organized as a movement and seek continuity, such as Israelis by Choice (immigrants largely from North America and Western Europe who fear that Israeli democracy will be shattered). An important shift in political strategy has occurred in a number of the groups, from affecting government policy to establishing longer-term alliances and cooperative working arrangements with Palestinians. In turn, as the uprising continued, there has been greater willingness on the part of Palestinians to become directly involved with Israeli protest movements. Regular meetings have been arranged between groups of Israelis and residents of Palestinian towns such as Beit Sahur, Jericho, and Ramallah. Some Israeli peace groups make weekly visits to Palestinian refugee camps to express solidarity.

The efflorescence of nonparliamentary protest/peace groups in Israel has not been matched by similar activity on the right, although some organization has occurred. Gush Emunim (Bloc of the Faithful) has reactivated itself, working largely in cooperation with Israeli settlers through the Council of Judea and Samaria. Mothers for Israel is closely linked to Gush Emunim. Moledet (Homeland) is a new right-wing ultranationalist party advocating expulsion.

Israel has suffered both indirect and direct costs as a result of the *intifadah* and the state's attempts to repress it; the most obvious are international attacks on Israel's role. The UN Security Council voted unanimously against Israel's deportations (January 5 and 14, 1988—Resolutions 607 and 608), and earlier had deplored Israel's policies and practices in the occupied territories and affirmed the applicability of the Geneva Conventions (December 22, 1987—Resolution 605). UN Under-Secretary-General Marrak Golding was sent to assess the situation in January 1988 and submitted a report highly critical of Israel (Document S/19443, January 21, 1988). In early March the European Parliament in Strasbourg voted against three trade and financial protocols which would have been financially beneficial to Israel, citing Israel's repressive activities in the occupied territories. On September 13, 1988, Yasir Arafat, the PLO chairman, addressed the socialist members of the European Parliament in Strasbourg at their invitation. At its annual conference in Blackpool the British Labor Party denounced Israel's "iron fist" policy in the occupied territories, urged withdrawal from the territories occupied in 1967, and, in a gesture of solidarity, called for a PLO speaker at the 1989 conference.[45] There were numerous other signs of the costs to Israel's image internationally.

The economic and psychic costs to Israel have also been marked. Army reserve duty for all men twenty to fifty-five was lengthened from 30 to up to 65 days per year at the height of the *intifadah* in order to provide the 10,000 to 20,000 troops deployed on a daily basis in Gaza and the West Bank. This entails the loss to the civilian economy of many worker-days.[46] The U.S. embassy in Tel Aviv estimated the direct military and police costs at some $120 million per month, or almost $1.5 billion annually. Tourism, one of Israel's largest money earners, has been seriously hurt by the uprising—down by 20 percent from the previous year.[47] As Shlomo Maoz, economic editor of the *Jerusalem Post*, commented: "The damage to the tourism sector could total hundreds of millions of dollars in lost revenue."[48] Maoz also reported that the presence of Arab labor from the territories dropped by 30 to 40 percent, leading to an expected 15 percent decline in the building sector alone.[49] The *intifadah* was responsible for a 1.5 percent loss of total GNP, according to Finance Minister Moshe Nissim. A 50 percent drop in exports to the territories, which normally ran at $1 billion per year (equal to 10 percent of the total exports), was the major cause of a 3.5 percent decline in industrial production during the first quarter.[50] Direct and indirect economic costs add structural pressures to Israel's decision about whether or not to maintain the occupation—the status quo.

A final assessment of the full impact and extended implications of the *intifadah* will only be made with the passage of time, but the immediate consequences are already significant. A new and crucial phase in the Israeli–Palestinian conflict has been entered, with the actual confrontation returned to the soil of Palestine/ Israel. Israeli military control of the occupied territories has been shown to be quite vulnerable even at the significant level of force that Israel has used so far. The Palestinian nationalist movement in the territories has built a remarkable organization, possessing discipline and endurance, and the movement outside has been energized to develop new diplomatic and political efforts. The Palestinian question is high on the international agenda and has maintained a crucial prominence. The United States, the Soviet Union, European nations, and the UN have all been involved. Within Israel the critical debate over the future of the occupied territories, forced on a reluctant public, became the central issue of the election, and will almost certainly intensify as the full costs become apparent and the necessity for hard choices becomes obvious. The need for clear and direct communication between the Israelis and the Palestinians, as both search for the means to honestly meet their mutual needs, has never been more urgent.

4

The Palestinians

The 1970 AFSC study, *Search for Peace in the Middle East*, offered an important though modest assessment of how to deal with the "Palestine question."

> Recognition in practical form of a way to build community and to establish the political rights of the Palestine people is a necessary early step toward solution of the area's problems. This must be achieved straightforwardly and honestly, with full cooperation of the international community, of Israel, and of the Arab states.[1]

Almost two decades have passed and the recommendation is largely unfulfilled. While some things remain unchanged and the majority of Palestinians still live under occupation or in diaspora, there have been important developments in the Palestinian nationalist movement; a vision of pragmatic nationalism mixed with a passionate concern for justice is emerging.

But first the people. Who are and where are the Palestinians today? What elements of their lives shape the politics of their movements and the statements of their leaders? Two recent distinct experiences are critical in every Palestinian's consciousness: occupation and dispersion. Although no complete census has been taken of the Palestinians, estimates suggest that they number over 4 million. Of these, approximately 645,000 live in Israel and have become Israeli citizens since the 1949 truce. An additional 125,000 live within the expanded municipal boundaries of Jerusalem annexed by Israel shortly after the June 1967 war; most of this group have not taken Israeli citizenship, although eligible for it, since they reject the legitimacy of the annexation of Arab East Jerusalem and adjoining areas. Another 1,068,000 live in the West Bank and 633,000 are in the Gaza Strip. The largest group (about 1.3 million) living in the diaspora is in Jordan. Smaller Palestinian communities are spread throughout the Arab world; approximately 400,000 in Lebanon, 180,000 in Syria, 170,000 in Kuwait, with others in Egypt, Saudi Arabia, the Gulf states, Iran, Libya, and Tunisia. Upward of 50,000 are spread throughout the United States, Europe, and South America.[2] Approximately 20 percent of the Palestinians not living in Israel itself are still residents of the two categories of refugee camps established under the aegis of the United Nations Relief and Works Agency (UNRWA) to care for refugees who left their homes during the 1948 war. Initially it was thought that these would be temporary shelters.[3] These camps are located in Lebanon, Jordan, Syria, the West Bank, and the Gaza Strip. From those who entered the camps in the aftermath of the 1948 war, a whole generation has been born and raised and has had children of its own within the confines of the camps.[4]

PALESTINIANS IN ARAB LANDS

No single description would fit the experiences of Palestinian communities in different parts of the Arab world. They form different proportions of the populations in their host lands, ranging from 60 percent in Jordan to below 1 percent in Iraq, so that the importance of their political and social roles varies. Although Palestinians share Arabic as a common language and Islam as a common religion (except in Lebanon, Galilee, and the West Bank, where there are large Christian minorities), in the various societies in which they reside they have established very different social and political organizations and have different means of taking in and integrating Palestinians. In Jordan many had achieved full citizenship and participated in the affairs of the state (including even Cabinet membership), a result of the annexation of the West Bank by the Kingdom of Jordan after the 1949 armistice agreement. The status of the several different groups of Palestinians in the kingdom was put in some question by King Hussein's action of severing administrative and legal ties with the occupied West Bank. In other countries, however, they remain refugees or, even in the second generation, outsiders. Many live in camps or in city districts or neighborhoods which are effectively separate, and they are often discriminated against. Like other foreign nationals, they may engage in business in the Gulf and Arabian states, but a national must be either the senior partner or the business registrant. Palestinians, aware of European history, often compare their present status to that of the Jews in the ghettos of Europe. In many societies they have come to fill the role of expatriate professionals, teachers, technicians, and skilled artisans.

Because of their nationalism and the democratic and revolutionary elements of some parts of their movement, Palestinians have been politically suspect in many Arab lands and sometimes have been imprisoned for political reasons. Thus, while the Palestinian political movement has been supported for its external activities, it has been closely circumscribed in Arab host countries.

In addition, some Arab states have used or controlled Palestinian nationalist groups for their own ends. There are Syrian-, Iraqi-, and Libyan-backed Palestinian organizations; within Lebanon, the political and military operation of the PLO is mediated and constrained in large measure by the Syrian military presence. Indeed, the first Syrian involvement in the Lebanon civil war in 1976 was a battle against the PLO and the Lebanese-Muslim-Leftist alliance. Since 1982 Syria has opposed the Arafat-led PLO and directly aided several Syrian-backed Palestinian factions and anti-PLO Lebanese militias.

One Palestinian scholar who lives in the United States, Edward Said, has expressed concern with "the form of Palestinian survival." Divided, dispersed, without territorial sovereignty, distrusted, demeaned, faced by hostility everywhere, Palestinians face a problem of maintaining their identity. He comments: "A child born since 1948, therefore, asserts the original connection to lost Palestine as a bit of symbolic evidence that the Palestinians have gone on regardless: He or she would have been born there but for 1948."[5] The dispersion and the refugee camps keep alive an image of the whole of the old Palestine.

The assumption of the 1950s, widely held in the United States and elsewhere, that somehow the Palestinians would literally be absorbed into the Arab states has given way to the realization that the Palestinians are stateless exiles. The dynamics of the Middle East nationalist development have worked to increase rather than diminish Palestinian nationalism. It is even possible that the Palestinians might be accepted more easily as long-term residents in Arab lands if they had a passport and nationality of their own. Most Palestinians insist on their heritage and nationhood and claim that they do not seek permanent residence in the Arab countries.

THE OCCUPATION

The other commanding Palestinian experience since 1967 has been life under occupation. The largest single group of Palestinians now lives in day-to-day interaction with the Israeli military government. There are extensive refugee camps in the West Bank and especially Gaza, and it is in the Palestinian cities, towns, villages, and camps that there is the greatest sense of urgency to remove the occupiers. Widely accepted UN Security Council Resolutions 242 (1967) and 338 (1973), calling for withdrawal by Israel from recently occupied territories and for peace and secure borders, have been seen by some Palestinians as adding a special legitimacy to their claims for self-determination in the West Bank and the Gaza Strip.[6] But the Palestinians have been politically cautious about relying solely on these resolutions, since in them Palestinians are treated only as refugees and the explicit right of self-determination is never mentioned. The very nature of the occupation has created an international politics, an Israeli politics, and a Palestinian politics that influence the course of the development of Palestinian nationalism.

For the Palestinians who had sought the return of their entire homeland, the occupation of the West Bank and the Gaza Strip has raised a pressing question. Can they afford to wait out some grand solution to the problem of all of Palestine or will the continued occupation of the territories mean such irreversible change as to make them in fact part of Israel itself? Palestinians today find themselves at a critical juncture—to enter negotiations with Israel or to disdain them. All the signs of recent years confirm that there is a growing acceptance of the wisdom of entering negotiations with Israel that will lead to an independent and peaceful Palestinian state in the territories of the West Bank and Gaza. The resolutions of the most recent Palestine National Council meetings (April 1987 and November 1988), public statements by the leadership of the Palestinian nationalist movement, including Chairman Arafat's UN speech of December 1988, and the clear desires expressed by the activists of the *intifadah* confirm this assessment. The declaration of an independent, albeit still occupied, state in the West Bank and Gaza on November 15, 1988, was the culmination of a decade and a half of political change and compromise. The question those living under occupation ask is: "Will even this limited dream be fulfilled?"

THE PLO AND THE PALESTINIANS

Israeli leaders have often tended to belittle ideas of Palestinian national identity or to deny the existence of the Palestinians. "Who are the Palestinians?" Golda Meir asked. Begin called them the "Arabs of the Land of Israel." But in the Camp David accords, Begin initialed a document referring to the "legitimate rights of the Palestinians."[7] Now, with the full and broad support of the Palestinian people, the focus for discussion has become the Palestine Liberation Organization (PLO) and its role in the political life of the Palestinians. The United States declared that it would not deal with the PLO until it met certain conditions—recognition of Israel's right to exist, renunciation of terrorism, and acceptance of UN Security Council Resolutions 242 and 338. For Washington those were met by Arafat's December 1988 statements. Israel, however, has persisted in its refusal to consider the PLO a candidate for negotiations. For most Palestinians the PLO is *the* representative of their nationalist goals, especially in the international arena, and the Arab states, across the political spectrum, have declared that the PLO is the "sole legitimate representative of the Palestinian people."[8] The Soviet Union and many nations of the Third World accorded formal diplomatic status to the PLO, extended by many to the new Palestinian state, and most Western European nations now maintain some form of quasi-official relations with the PLO. At this time it is an illusion to maintain that some other group exists that can speak on behalf of the Palestinians or engage in any serious negotiations for Palestinians without the involvement or endorsement of the PLO. While there is not always unanimity within the PLO, it remains politically the strongest group by far among the Palestinians.

The history of the Palestinian nationalist organization is complex and interesting to those concerned with the manner in which religious, nationalist, political, social, regional, and personal factors interact to create Third World liberation movements. It is important to take into consideration the broad outlines of the history of Palestinian political organizations and to understand both the constraints they live with and the opportunities they share.

The PLO had its origins in January 1964 at the Cairo Summit of Kings and Presidents of the Arab states. The meeting had several purposes. Inter-Arab rivalries and the use which different states made of separate Palestinian groups for their own ends were troubling. The Arab states recognized the new organizational role that Palestinians would play in the resistance to Israel. The Palestine Liberation Organization was then formed to be the organizational umbrella for Palestinian liberation. There is little doubt, however, that Egyptian President Nasser continued to be the commanding influence.

After the Arab defeat in the 1967 war and the concomitant destruction of the legitimacy of much of the existing Arab leadership, the Palestinians realized the limits to their reliance on the Arab states. The 1967 defeat also reshaped Arab and Palestinian thinking about any resolution of the Palestinian question. The broader revolutionary purposes which had previously been a focus of Arab nationalist movements from Egypt to Iraq were overshadowed by the resurgence of Palestinian nationalism.

One recent study lists more than twenty Palestinian resistance groups. Among these, Fatah (Palestine National Liberation Movement) is the oldest, largest, and most influential. While it is only one of many groups of the PLO, it accounts for at least 70 percent of the membership of the umbrella group, and its leadership has assumed effective control. Fatah's membership runs the spectrum of belief and social orientation in the Palestinian community. It is more conservative than other groups and reflects a generally Arab orientation, broadly construed Islamic religious beliefs, and a politically nonaligned stance. It contains segments that are Christian and also a strong secular, socialist wing.[9] Some eight groups along with Fatah now make up the PLO. Yasir Arafat, the Fatah leader, is chairman of the PLO executive committee. In the wake of the 1967 war, the PLO filled a vacuum. To outsiders, the PLO took on the semblance of a "government-in-exile," although for many years it rejected that political role. Known in the media primarily for guerrilla activities and terrorism, the PLO has assumed responsibility for many aspects of Palestinian life, especially in refugee communities. It has established a social service system and formed a Palestinian branch of the Red Crescent (headed by a physician, the younger brother of Yasir Arafat); it created schools and operated an industrial cooperative (SAMED) in Lebanon prior to 1982.

The PLO offered a political defense for its resort to terrorism, arguing that it "gives our cause resounding coverage—positive or negative it mattered little."[10] The "terrorism" or military action (as the PLO calls it) question has been vigorously debated within the councils of the PLO, and a broad shift away from nonmilitary targets has been accepted and indeed all "terrorism" renounced. In principle, the PLO core had already adopted a policy of limiting its use of military action against Israel to military targets in the occupied territories and in Israel itself before Arafat's Geneva declarations. This principle is reinforced by the fact that the PLO's military infrastructure was largely shattered during the Israeli invasion of Lebanon in the summer of 1982.[11] The need for legitimate diplomatic and political activity acceptable to the international community further constrained the resort to either guerrilla warfare or terrorism. At the November 1988 PNC meeting, a clearer renunciation of terrorism was included in its historic statement.[12]

In the aftermath of the 1973 Arab–Israeli war, an Arab summit at Rabat, Morocco, in 1974 strengthened the PLO role and designated it as the "sole legitimate representative of the Palestinian people." This further legitimization of the Palestinian movement had several important results. It strengthened the hand of the PLO at the international level, and sanctioned it to speak for the Palestinians and to assert greater control over all aspects of the movement. This was of particular interest to all Gulf Arab oil states, the most important financial supporters of the PLO, who wanted to assure a responsible Palestinian movement. The Arab states, having achieved new self-confidence based on wealth from oil and what they conceived to be a positive military performance in the 1973 war, asserted what one observer described as a "metaphysical right" to the West Bank and Gaza.[13] This Arab support for the PLO has been interpreted as sanctioning a conservative and largely nonrevolutionary nationalism for the Palestinians.

Other elements served to shape the attitude of growing pragmatism toward the Arab–Israeli conflict in the Palestinian movement and the PLO, as well as in the Arab world as a whole. Walid Khalidi, a leading Palestinian political scientist, points to a growing awareness of the extent of the commitment the United States was willing to make to the security and well-being of Israel and conversely the limited and quite cautious Soviet support of the Arabs against Israel.[14] This realization was one influence in President Sadat's decision to break ties with the Soviets. Khalidi also points to "the growing Palestinian awareness of what the revolutionary armed struggle can and cannot achieve." This trend toward political action rather than revolutionary struggle gained greater emphasis after the PLO's withdrawal from Lebanon in 1982 and from the clear new policies emerging in the Soviet Union following Mikhail Gorbachev's rise to leadership in 1985.

The PLO has been further legitimated by the extent to which it received support from Palestinian communities in the West Bank and the Gaza Strip. As the occupation continued after 1967, the local Palestinian leadership that had been tied to Jordan during the two decades from 1948 to 1967 began to grow weaker. Jordanian influence suffered further erosion following the September 1970 clash between Jordan and the PLO, during which the PLO military and political leadership was forced to leave Jordan and move to Lebanon. The influence of Jordan as spokesman for Palestinian interests decreased. A very detailed poll of West Bank and Gaza public opinion, in July and August 1986, sponsored by *Newsday*, the Australian Broadcasting Corporation, and the East Jerusalem daily *Al-Fajr*, demonstrated the very weak support for Jordan (3 percent) as compared with the PLO (93 percent).[15] The Israeli occupation helped create a distinct Palestinian consciousness in the territories and gave focus to a struggle against the occupier. When traditional Palestinian leaders failed to win political concessions from Israel, they were replaced by more explicitly nationalist leaders. As one Israeli analyst assessed the situation: "Israeli policy with regard to the question of Palestinian leadership proved to be counter-productive."[16] Limiting local leaders to purely municipal affairs, deporting over 2,000 leading Palestinians, banning public political meetings, and expecting broader Palestinian issues to be handled by the Jordanians thoroughly undermined the credibility of the traditional West Bank leadership. This trend reached a dramatic climax during the uprising in the occupied territories which began in December 1987. By the end of July 1988, King Hussein bowed to what had become obvious: he could not represent the Palestinians of the territories. As a senior figure in the palace in Amman noted in September 1988: the uprising was not only against Israel but also against the pro-Jordanian leadership of the West Bank; it represented a form of "class warfare."[17] The Israeli acceleration of land expropriation and Jewish settlements in the territories only strengthened these trends. During the late 1970s and the 1980s the PLO continued to rise to broad recognition and legitimacy in the Arab world as well as internationally. It was through the political interests of the Arab states and the Palestinian people that the PLO came to be accepted as the obvious and sole coordinator of Palestinian unity.

In 1976 the Israelis set municipal elections for the West Bank with the clear hope that a moderate leadership not linked to the PLO would emerge and provide an alternative Palestinian voice in the occupied territories.[18] Initially, the Palestinians rejected participation in the electoral process as part of their boycott of Israeli rule, but at the last moment they relented. They elected to municipal office an almost complete slate of Palestinian nationalist leaders, many fresh political faces, and primarily PLO supporters. Seventy-two percent of the eligible electorate went to the polls and overwhelmingly supported the new nationalist leadership, a victory that stunned the Israeli government.[19] Bassam Shak'a, the new mayor of Nablus, made the point: "The elections proved clearly that the Palestinians believe their sole legal representative to be the PLO."[20] Israel had underestimated the growing nationalism of the Palestinians and ignored the changes taking place in the second Palestinian generation. Educated and independent, this generation was ready to break with an earlier compliant generation and to vote for new leadership. The Israeli unwillingness to understand that Palestinian nationalism and support for the PLO were potent forces was continued by the Likud government when it came to power in May 1977. Begin's government, with its ideological commitment to maintain sovereignty over the occupied territories, which it referred to by their biblical names, Judea and Samaria, rejected territorial compromise. It further sought to prevent Palestinian self-expression. The pro-PLO leadership in the West Bank gained popular support; it was strengthened by Israel's repressive acts, and became an increasingly important political voice in both the international Palestinian nationalist movement and the PLO. But within several years all but one of the elected mayors (Elias Freij of Bethlehem) had been deposed or deported.

Public support for the PLO leadership also came in statements and resolutions from West Bank voluntary societies, student groups, and professional organizations. In September and October 1978, in response to the search for some alternate Palestinian leadership to join in the Camp David process, the Arab Graduates Union, the Union of Professional Societies, students at the Teacher Training Institute in Ramallah, Bir Zeit University, and An-Najah University adopted a resolution reaffirming the unity of the Palestinian people and maintaining that the PLO is their sole legitimate representative. They also rejected Begin's "self-rule" proposal and called instead for self-determination, national independence, and Israeli withdrawal from the occupied territories and East Jerusalem.[21]

It is important to note that even during this period political consciousness had changed and the Palestinian statements generally limited their calls to Israeli withdrawal from the West Bank and Gaza, with Palestinian self-determination to be exercised only in these areas. Hebron mayor Fahd Qawasmi, even after he was deported, explicitly indicated that his vision was of Palestine living alongside Israel: "When I say I support the idea of two states this means mutual recognition and normalization."[22] But he cautioned that he was expressing a personal view and that he could not speak for the PLO. Nonetheless, his politics and his constituency were an important influence on PLO decision making. As we have seen, this trend has gained clear political dominance and has now become basic Palestinian nationalist policy.

What does the PLO believe? Yasir Arafat suggested the pattern of policy change through which his organization has gone. In an interview with *The New York Times*, May 8, 1980, he is quoted: "We are the only victims who have offered two solutions; in 1967 we suggested a democratic secular state, but people said we wanted to demolish Israel, so we offered another solution. We said that we have the right to establish our independent state in any land from which the Israelis withdraw or we have liberated."[23] This became the familiar formula that Arafat and much of the rest of the PLO have used in recent years. In the years 1982 through 1988 this position has been sharpened. In the several stages of the on-going peace process, the Palestinian commitment to the limited goal of an independent state in the West Bank and Gaza gained more formal acceptance, culminating in the flurry of political and diplomatic activity in late 1988 in wake of the *intifadah*. The resolution adopted by the Palestine National Council on November 15, 1988, details the new political program: an independent Palestinian state, the acceptance of UN Security Council Resolution 242 and Resolution 338 as the basis for negotiations in an international conference, and the acceptance of the partition of Palestine into two states. On a number of occasions the PLO has accepted the concept of security provisions, including joint superpower guarantees, demilitarized zones, and UN peacekeeping forces within the Palestinian state.[24] These issues, including careful consideration of security concerns, have been discussed in ever-greater detail by Palestinians regarded as close to the PLO.[25]

In recent years Yasir Arafat and other leaders of the PLO have moved from their very restricted contacts with Israelis and have engaged in discussions with numerous Israelis, not limited to "progressive forces," but including many active Zionists. (Ironically, Israel recently sought to block this trend by declaring it illegal for Israelis to engage in direct contact with PLO officials and has brought several individuals to trial.) On the politically sensitive question of explicit recognition of Israel, the PLO maintained a studied ambiguity until late 1988. As Arafat put it on numerous occasions, recognition was the Palestinian "trump card," which he would not play without some form of recognition in return. This finally came in the form of Washington's willingness to engage the PLO in substantive dialogue, but the pattern and movement of policy had been evident for some time as the PLO slowly moved toward a new and pragmatic policy of explicit recognition of Israel. The *intifadah* had a strong influence in propelling this policy to a conclusion.

Critics of the PLO can and do point to the Palestine National Covenant, written in 1964 and amended in 1968, which declared the original UN partition of 1947 illegal (Article 19) and called for the liberation of Palestine and the elimination of the Zionist presence in Palestine (Article 15).[26] In response, Palestinian leaders claim that the history of decisions taken subsequently by the Palestine National Council (often referred to as "Parliament-in-Exile") has superseded the earlier Covenant.[27] The accumulated evidence suggests a shift in the PLO and Palestinian position from the extreme claims of 1968, when the revised Palestinian Covenant was adopted, to the more forthcoming and pragmatic statements of the 17th PNC (Amman, November 1984) and the 18th and 19th PNC (Algiers, April 1987 and November 1988). The latter two both accept the terms of the Arab Peace Plan agreed to at Fez, Morocco, in September 1982, which provided for "guarantees for peace for all the states of the region, including the independent Palestinian state."[28] The 1988 session went further in accepting UN Security Council Resolution 242 and partition. This was capped by Arafat's explicit recognition of Israel's right to exist in his Geneva UN address and press conference in December 1988. Careful consideration of the changing political base and the altered sense of current realities strongly suggests that the newer conceptualizations—a limited Palestinian state in the West Bank and the Gaza Strip—were not merely tactical formulations. Basic shifts in the PLO stance have developed over time.[29] By reversing their former position as enunciated in the Covenant and accepting the legitimacy of the 1947 UN partition resolution (181) and placing this in the context of Resolutions 242 and 338, the PLO has sharply limited its claims for self-determination to the occupied territories and accepted the internationally sanctioned boundaries of Israel. In the context of these profound political shifts the Covenant has been functionally replaced. It may well be formally replaced by the documents drafted to establish a provisional government. This move would lend even greater clarity to Palestinian nationalist intentions.

These changes did not come quickly, though they were obviously entertained for several years after the 1967 war. In 1972 King Hussein of Jordan proposed retrieving the West Bank and federating it with Jordan. During this period, the Palestine National Council rejected the suggestion of a ministate for Palestine.[30] In part its resolutions rejecting this were implied criticisms of King Hussein. But it was probably his suggestion that triggered the new Palestinian attitudes. The Palestinian leadership was fearful that if the West Bank was returned to Jordan, the Palestine question would be perceived to be resolved and the PLO would have forfeited its role in deciding the fate of its people.

A significant change in the PLO position can be dated from the period immediately following the 1973 Arab–Israeli war. As early as November 1973, Eric Rouleau, veteran Middle East correspondent for *Le Monde*, described new attitudes among the PLO leadership. Fatah leaders, including Arafat, told him that they needed time "to prepare the grass roots psychologically for recognizing a state whose destruction they have pledged for over a quarter of a century."[31]

The 12th meeting of the PNC in June 1974 saw the first signs of an official reformulation. A resolution, still couched in the language of self-determination for the whole land, spoke also of establishing an "independent combatant national authority over every part of Palestinian territory that is liberated."[32] A variety of statements and resolutions by Palestinian leaders continued for several years to present a mosaic of ambiguous views. The concept of a democratic secular state in all of Palestine was dropped, however, and instead "an independent Palestinian state" became the goal. Said Hammami, the PLO representative in London, noted in 1975 that "the Palestinian Arabs must recognize the fact that there is an Israeli people and this people has a right to live in peace in what they consider to be their own country."[33] (Said Hammami was later assassinated by an Iraqi-sponsored squad.) About this same time, Dr. Issam Sartawi, an independent among the PLO leadership, began discussions with Israeli moderate Zionists, initially under the aegis of former French Premier Pierre Mendès-France and later with the aid of Austrian Prime Minister Bruno Kreisky. (It is sad to note that Sartawi was also assassinated, in April 1983, while attending a meeting of the Socialist Internationalist in Portugal, presumably by agents of the extremist Abu

Nidal faction.) These contacts continued despite criticism from some Palestinian "rejectionists," who refuse any dealings with Israel. A PNC resolution of July 1981 sought to restrict contacts to progressive Jews and anti-Zionists. This was altered by April 1987 to allow contacts with Israelis who would support the cause of Palestinian self-determination (Resolution III-7). Another change, although ambiguous, came in March 1977, at the 13th PNC meeting. Resolution 11 expressed the Council's determination to pursue the struggle to establish their independent national state.[34] However, they still rejected explicit recognition of Israel as a price for a settlement of the conflict. Unofficial attempts to have the United States and the PLO engage in a dialogue began in this period and have continued since, with success coming only in December 1988. The U.S. formula for permitting itself to override its commitment to Israel not to negotiate with the PLO was to secure PLO recognition of Israel's right to exist, its acceptance of UN Security Council Resolutions 242 and 338, and its rejection of terrorism. Out of the 19th PNC meeting also came intensive diplomatic efforts by the PLO to gain international political support. The results over the years, from the Palestinian point of view, have been highly successful, and some 105 nations have recognized the PLO and given it a status equivalent to that of a government-in-exile. The move to gain recognition for the newly declared independent state of Palestine proved to be more difficult. While over seventy nations responded fairly rapidly (largely from the Arab world, nonaligned nations, and the socialist bloc), other countries made generally positive statements but held back from recognition. Israel launched a diplomatic campaign to head off recognition and the United States urged its allies and friends to reject the new state.

Among important international diplomatic efforts in 1977 was an October joint statement of the United States and the Soviet Union drafted by Secretary of State Cyrus Vance and Foreign Minister Andrei Gromyko. While it is not a Palestinian document, it has frequently been referred to by Palestinians as an acceptable basis for peace. Israeli withdrawal to the approximate pre-1967 borders was envisioned as part of a comprehensive settlement that assumed the need for Israeli security and the legitimate rights of the Palestinian people. The statement included several proposals, including demilitarized zones, UN troop involvement, and joint superpower guarantees to protect the borders of all nations in the region. The Palestinians were to be represented at a Geneva conference.[35] Israel objected vigorously to the formulation, and within a month Egyptian President Sadat made his surprising visit to Jerusalem. The Camp David meetings and subsequent accords made the statement moot and marked a significant shift in the U.S. approach to support bilateral, step-by-step negotiations, and effectively cut the Soviet Union out of the peace process.

The Palestinians gathered at Tripoli in December 1977 in response to the Sadat mission and issued a statement, belligerent in tone, and seeming to pull back from diplomatic efforts. The representatives, including those from Palestinian rejectionist groups, did, however, agree to "strive for the realization of the Palestinian people's right to return and to self-determination within the context of an independent Palestinian state on any part of Palestinian land without reconciliation, recognition or negotiations as an interim aim of the Palestinian Revolution."[36]

The PLO was clearly fearful of being closed out of any peace process and thus hardened its position and rejected the legitimacy of the Camp David process. In part at least, these fears were confirmed by the restrictive autonomy proposal that Begin announced after Sadat's visit. It is also important to note, however, that the PLO explicitly included in this strident statement the concept of an independent state on part of the land of Palestine. Reinforcing this statement were not only international agreements for outside support but strong approval of the West Bank Palestinians and those in the PLO who firmly agreed to a limited Palestinian state. The rejectionist groups in the PLO expressed their views in the formal resolutions of January 1979. Palestinian nationalism has many faces. The language in the resolutions of the parliament-like PNC has something in it for everyone. However, in the commentaries and public statements of the PLO leadership and their close supporters more subtlety is introduced, and to understand the PLO and Palestinian policy, it is necessary to read these with care.

In 1979–80, senior PLO leaders, including Yasir Arafat and Khalid al-Hassan, became involved in a series of initiatives in Europe, ranging from meetings with Chancellor Bruno Kreisky of Austria and former German Chancellor Willy Brandt to contacts with then French President Valéry Giscard d'Estaing and British Foreign Minister Lord Carrington. The PLO brought to these meetings a plan for Israeli withdrawal from the occupied territories and a UN–PLO-coordinated plan for self-determination by the Palestinian people, including the right to establish a state. Of particular interest in this plan, prepared initially by al-Hassan, was the involvement of the UN, the United States, the Soviet Union, and member nations of the European Economic Community. In addition, al-Hassan proposed that the UN Charter and Declaration of Human Rights and "all UN resolutions regarding the Palestinian issue and the Zionist-Palestinian conflict" be the basis of any solution. He also referred to several anti-Zionist General Assembly resolutions. Acceptance of UN Security Council Resolution 242 was implied but not made explicit. The critics noted, however, the plan's inclusion of "the principle of the right to pursue through democratic means the reunification of Palestine in a single Palestinian state."[37] This statement showed pragmatic realism, accepting a limited state in the short run while holding out the right to renegotiate reunification of Palestine in the future. By stipulating that "democratic means" were those to be used to achieve what Arafat in his UN speech of 1974 called his "dream" of a unified Palestine, the PLO was responding to Israeli fears of violence and to international concern for peaceful resolution of the conflict. The PLO in this statement is implying that any further claims must be negotiated and not pursued by force. This "dream" of an ultimately unified Palestine has been conspicuously dropped from PLO statements and speeches in recent years. There has been no sign of it in resolutions passed at recent meetings of the PNC.

The European Community meeting in Venice on June 13, 1980, responded to the Palestinian contacts with a statement on how to resolve the Arab–Israeli conflict. As a result of American entreaties to the European Community not to undermine the Camp David process, the "European Initiative" that emerged was quite mild. It endorsed a role for the United Nations and supported the concept of Palestinian self-determination. While viewed as generally sympathetic to the Palestinian cause, the European statement did not explicitly support a Palestinian state; and while not recognizing the PLO, it did say the PLO should be associated with the solution.[38]

A review of the evolution of PLO policies leaves us with the feeling that each full step forward has been followed by a half step back. However, there is a consistent theme—support for an independent state. What about its borders, or its relations with Israel? In the middle of one of the debates at the PNC in March 1977 when Dr. Issam Sartawi was sharply criticized for holding meetings with Zionist members of the Israel Council for Israeli–Palestinian Peace, Arafat, addressing a Palestinian audience, supported Sartawi for his work with an Israeli group. He said, "Are you willing to live together with the Jews? If not, you are using false slogans, since the day the Palestinian state will be created, we shall have to live with the Jews side by side and in peace."[39] Pragmatic language and politics have come to mark PLO discussions. In an important statement, written by Bassam abu Sharif (a close adviser to Yasir Arafat) and circulated at the Arab League Summit at Algiers in June 1988, some of the most far-reaching claims were made:

> Israel's objectives are lasting peace and security. Lasting peace and security are also the objectives of the Palestinian people. No one can understand the Jewish people's century of suffering more than the Palestinians. . . . We feel that no people—neither the Jewish people nor the Palestinian people—deserve the abuse and disenfranchisement that hopelessness inevitably entails. We believe that all peoples—the Jewish and the Palestinian included—have the right to run their own affairs, expecting from their neighbors not only non-belligerence, but the kind of political and economic cooperation without which no state can be truly secure. . . . The PLO . . . does accept Resolutions 242 and 338. What prevents it from saying so unconditionally is not what is in the Resolutions, but what is not in them . . . the national rights of the Palestinian people."[40]

Sharif's words were greeted at the time with great interest and applauded by many in the United States (including a small group of prominent leaders of the Jewish community) and welcomed as a good sign by the Israeli peace movement. They were shrugged off by the Israeli government. While the rejectionist Palestinians, largely in Damascus, vigorously criticized the statement for its conciliatory tone, it initially gained only indirect support from Arafat himself. The statement did indicate the seriousness with which peace moves were being pursued within the Palestinian nationalist leadership. Arafat followed this initiative with his September 1988 speech to the European Parliament, and while not as explicit in its conciliatory proposals, it marked a continuation of the new diplomatic efforts. But this was all preparation for the politically important decisions that were taken at the 19th PNC meeting in Algiers in November 1988. While their tone was not as conciliatory and informal as the language used by Bassam abu Sharif, the politics of the PNC resolutions was identical to that of his statement.

Much of the PLO and its leadership has moved steadily, if cautiously, from the maximalist positions of the mid-1960s in the direction of accommodation. The organization has dropped its insistence on the armed liberation of all Palestine and has talked of and utilized political action as the means to achieve their ends. The explicit willingness to meet with Jewish and Israeli groups from inside and outside Israel has not only widened contacts but given the process of peacemaking human dimensions. The AFSC has been directly involved with many of these informal meetings and has been, on each occasion, deeply impressed to see former combatants from both sides struggle together to identify acceptable paths to peace.

In August 1981, Crown Prince Fahd of Saudi Arabia released an eight-point peace proposal (drafted jointly with the PLO) drawn largely from previously adopted United Nations resolutions—notably UN Resolutions 242 (Security Council) and 3236 (General Assembly). In summary, its points included:

- Israeli withdrawal from all territory occupied in the 1967 war
- Removal of Israeli settlements from the West Bank and other occupied areas
- Guarantees of freedom of worship for all religious sects in the Holy Land
- Recognition of the right of 2 million Palestinian refugees to repatriation and compensation for those who choose not to return
- A UN trusteeship in the Palestinian-populated West Bank of the Jordan River and the Gaza Strip during a transition period of a few months
- Establishment of an independent Palestinian state, with the Arab sector of Jerusalem as its capital

- Affirmation of the "right of all countries of the region to live in peace"
- Guarantees of the implementation of these principles by the United Nations or some of its members (presumably the United States and the Soviet Union)[41]

The inclusion of the intent of UN Security Council Resolution 242 guaranteeing the right of all states "to live in peace" was an inclusion of the diplomatic language for recognition of Israel. The explicit reference to Israel's withdrawal from the territory occupied in 1967 and the mention of no other territory also implied recognition of Israel within the pre-1967 borders. While no element in the Saudi proposal was new, Crown Prince Fahd's bringing them all together put forward an Arab negotiating position. Saudi Arabia, while an important state in the region and a key supporter of the PLO, had to be joined by other Arab countries if its proposals were to become a realistic basis for solving the Palestinian question. The failure of the plan to win acceptance at the Arab summit at Fez, Morocco, in November 1981 was not attributable to the merits of the proposal but indicated political divisions among the states. In this instance, Syria withheld its agreement. Just a year later, a few weeks after the PLO was forced to withdraw from its positions in besieged Beirut, the Twelfth Arab League Summit was hastily convened at Fez, and on September 9, 1982, a unanimous Arab League (Syria included) accepted the Fez proposals, in slightly amended fashion, as their own. This represented the first joint Arab peace plan and was seen as a political victory for the PLO even as it recovered from the military defeat in Lebanon.[42] The PLO was reconfirmed as the "sole legitimate representative of the Palestinians," and when it reasserted the diplomatic role over the military, the moderates or centrists of the PLO were strengthened. Jordan's role was constrained by the plan in part to blunt the influence of the Reagan initiative which had been announced only one week earlier and had featured the "Jordanian option" as its centerpiece. The call to have member states of the UN Security Council oversee the Arab Peace Plan reflected both displeasure at the way the United States had tilted toward Israel and a desire to involve the Soviet Union to counter the American position. Article 7 was extremely important since it implied, even if indirectly, recognition of Israel. The plan was taken to the capitals of the five permanent members of the Security Council by a seven-member team led alternately by King Hassan of Morocco and King Hussein of Jordan, and including a senior Palestinian representative appointed by Yasir Arafat. While little direct support was gained, the Arab Peace Plan, by its implied minimum support for some elements of the Reagan initiative, gave U.S. diplomatic efforts some room for maneuver.

A series of diplomatic and political efforts followed the presentation of the Fahd plan in the early summer of 1981. Several days after the Saudi proposal was made, Yasir Arafat termed it "a good beginning for lasting peace in the Middle East." Several months later, on October 30, 1981, in a full-page interview in the leading Beirut daily, *An-Nahar*, Arafat explained that he supported the proposals because they call for "coexistence" between Israel and the Arabs. He also linked the Saudi proposal to points included in the Palestine National Charter.[43] As part of an attempt to push the diplomatic efforts further, during the summer of 1981 the PLO engaged in indirect negotiations with Israel for a cease-fire in southern Lebanon. This initiative, which brought a full and enforced truce to the northern border of Israel and the southern border of Lebanon, remained intact for almost a year, until it was broken largely by Israeli action in the weeks preceding the large-scale Israeli invasion of Lebanon in June 1982. During the very months of the cease-fire's success, Israeli Minister of Defense Sharon was secretly planning a war on the PLO and Lebanon. Detailed examination of the preparations has been given by noted Israeli defense editor Ze'ev Schiff and journalist Ehud Ya'ari.[44] Thus while the PLO demonstrated its willingness under some circumstances to engage seriously in the diplomatic and political processes necessary for peacemaking, the Israelis at the time had no intention of extending the American-brokered cease-fire.

Menachem Begin's government quickly rejected the Saudi proposal and denounced the Fez peace plan when it was restated in September 1982. Several Labor Party leaders, while rejecting the Saudi proposal for a Palestinian state, did, however, note Saudi Arabia's implicit acceptance of Israel in the region. The difference in PLO and Israeli government reaction is important. For if the trajectory of Palestinian policy has led it steadily toward limiting its claims to the territory of the West Bank and Gaza organized as an independent state alongside Israel, the Israeli government policy, especially since 1977, has hardened appreciably, now claiming permanent sovereignty over the West Bank and the Gaza Strip. The Saudi proposals also were greeted with suspicion or denounced by the rejectionists in the Palestinian movement, although many had to follow Syria's lead in accepting, even if grudgingly, the Arab Peace Plan when it became Arab League policy at the Fez summit.

RESOLVING THE PALESTINIAN ISSUE

Can the impasse be broken? Can the Palestine question be resolved? Perhaps, if the key parties with an interest in the outcome take steps to seek a solution rather than to block one.

The United States may have lived with the illusion that Camp David is enough and that someone other than the Palestinians can speak for them, but the United States can, if it chooses, play a vital role in bringing the Palestinians into the political discourse from which peace may emerge. The United States need not agree with the PLO or believe that its current political expressions are sufficiently forthcoming, but U.S. initiation of direct contacts with the PLO in December 1988 could prove to be a critical turning point in Middle East negotiations.

The United States should be ready to deal honestly and justly with both Israel and the PLO. This realistic view had been gaining support from many political quarters in the United States, including those who previously opposed a U.S.–PLO dialogue, although it took thirteen years to overcome the 1975 Kissinger agreements to isolate the PLO. In the summer of 1981, after he had left office, Zbigniew Brzezinski, President Carter's national security adviser, advocated opening up direct discussions with the PLO, pointing to changes that have occurred in the Middle East. "We have to take account of changing attitudes in the Arab world . . . the view that Israel must be accepted," he said.[45] Brzezinski drew an analogy to France's refusal to talk to the National Liberation Front of Algeria in the 1950s during the Algerian war for independence. Today the government of Algeria, one of the most responsible in North Africa, Brzezinski said, is led by former leaders of the Front.

Hermann Eilts, the former U.S. ambassador to Egypt, has also urged direct dialogue: "Only through open U.S. contacts with the PLO leadership will it be possible to gauge whether the PLO would be willing and able to participate responsibly in broader peace negotiations."[46] This point of view gained additional support from former Presidents Ford and Carter, who, on returning from the funeral of President Sadat in October 1981, jointly expressed the conviction that the United States should enter into direct contact with the PLO as an element in resolving the Israeli–Arab impasse.[47] While the most recent Brookings report—*Toward Arab-Israeli Peace* (1988)—still waffles on the issue of PLO participation, it does "recognize that Palestinians are unlikely to come forward to negotiate with Israel without having an implicit or explicit endorsement of the PLO" (p. 31). The senior editor of the report, former National Security Council Middle East staff director William Quandt, is more forceful in his own assessment that the PLO must be dealt with by the United States if there is to be any hope for progress in negotiations.[48] U.S. talks with the PLO cannot be expected to bring immediate solutions to Middle East problems, but they can induce a sense of new realities for both the Israelis and the Palestinians.

Israeli settlements in the West Bank and the politics behind them have been severe obstacles to developing options for a peaceful accommodation with the Palestinians. The obduracy of the Israeli right wing and the influence it has wielded on successive Israeli governments present one of the strongest challenges to successful peacemaking. The threats of Likud and its allies on the right to vastly expand settlements should they achieve enough political power should not be easily dismissed. The United States, by not objecting to the indirect use of its military and economic aid for Israeli settlements and maintenance of the occupation, becomes a silent partner in thwarting the intent of UN Security Council Resolution 242, which calls for Israel's withdrawal from these lands.

The U.S. government must express its opposition to land expropriation, the creation of new settlements, seizure of water resources, deportations of civic leaders, and those other moves aimed to ensure long-term Israeli control of the West Bank and the Gaza Strip. It must also take direct steps to assure that U.S. aid is not related to this policy; the expenditure of funds given to Israel should be under regular American scrutiny, and the normal forms of prior approval and accountability, which have been waived by Washington for Israel alone among aid recipients, must be rigorously applied so that U.S. opposition to Israeli conduct in the occupied territories cannot be brushed aside. Further, the United States could reduce aid in proportion to Israeli expenditures for West Bank and Gaza occupation and settlements as a concrete if limited expression of disagreement with Israel's claim to full sovereignty in the West Bank and Gaza. Such expression is particularly important as Israeli society and its government confront the hard but essential choices that must be made following the 1988 elections.

U.S. policies in relation to Israel and to the Palestinians should reflect a true intent to achieve peace based on the principles of self-determination for Israelis and Palestinians and mutual security for Israel and for Palestinians in their national state-to-be. The Arab countries have the opportunity to play a crucial role in bringing Israel and the Palestinians to the negotiation table. General and vigorous support for the proposed international peace conference involving Israel, the PLO, and the concerned Arab states, under the auspices of the five permanent members of the UN Security Council, will help establish a sound pre-negotiation environment. The Arabs must understand that Israel will mistrust any such proposal and so must be ready to reiterate their intentions and pursue negotiations openly and forcefully. They will have to be explicit in communicating to the Israeli people their respect for Israel's right to a secure existence.

The European initiatives and the important rapport European nations have established in the Arab world give the Europeans the opportunity and responsibility for bolstering a new peace process. As Walid Khalidi has noted, the Europeans could constructively focus attention on the two principles of "reciprocity" and "coexistence"—that is, on mutual recognition and mutual security.[49]

While Israel's current policy of claiming full sovereignty over the occupied lands seems to foreclose any solution to the Palestinian question, the willingness expressed by the Labor Party to participate in an international peace conference and to ultimately negotiate an exchange of some "land for peace" leaves options open. That significant public support can be mustered behind territorial compromise has been demonstrated in public opinion polls, even during the *intifadah*. At the end of October 1988, 65 percent of Israelis polled favored some form of territorial concession in return for peace.[50] Israeli actions either supporting compromise and reconciliation or blocking it are of critical importance. Continued repressive measures in the occupied territories, attempts to expand Israeli settlements and create additional infrastructure of annexation, and the total rejection of Palestinian nationalist leaders all block moves toward agreement. By contrast, a willingness to engage in mutual recognition, establishing realistic terms for negotiating with PLO leaders, and giving credence to the pragmatic moves and statements of PLO leaders could significantly promote the process of peace. Is the call for reciprocal recognition one that could begin the process? Israel could take up the negotiating proposals of the Arab states, with their implied recognition of Israel, and the new Palestinian proposals and use them to fashion an agenda for further exchange.

The PLO has begun to act to unblock the impasse by finally making explicit much of what it had left implied in its prior statements; the PLO should set out the implications of its recognition of Israel and be willing to engage in the long-delayed negotiations. A sound PLO–Arab proposal should offer peace, recognition, and security to Israel in return for Israeli withdrawal from the occupied territories and an independent and secure state for the Palestinians. Israeli–Palestinian relations are at a critical turning point. The dynamics of the recent past in the occupied territories, in Israel, within the PLO, in Jordan, the steps taken by the Soviet Union at the international level, and the new move by the United States all make the achievement of a just and lasting peace seem more possible. The crucial element remains the political will to take the steps of risk, but real opportunity exists. In this there is a particular role for an enlightened, fair, and compassionate U.S. policy.

5

Options and Proposals

Any resolution of the Arab–Palestinian–Israeli conflict must include a solution to the Palestinian issue acceptable both to the Palestinians and to the Israelis. The situation has existed for many years, and rather than improving, it gets more serious and takes on more importance with each passing year. Various options have emerged to deal with the conflict. But all options and proposals must not only be politically acceptable; of even greater importance, they must offer a just and stable peace: mutual self-determination, mutual recognition, and mutual security. Only in this way will two parties achieve a mutually acceptable settlement.

SECURITY

It is impossible to discuss plans for resolving the Israeli–Arab/Israeli–Palestinian conflicts without dealing with security. What was initially conceived of as the problem of security for an Israel surrounded by hostile forces has over the past four decades become a problem of mutual security. The change in military balance, perceived and real, and the changed tactics of the several parties to the conflict make the issue objectively more manageable even though passions and fears remain. It is important to recognize that the concept of security is broader than military defense, and indeed other aspects of Israel's relations with the Palestinians and neighboring Arab states may well have become equal in importance to the largely military factor.

Security is a central concern of every Israeli citizen. The country is small, and wherever one may be, the borders are close. Five wars in four decades lend credence to Israel's claim that security is a compelling issue. Israel traditionally has relied on its military prowess and its sophisticated weapons to counter any enemy. It has depended upon a deeply committed citizenry, willing to fight when called to war and willing to spend a significant portion of its civilian life in making ready for war. When the state was formed in 1948, the defense perimeters were established by placing settlements at key points along its borders. Israelis now face the question of how to achieve security in an era of aircraft that travel faster than sound, long-distance missiles, and high-firepower weapons. The added question of the *in*security created by long-term and repressive occupation of an unwilling population cannot be overlooked; this is especially true in light of Israel's need to deploy tens of thousands of troops to contain the *intifadah*.

The Israelis have developed and become strongly attracted to the military concept of "strategic depth." By this is meant "the space between the furthermost line at which a country may maintain military forces for its defense without impinging upon the sovereignty of another country and its own vital area."[1] To defend its "vital areas" (areas which if occupied end the sovereignty of the state) in an era of modern weapons against enemies that possess an advantage in manpower, Israel has depended upon rapid, large-scale mobilization, high-technology weapons and intelligence systems, preemptive strikes, and surprise. Israel's strategy has been to fight in territories other than its own to compensate for the lack of strategic depth and the proximity of its major population centers to its borders.

The 1967 war was a classic example of this strategy. It was also, in military terms, supremely successful. While it left Israel with the additional territory envisaged in the doctrine of strategic depth, it also left the country with political, diplomatic, and human problems of great magnitude. Did the greatly expanded borders resulting from the 1967 war provide security when the new territory could be protected only by fielding a permanent army of occupation? This question is vigorously debated in Israel, even among those most directly involved in and knowledgeable about military matters. Challenging the predominant view, retired general Mattityahu Peled argues that the expanded defense perimeters are actually wasteful and that Israel's security is undermined rather than served by them. He points to the much greater expense and greater troop commitment necessary to maintain the extended borders. General Peled, the commander of logistics for the Israeli army during the 1967 war, claims that the pre-1967 borders gave Israel greater security because they allowed a more effective disposition of Israeli forces in relation to Arab forces.[2] Recent statements by members of the Council for Peace and Security (retired generals and colonels) have lent credence to this claim.

On Israel's western borders with Egypt, the security issue has been resolved. General Aharon Yariv, director of Israel's Jaffee Center for Strategic Studies at Tel Aviv University and chair of the Council for Peace and Security, notes that in withdrawing from the Sinai, Israel has found ways, relying on special arrangements, to ensure its margin of security. The treaty with Egypt created "demilitarized areas, where only limited forces may be stationed, buffer zones, and the presence of an international force or that of a third country, as well as a variety of guarantees."[3] Aware of potential weaknesses in arrangements of this sort, Yariv suggests some additional elements to strengthen them. First, he believes it is necessary to be clear about what would constitute a violation of security arrangements and bring a return to war footing. In addition, Yariv proposes that it is possible to compensate for lack of strategic depth (space) by early-warning depth (time). He discusses the real gains to Israel possible through a reduction of Arab hostility that would result from Israeli withdrawal from the occupied areas. Egypt, he believes, provides a case in point.

The most controversial element in Israeli security concerns the Gaza Strip and, particularly, the West Bank. The question can be simply put. Can Israel give up its claims to sovereignty over the occupied territories and still maintain security? On this question there are sharp divisions within Israel. The Likud coalition and some key segments of the Labor Party respond negatively and act upon that response. A broad assortment of others, including both doves and military strategists, believe that the answer is "yes, if . . ." The Likud response is complicated by an element that has nothing to do with security, belief in the biblical vision of a Greater Israel and in an extended nationalism. This belief has been the compelling force behind Gush Emunim and other ultranationalist settlers' groups. It has become thoroughly mixed with the political positions of Likud, Tehiya, Tzomet, Moledet, and other political groups on the right who support permanent Israeli sovereignty over the occupied territories. For some it has led to a specific call for annexation of the West Bank and Gaza. Others, such as Yitzhak Shamir, Likud leader and Prime Minister, make the rhetorical claim that "there is no need to annex what is already ours"—Eretz Yisrael—considered by him to be God's gift to the Jewish people.[4]

Security is considered most vulnerable on Israel's eastern borders since the distance there from the pre-1967 borders to the Israeli heartland is the shortest. On the other hand, analysts point to the security risks involved in occupying and policing a hostile population. Former Defense Minister Ezer Weizman, while supporting the principle of using settlements for security, is realistic about the problems: "I object to the confiscation of Arab lands because the most important component of our security is the feasibility of peaceful relations with the Palestinians and with the rest of the region. Our future depends on it."[5] Shai Feldman, from Israel's Jaffee Center for Strategic Studies, also discusses an internal weakness generated by the occupation. He says: "Israelis raised fundamental questions about the purposes of their state and the nature of the road it was taking. Basic political and moral objections to Israel's foreign and defense policies were raised . . ." Doubts about government purpose undermine Israel's security because security depends on citizen soldiers whose motivation must be high. "Once its national consensus is lost, Israel's very survival is in question," Feldman notes. He believes that a return to the approximate pre-1967 borders would strengthen Israel and leave no doubt about its soldiers' motivation. "This by itself is a major factor to be considered in weighing the security risks associated with giving up control over the West Bank."[6]

Withdrawal from the West Bank would be accomplished, in Feldman's view, within the framework of a full national security plan. This would include links to the Western alliance, strong internal West Bank security, an international effort to ensure a viable West Bank economy that is linked both to Israel and to the pro-Western Arab states, and a strategy of nuclear deterrence. Each of these involves problems, but the nuclear strategy is the most likely to raise serious new questions. In another paper, prepared after the 1981 Israeli raid on the Iraqi nuclear reactor, Feldman stresses the importance of rapidly resolving the Arab–Israeli conflict in order to avoid a Middle East nuclear arms race. General Yariv adds that alongside a peace agreement there should be an area-wide agreement to control nuclear proliferation.[7]

Another Israeli analyst, Dr. Avi Plascov, produced a lengthy and detailed study of Israeli alternatives in dealing with a Palestinian state. In his research, conducted at the London International Institute for Strategic Studies, he concludes that a militarily restricted, independent state of Palestine is acceptable if the Palestinians and the Arab states drop their broader territorial claims. Only through politics will Israel ultimately gain security. "New military technology," he writes, "tends to diminish the value of buffer zones and the virtues of strategic depth and it is only predictable behavior and good will—not the security arrangements as such—which can provide the parties with security. Yet, because the political arrangements will be fragile, security arrangements are of paramount importance."[8] In the years since Plascov wrote in 1981 the accelerated introduction into the Middle East of over-the-horizon missiles and chemical weapons has further reduced the value of buffer zones and increased the importance of reliable peace treaties and workable security agreements. The rocket bombing of Teheran and Baghdad and other cities during the Iran–Iraq war provides a sobering example of the meaning of these new technologies and their growing ubiquitousness in the region.

A variety of security arrangements have been examined and suggested by Israelis. Shai Feldman proposes several low-manpower, primarily technological arrangements aimed at giving Israel warning time and protection against attacks from east of the Jordan River. He also argues for not permitting other Arab military forces to enter Jordan, to keep them distant from Israel. In addition, heavy armament, either Jordanian or Palestinian, should be prohibited on the West Bank.

A comprehensive view of the militarily related issues of importance to any agreement for West Bank withdrawal was proposed by Meir Pail, former Knesset member and reserve officer. Pail called for Israeli evacuation in stages, with Arab authorities in the territories establishing local police and security forces equipped with the number and types of arms determined by negotiation. Neither Israeli nor Arab offensive weapons and forces would be allowed in the area; fortifications and minefields would also be prohibited. Except for the existing Kalandia Airport, large fields would be prohibited. Mixed Israeli–Palestinian observation units would be posted in strategic locations in the Jordan Valley and on the Gaza border, and a joint Israeli–Palestinian–Jordanian border patrol would prevent terrorist infiltration. Such a plan, Pail believes, would not endanger Israeli security; it has the potential of increasing it by encouraging genuine peace initiatives.[9]

General Peled adds to these arguments that the establishment of a Palestinian state on the West Bank might give Israel a better strategic position than it enjoyed in the pre-1967 period: any negotiated Palestinian state would perforce be militarily weaker than Jordan was when it held the West Bank. He notes that Jordan had tacitly accepted restrictions on armor and antiaircraft systems in the earlier period, accounting in part for its inability to match Israeli force during the 1967 war and for its consequent loss of territory. Similar military restrictions could be instituted by the terms of a peace treaty. Any political misuse of its military forces by a new Palestinian state would result in war, threatening the loss of all the gains the new state might have achieved.[10]

Another Israeli scholar, Mark Heller, in a far-reaching analysis of the implications of a Palestinian state in the West Bank and Gaza, concludes that "it is most unlikely that a Palestinian state would constitute, in the foreseeable future, a serious independent military threat to Israel."[11] For him it is not so much the technical military elements which would be Israel's greatest insurance (although they should be put in place) but rather "the Palestinian calculation of probable consequences, beginning with Israeli counter fire and ending with massive retaliation." Limiting forces, banning heavy weapons, joint Palestinian–Israeli observation teams at strategic points, and limitations on local military production and deployment are among the security arrangements that Heller would seek in a negotiated settlement.

The main point is clear; prominent Israeli analysts maintain that military security is not a compelling argument against Israeli with-drawal from the occupied territories and that appropriate security safeguards can be identified and should be included in a negotiated settlement.

In a very important article published in *Foreign Affairs* in July 1978, Walid Khalidi, a leading Palestinian intellectual, outlined his conception of a Palestinian state living side by side with Israel. His appraisal of such a state's foreign and military policy was based on a realistic assessment of options and provides a Palestinian counterpoint to the Israeli views outlined above. The Palestinian state he described would not be aligned with the superpowers and other states, particularly militarily. He uses Austria in Central Europe to illustrate his point. The state, while obviously without sophisticated weapons, would require security forces able to meet its needs and to deal with cross-border adventurism. United Na-tions forces would supplement the local forces at borders and air-ports. Khalidi goes so far as to suggest the numbers of weapons a new state might have as compared with Israel and Jordan.

Professor Khalidi provides serious points for discussion. For Palestinians who seek to establish an independent and viable state in the West Bank and the Gaza Strip, he calls for full acceptance of legitimate Israeli interest in security. He also insists that the new state would have security problems to contend with as well. He points out that if Tel Aviv is fifteen miles from the West Bank, the reverse is also true. The West Bank and the Gaza Strip are easily accessible from Israel and too easily observed for much to be hidden. Palestinian territory is vulnerable to attack from Israel. Its skies are visible from Israel. Khalidi puts it graphically: "The terrain on both sides of the Jordan River is an ideal burial ground for armor." He closes his analysis with the observation that "any PLO leadership would take the helm in a Palestinian state with few illusions about the efficacy of revolutionary armed struggle in any direct confrontation with Israel. They would be acutely aware of its costs. They would have little incentive on national or cor-porate grounds to incur it."[12]

If security is an important element in Israeli thinking, it has a similar status for the Arab states and particular meaning for the Palestinians. The Israeli invasion of Lebanon and the siege of Beirut in the summer of 1982 offered vivid proof of Israel's willingness to use massive military force for largely political ends; Israel's bombing raid on the Osirak nuclear reactor on the outskirts of Baghdad in June 1981 showed Israel's determination to preempt any potential technological challenge; the two raids on the PLO headquarters in Tunis, one a bombing attack on offices and the other the assassination of Abu Jihad, the PLO's second-in-command, in April 1988, demonstrated that national boundaries and distance are not barriers to military operations; the bombing of Palestinian and Lebanese sites in the south of Lebanon illustrates Israel's willingness to preempt, punish, or warn by using military firepower. Thoughtful security agreements will have to satisfy the several parties at risk.

The fear of terrorism from an independent Palestinian state deserves to be dealt with explicitly. It has often provided Israel with justification for military strikes and for rejection of an independent Palestinian state. Shai Feldman notes that while terrorism represents great personal tragedy, it is not "a major strategic threat."[13] A strategy which is otherwise sound should not be rejected, he argues, because it fails to solve the problem of terrorism. Feldman's conclusion, similar in spirit to the one offered by Khalidi, is that Israeli withdrawal from the West Bank, by allowing a resolution of the Palestine question, would actually lead to a decrease of terrorism.

The arguments of Israelis and Palestinians outlined above suggest that the security of both peoples would be as well or better served by political measures than by reliance on military strength, even as agreements are negotiated to minimize military threat and instability. While the slogan "peace through security" is frequently heard, it is important to note that true security is realized only through peace.

TERRORISM

Terrorism and violence have been so interwoven with other parts of the Arab–Israeli conflict that only those involved in seeking settlement of the strife between Israelis and Palestinians deal fully with the problem. No one can say for the Israelis that the intrusion of Palestinian guerrillas across Israel's borders is not terrifying; no one can say for the Palestinians in Lebanese refugee camps and villages that air strikes by Israeli planes are not terrifying. For the American Friends Service Committee, terrorism and violence, whether conducted by individuals acting alone, by small guerrilla groups, or by the military forces of a state, are morally unacceptable. There is long-standing Quaker tradition opposed to violence, and the AFSC still "utterly rejects all wars and fighting with outward weapons . . . for any cause . . ." In the case of the Middle East, the AFSC has been equally clear and its representatives have remonstrated with Palestinian, Israeli, and Arab leaders to urge that all parties turn away from the use of murder to gain political ends. We have been unwilling to accept the rationale that legitimates some violent acts and condemns others. We find repugnant the idea that humane rules of war can be established that allow some weapons to be used in killing putative enemies but outlaw other weapons. For in every instance we are talking about the inflicting of death by human beings on other human beings.

Of course, the Middle East has not been alone in resorting to terror and violence. But the legacy of terror in the Arab–Israeli conflict, dating back decades and practiced at times by both sides, has frustrated the peacemaking process. As we have examined the record of this legacy, even recognizing the instances where each side resorted to violence to set right an obvious injustice or wrong, we find it particularly intolerable that any movement or government should take revenge on the unarmed and on children.

We believe that in the long run peace must be built upon the ability to transcend the past and forgive the enemy. This is hard enough to achieve among the soldiers who fought in the armies of opposing nations. It is much more difficult to wipe out the memories of cruelty or wanton murder. Jews in Israel and around the world know the Holocaust in a special way and remember the murder of the innocents—a memory that cannot be removed. For Palestinians and Israelis today it will be difficult to forget the killing of the innocents on both sides, the terror of the Palestinian attack and the Israeli reprisal, the shooting in a kibbutz or school, the roar of jets bombing a refugee camp, or the brutal beatings in the occupied territories. As David McReynolds of the War Resisters League wrote to the AFSC: "The legacy being built is one that, murder by murder, makes a peaceful settlement more difficult."

The author of this report and the AFSC urge soldiers and terrorists alike to let the guns fall silent, to free innocent civilians from their role as hostages to violence and to seek instead political solutions to the deeply vexing problems that face the Israeli and Palestinian people. In addition, we urge those who condemn the violence to recognize the wisdom advanced by one Israeli, Simha Flapan, a longtime advocate of just and peaceful relations between Palestinians and Israelis:

> In the long run, the eradication of terrorism is possible only by elim-inating the condition that breeds it. Palestinian terrorism is a result of statelessness and a refugee existence. Only a political solution that offers the prospects of statehood, of a normal economy and a productive life for the Palestinians might put an end to terrorism.[14]

And, it should be added, in the long run Israel's reprisals and preemptive strikes may be ended only by eliminating the conditions that breed them. Recognition of Israel's right to exist and assurance of its security are essential elements of any political solution with the Palestinians.

THE STATUS QUO/ANNEXATION

Since 1967, Israel's policy has been to maintain the status quo in the West Bank and Gaza. Israel has not sought to change its position as occupier of these captured territories. This policy has been seen as advantageous. Borders viewed by some as militarily more defensible have been achieved along the whole eastern front, and Israel's major population centers are farther from potential military attackers. Originally by default, and more recently by design, the occupied territories have become integrated to a great extent into the political economy of Israel. For the short term, at least, Israel has considered the status quo to be less risky militarily and more advantageous in other ways. Through extensive Jewish settlements, primarily in the West Bank, it has permitted partial realization of the biblical imperative to reinhabit all the land of Eretz Yisrael that is claimed by some Israelis. Maintaining the status quo has allowed Israel to avoid confronting the problem of direct negotiation with the Palestinians.

To date, Israel's leaders have refrained from making any explicit call for annexation of the West Bank and Gaza, though many see the settlements policy as de facto annexation. During Prime Minister Begin's first term, however, the Knesset formalized de facto annexation of an enlarged East Jerusalem, incorporating a Palestinian population now estimated to be 130,000, and later annexed the Golan Heights.

In the long run, and perhaps (in light of the uprising begun in December 1987) in the short run as well, the status quo and de facto annexation are untenable and suffer from all the disadvantages of outright annexation. The long-term occupation has threatened to undermine democratic principles within Israel and has sharply increased the hostility of the Palestinians. De facto annexation and prolonged occupation would, through the demographic changes already noted, threaten the Jewish character of Israel itself.[15] If West Bank and Gaza residents were given the vote, as democratic tradition would require, the character of Israel as a Jewish state would change. If Palestinians were denied the vote and other rights of citizenship, Israel would create a second class of citizenship and a major denial of democracy. The demographic issue is of great concern to Israel's Labor Party and was one of the chief reasons advanced by Shimon Peres for Israeli participation in an international peace conference. The principle of trading land for peace was forcefully argued during the national elections in 1988. The Likud coalition's response has been to maintain that the Arab populations will ultimately emigrate if Israel keeps the West Bank and Gaza and further integrates them into a Greater Israel.[16] Ariel Sharon has publicly advocated programs and policies to encourage, even force, Palestinians to move from the territories. Indeed, planned expulsion of the Palestinians is now discussed openly and has been advocated by many on Israel's political right.

Maintaining the status quo has negative demographic implications for Israel, presents moral and ideological difficulties, and projects an image of Israel as a recalcitrant rather than peace-seeking state, unwilling to move toward solutions of the Palestinian question. Formal annexation would compound all these negative elements.

AUTONOMY/SELF-RULE

The proposal for a form of Palestinian self-rule was Prime Minister Begin's response to President Sadat's dramatic Jerusalem initiative of 1977. Autonomy for the Palestinians became the second part of the Camp David framework and the focus of drawn-out negotiations between Egypt, Israel, and the United States. The Palestinians were not part of the negotiations and no significant attempt had been made to solicit their views during the formal negotiations. Even Jordan, which was expected ultimately to play a role in the autonomy process, was not involved in the negotiations and was only informed of the results after their conclusion. While Israel, Egypt, and the United States remain committed to autonomy by the terms of the treaty, the decade of inaction and the changes of Palestinian political culture leave the formal proposals largely abandoned.

Autonomy is the one option that had fairly broad support in Israel. (One version of it was proposed early in 1989 by Prime Minister Shamir.) Israel interpreted autonomy in a much narrower way than either Egypt or the United States. Begin envisioned autonomy *for people*, not *for land*. He proposed to establish an administrative council comprised of Palestinians in the occupied territories that would be responsible for education, culture, religion, industry, trade, commerce, agriculture, transportation, housing, and health.[17] It would manage the day-to-day affairs of the Arab inhabitants. However, the Israeli scheme includes restrictions on the council's powers. The education department of the territories would remain subject to Israeli control, the finance department could not issue currency, the agriculture department would not control either the land or the water, while tourism authorities would not have jurisdiction over the historic and holy sites of East Jerusalem.[18] Jerusalem would remain united and the capital of Israel with no provision for Palestinian control over Arab East Jerusalem. The territories under Begin's autonomy concept might have an anthem, a flag, and a local police force, but Israel would maintain sovereignty.

Defense and foreign affairs would be under Israeli control. The Israeli military government which currently administers the territories would be withdrawn, but not dissolved. It would be ready to intervene if the administrative council, in the eyes of the Israeli government, proved incapable of controlling the area. The Israeli Defense Forces would be redeployed and become less visible, posted instead in "specific security locations." The borders of the territories, which would be considered Israel's borders during the five-year transition period called for in the Camp David agreement, would be controlled by Israel. Jewish settlements in the area would remain under the jurisdiction of the Israeli government, not the local administrative council. There would be no restriction on the formation by Israelis of new settlements. Rather than calling upon the UN or other international agencies, ultimate authority for the territories during the transition would be held by Israel; Israeli sovereignty would be maintained. Moshe Nissim, then chairman of the Likud bloc in the 8th Knesset, commented: "We are speaking of self-rule, not of statehood." Autonomy is, in this interpretation, an explicit alternative to self-determination and an independent state.

The Begin autonomy plan was to be a means of offering the Arabs in the territories the maximum degree of self-rule believed to be consonant with Israeli security and Israeli sovereignty. By retaining control over foreign affairs and defense, controlling land and water rights, keeping limits on the administrative council, and reserving the right to intervene if it deemed necessary, Israel would be in a position to block any future moves in the territories toward independence.

This approach would free Israel from administering the affairs of a population which resents its presence. With a shift of authority in a number of fields from the military government to the elected Arab residents, clashes between the inhabitants and the authorities might be reduced. Israel would, however, continue to enjoy the defense advantages afforded by de facto boundaries along the Jordan River and on the Golan Heights. Israel would also maintain the economic advantage built up over the years of occupation.

In the Camp David framework, autonomy was to be a transitional arrangement. Progress toward autonomy under the Camp David process had been understood by Israel to be a quid pro quo for peace with Egypt, which both parties are reluctant to jeopardize. Israel and Egypt, however, have strikingly different views about autonomy. The Begin government gave signs from the beginning, and made them more explicit after the 1981 election, that restricted autonomy would be permanent rather than serve as a transitional arrangement.[19] This view was strengthened by Begin's successor, Prime Minister Yitzhak Shamir, who originally voted against the Camp David accords and only late in his second round as Prime Minister reverted to his interpretation of the Camp David formulas as a means of opposing the somewhat new options proposed by U.S. Secretary of State George Shultz in the spring of 1988. Shamir totally rejects ceding Israeli sovereignty over the territories and talks vaguely of autonomy for West Bank and Gaza residents and refuses to be drawn out on the terms of such self-rule. Egypt, on the other hand, conceives of autonomy as being a step toward Palestinian self-determination and the creation of a Palestinian state. The Israeli Labor Party supported autonomy as one of several possibilities for a transition leading to a territorial compromise with Jordan involving the partition of the West Bank.[20] This sharp divergence in views on the ultimate disposition of the territories after the five years of autonomy and on their administration during the transition left the Israeli–Egyptian negotiations in total deadlock and they were ultimately abandoned. The Palestinians completely rejected the autonomy scheme as envisaged in the Camp David accords and in the later interpretations of Prime Minister Shamir. Their goal is an independent state and the most they concede is a brief transition period strikingly different from the Israeli-proposed autonomy concept.

The United States has interpreted the nature of autonomy and the powers of the administrative council more broadly than Israel and in a manner quite similar to Egypt. During the Carter administration, the United States interpreted the Israeli settlements policy in the occupied territories as illegal under international law and counterproductive for the peace process. Early statements of the Reagan administration seemed to diverge from this judgment and left U.S. policy unclear during Reagan's presidency. The administration did not, however, formally break with the commitment to Camp David. In the last year of the Reagan administration, in response to the Palestinian uprising, Secretary of State Shultz proposed a formula for speeding up the transition period (three years) and opening negotiations for the final disposition of the occupied territories even as the transition period began. The whole process was to be linked to a weak form of an international peace conference involving the parties to the conflict and the five permanent members of the UN Security Council. Palestinian participation was to be confined to membership in a joint Jordanian–Palestinian delegation and predicated on prior acceptance of UN Security Council Resolutions 242 and 338. Prime Minister Shamir's blunt response was to disagree with every word in the Shultz proposal except the signature! However, the initiative was strongly supported by Foreign Minister Shimon Peres.[21]

The restrictive definition of autonomy has meant that no one other than the three original signatories to the Camp David framework has accepted it and both Cairo and Washington differ with Israel in interpretation. Palestinian leadership in the PLO, West Bank and Gaza Palestinians, the Arab states, and the Western Europeans have rejected the proposal for limited autonomy, contending that it offers little or no promise for a solution to the Palestinian question. It is virtually certain that West Bank and Gaza residents would not agree to participate in the elections for an administrative council, carried out under Israeli control, even if Egypt and Israel finally agreed upon its powers and upon appropriate mechanisms for an election.

The three participants in Camp David shared a strong hope and expectation that Jordan and Saudi Arabia would accept the autonomy plan and participate in the Camp David peace process. The failure of either government to join and their criticism of the whole process undermined its chances for success. Without Jordan's assuming the role envisaged for it and without the cooperation of West Bank and Gaza residents, the autonomy plan, if pushed ahead, would be an "imposed" solution with all the difficulties this implies.

There is no real hope of success for the autonomy plan without significant changes in its projected goals and the inclusion of the Palestinians in the planning process. For Israel the restricted autonomy plan meets its desire to maintain control over the West Bank and Gaza while ceding some limited authority to the residents. The very restrictions and lack of a goal of Palestinian independence and self-determination after a period of transition reduce to close to zero the chances that an autonomy plan could gain adherents or be successful. In the hands of the current Likud leadership, autonomy has become a euphemism for continued Israeli control. It is worth noting, however, that even the Likud proposal contains the concept of separation, which is an essential prerequisite for partition. Labor has largely given up discussing autonomy, though its proposals would involve a transition period with some form of self-rule. The Israeli peace movement has more or less abandoned the proposal and embraced the idea of an independent Palestinian state with negotiations aimed at achieving that end.

THE JORDANIAN OPTION

The earliest of the Israeli plans for the West Bank and Gaza—the Jordanian option—was developed slowly during the occupation and was reformulated as part of the Labor Party position in the June 1981 elections and with only slight modifications it has remained a staple of Labor policy. In response to Egyptian and Jordanian urging, Labor acceded to the idea of an international peace conference as the favored venue in which to conduct negotiations with Jordan. The Jordanian option is based on two key elements. The first is that Israel should not permanently rule over the 1.7 million Palestinian inhabitants of the West Bank and Gaza. Second, Israel should seek to negotiate a territorial compromise with Jordan involving the partition of the West Bank that would turn significant segments of the West Bank and Gaza over to Jordan, while Israel would retain areas designated as necessary for security. In its initial form prepared by Yigal Allon, Israeli Foreign Minister from 1974 to 1977, the plan called for a ten- to fifteen-kilometer-deep security strip along the west side of the Jordan River.[22] On the basis of this early plan, successive Labor governments encouraged the establishment of settlements in the Jordan Valley reminiscent of the early Israeli efforts to define the original borders of Israel by building settlements. In addition, there would be border adjustments to the pre-1967 boundaries amounting to as much as one-third of the territory, including, for example, within the new borders the Etzion block of settlements, the Latrun salient, and the southern portion of the Gaza Strip.[23] Jerusalem would remain unified and under full Israeli sovereignty. In the north, the border with Syria would run along the ridge of the Golan Heights to avoid repetition of the pre-1967 shelling of Galilee settlements. The major populated areas of the West Bank and Gaza would be transferred to Jordan, and a land corridor would be opened connecting the West Bank and Gaza.

The primary argument advanced to support this plan is based on security. The readjusted borders and the advanced line on the Jordan River, it is argued, would enhance Israeli security. Jordan, under this plan, would assume responsibility for administration and security in the ceded territories, and Israel noted that King Hussein, a Western-oriented, "moderate" Arab leader, could be counted on to keep the area free from Soviet or radical destabilizing influences. Further, the combined Jordan–West Bank–Gaza state would be in a better position to reabsorb Palestinian refugees who return than a smaller West Bank–Gaza independent state. By transferring the populous Arab areas out of Israeli territory, the demographic threat to a Jewish Israel would be avoided. From the political point of view, the Jordanian option removed the necessity of dealing directly with the PLO, handing over that problem to King Hussein's government. It attempts to resolve the Palestinian problem permanently.

But there are serious problems which make the Jordanian option even less viable now than it might have been in the years immediately following Israel's occupation of the territories. The increasing politicization of West Bank Palestinians, their open support for the PLO, and their reluctance to become absorbed by Jordan provide strong internal resistance to any Jordanian solution which has not received prior assent from the Palestinian leadership. To add a significant hostile Palestinian population to the large Palestinian population already in the kingdom would undermine Jordanian internal stability. Indeed, just this consideration was in part responsible for King Hussein's decision of July 31, 1988, to give up administrative and legal ties with the West Bank. There would be little gain for the King and considerable political liability if he took on the thorny Palestinian question without full backing from the PLO and support from potential political rivals in Iraq, Syria, and Saudi Arabia. In accepting a partitioned West Bank along the lines proposed by Israel, he would have to give up his important and symbolic quest to return East Jerusalem to Arab rule.

Another complicating factor is that the Rabat Arab summit conference of 1974, the Baghdad resolutions of 1978, and the Fez plans designated the PLO as the "sole legitimate representative of the Palestinian people," clearly giving King Hussein no right to negotiate independently. This joint Arab recognition of the PLO reflected, in part, the fact that relations between Jordan and the PLO were strained since the Jordanians expelled the Palestinian guerrillas in 1970.

King Hussein has vacillated, changing his position on the Jordanian option. His representatives had intermittent contact with the Israelis throughout the 1970s and 1980s, culminating in a direct meeting between Israeli Foreign Minister Peres and the King in London in April 1987. There they agreed to terms for convening an international peace conference to deal with "all the aspects of the Palestinian problem."[24] Prime Minister Shamir rejected this plan and immediately moved to block its implementation. Israel in this instance spoke with two clear, sharply opposing voices. The Israeli Labor Party continues to espouse the plan. It should be noted, however, that Jordan's version of a Jordanian option differed significantly from Israel's as early as 1972, when King Hussein proposed a federation between Jordan, the entire West Bank, East Jerusalem, and any other Palestinian territories which chose to participate. Labor, then in power, rejected it. Jordan has continued to insist that the borders of pre-June 1967 would be the operative ones and that Arab Jerusalem would be the capital of the Palestinian portion of the federated kingdom.

The United States has continually supported plans which put Jordan at the center of negotiations (to the exclusion of the PLO) and has regularly supported Israel's restricted versions of a Jordanian option, including provisions which would limit the PLO's role in representing the Palestinian side in negotiations. The Palestinians and the Arab states agree that Jordan would have an important role in the establishment and viability of a West Bank and Gaza Palestinian state, when one is formed. There has been explicit talk of a confederation between Jordan and such a state (most recently in the November 1988 PNC resolution and Declaration of Independence). But such a confederation would have to be in the context of Palestinian self-determination and subsequent explicit consent to a link with Jordan. A badly partitioned West Bank, with continued Israeli military presence and security settlements, excluding East Jerusalem and barring Palestinian leadership from negotiations holds little promise for Jordan or for a solution to the problem.

UNILATERAL WITHDRAWAL

There is another idea that has been put forward by some Israelis—pulling back unilaterally. Unwilling or unable to negotiate with the PLO and the two other Arab states most closely involved, Syria and Jordan, and unwilling to bear the costs and the problems of occupation, the Israelis would, in this option, abandon the populated sectors of the territories and rely instead on their superior military force to ensure secure borders for the Jewish state. Moshe Dayan urged a partial and unilateral withdrawal on a number of occasions. Shimon Peres in early 1988 proposed a unilateral Israeli pullout from Gaza. This, after all, is the solution that Israel finally chose in 1984 to end its invasion of Lebanon. Involving no agreements with the Lebanese, it meant the establishment of a security zone in southern Lebanon manned by Lebanese mercenary troops and continued military sorties, both land and air, into Lebanon whenever Israel felt threatened. Defense Minister Rabin warned the Lebanese at the time that if Israel was threatened, the Israeli army would make sure that "life for them will not be worth living."[25] This unilateral scheme has another important aspect—the Israelis wouldn't have to deal with the Arabs and wouldn't have to trust them or respect them. Tom Friedman, a longtime correspondent for *The New York Times* in both Lebanon and Israel, calls this the tribal solution; it responds to the deep-seated distrust that Israelis have for Arabs' "visceral, almost primordial attitudes" that come from a century of conflict between the two peoples.[26]

There is a certain simplicity to the logic behind this plan—Israel has the power to carry it out at will and on its own terms. The territories would be left to those who could control them—the Unified National Leadership and the popular committees?—with Israel always in position to threaten and preempt. The internal lack of stability would not be Israel's problem. The parallel with Lebanon is clear. At one level, of course, it could work, at least in the short term. But it would leave Israel's conflict with the Palestinians and the Arab states unresolved, put off to some future date or generation. The security problem would continue and the potential for cross-border violence would persist. Again, the Lebanese parallel is a troublesome reminder. This plan is almost an invitation to long-term Palestinian irredentism, for if it satisfies the "tribal" attitudes of the Israelis, it also has the ability to stimulate and challenge a response in kind by the Palestinians. Stability would be exchanged for uncertainty; peace would be constantly threatened because none of the principles for a just and durable peace would be met. In fact, each would be violated.

AN INDEPENDENT PALESTINIAN STATE

An independent Palestinian state in the West Bank and the Gaza Strip is the other major option for solving the Palestinian question. It is the choice that has always met the stiffest resistance within Israel. Nonetheless, it has recently been given serious attention there and has clearly received almost unanimous support from Palestinians.

In the wake of the 1973 war, Aharon Yariv, former chief of Israeli Military Intelligence, and Victor Shemtov, former Minister of Health and head of the Mapam Party, suggested in June 1974 a way to break the deadlocked Palestinian issue. Israel, they said, should enter negotiations with any Palestinian group that would give up terrorism as a means of achieving its political goals and that would accept UN Security Council Resolution 242. The Yariv-Shemtov formula, as it became known, implied reciprocal recognition between Israeli and legitimate Palestinian leadership and accepted the proposition that Israel could not decide unilaterally who should represent the Palestinian people.

The idea, put aside during the Camp David process and subsequent autonomy negotiations, recently has been much more fully developed by its originators and by others. Shemtov, like many connected with the Labor alignment, prefers a "Jordanian solution"; he suggests, however, that Israel should indicate its willingness to accept Palestinian self-determination if it is designed not to jeopardize Israel's existence or security.[27] An independent Palestinian state only would exist within the context of the self-interest of neighboring states such as Israel and Jordan. He believes that the Israeli military could withdraw from most of the West

Bank provided that it is demilitarized and is involved in broad economic cooperation with Israel.

General Yariv and his associates have directly confronted the issue of Palestinian self-determination and statehood. They fear that failure to deal satisfactorily with the Palestinian issue will serve to unify the Arabs in their opposition to Israel and bring Israel again into total confrontation with a hostile Arab world. Further, they are concerned about the deepening international isolation of Israel, which may ultimately weaken it militarily. They are particularly worried by the strained relations between Israel and the United States and the decrease in arms supplies and financial support that could result. In addition, members of Yariv's group have pointed to the traditional concern of weakening the Jewish nature of the state if the large Palestinian Arab populations of the West Bank and Gaza are directly or indirectly linked to Israel. They have also noted the tensions within Israel arising from the presence of a military occupation government dealing with a hostile population, tensions which have risen markedly during the *intifadah*.

The Yariv group suggested that part of the "package," including a Palestinian state, should involve Israeli integration into the U.S.-led military alliance in the Middle East. But the core of its security argument is even more direct. Yariv noted that Israel's Arab neighbors have moved away from total rejection toward a policy of "reluctant acceptance" of Israel. The strategic implications of this shift allow the development of a flexible strategy involving both military and political elements. This strategy compels Israel to deal with the Palestinian question; it holds promise of preventing total conflict with the Arabs and reducing international isolation, thereby improving Israel's military situation. Autonomy in this view should not be used to keep Israeli sovereignty in the territories, but rather should be the means of solving the Palestinian question. For Yariv, self-determination would come gradually; the timing could be negotiated. While he does not accept the notion of a "Jordanian Palestine" (attributed to former Defense Minister Ariel Sharon and others), Yariv believes that Jordan should be involved in the process of self-determination. Jerusalem would remain the undivided capital of Israel, but Yariv would go far to see ways of satisfying Arab interests in the city. Palestinian refugees would not be repatriated to Israel, as some Arab proposals have suggested, but would be handled during gradual implementation of self-determination, presumably within the Palestinian territory or in other Arab states. Security is an important issue for the Yariv group and focuses primarily on borders and demilitarized zones to be agreed on by all parties. In this it reflects the experiences of the Israeli–Egyptian agreements for security arrangements in the Sinai following Israeli withdrawal.

Yariv is uncertain, indeed pessimistic, about the willingness of the PLO to accept the proposals he advances. He also believes that it is impossible to ignore the PLO and he would welcome negotiations with Yasir Arafat should the Palestinian leader be willing. While he did not demand that the PLO recognize Israel prior to entering formal negotiations, he would insist that it find some means of annulling those clauses of the Palestinian Covenant which call for the destruction of Israel.[28]

Although he is doubtful that any of the contact that Israeli moderates and peace groups have had with the PLO has produced any results to date, Yariv believes there is room for Israeli initiatives, in private, which would permit exploration without either side committing itself. These ideas, in an updated form, are at the core of a new study published by the Jaffee Center in March 1989. After critically examining a variety of options the authors, in an appendix, conclude that the establishment of an independent Palestinian state, following a longish transition period, offers the most stable resolution of the conflict.

A formulation of this sort developed by Yariv and his associates and additional proposals advanced by other parties run head-on into the strong opposition of Likud and its right-wing allies and hawkish segments of the Labor Party. A move toward Palestinian independence would face a strong challenge from the Jewish settlers in the territories and from their political allies, especially the right-wing and religious parties which have often held the swing votes in the Knesset necessary to form a coalition government or to maintain it in power. Since 1977 the religious parties have lent their support to Likud and have thus strengthened its already firm opposition to territorial compromise in any form and especially if it led to a Palestinian state. At least two of the religious parties are not opposed on principle to territorial compromise.

Support for Palestinian self-determination with proper security provisions is widespread among Israeli doves. It might also win acceptance from the leadership of the Labor Party if security issues were dealt with firmly enough and Labor accepted King Hussein's refusal to bring Jordan into the Labor Party version of the Jordanian option. The independence option is based on Labor's concern about losing the Jewishness of Israel by maintaining the status quo; whether Labor could overcome its long-standing reluctance to deal with the PLO remains an open question. It depends to some significant degree on how the PLO develops its own proposals for an independent state and how fully these proposals respond to Israeli concerns and fears. It will also be shaped by the responses in Europe and the United States to PLO peace initiatives.

A serious and increasingly loud call for Israel to examine the question of a Palestinian state has developed within an important segment of American Jewish leadership. Rabbi Arthur Hertzberg, a past president of the American Jewish Congress, has argued cogently for Israeli acceptance of the establishment of a Palestinian state in the West Bank and the Gaza Strip.[29] The arguments are similar to those noted above, with particular emphasis on the demographic factor—the potential for Arabs to outnumber Jews in an expanded Israel and for the Jewish character of the Israeli state to be lost. He also suggests that there may be a greater danger to Israel if a Jordanian solution is achieved and the occupied territories are partitioned and divided between the two countries. In a Jordanian state of this sort, Hertzberg warns, there is a likelihood that the Palestinians would topple King Hussein, take over Jordan, and open the door fully to Palestinians from the refugee camps in Lebanon. No treaty arrangements would be in place to bring restraint and such a situation could lead to challenges to Israeli and U.S. interests in the region. In Rabbi Hertzberg's view, concern about the Palestinian diaspora's intentions to return to Palestine is the major reason for Israel to be interested in creating a Palestinian state. Israel would be in a position to insist on security safeguards it believes to be essential. Hertzberg's argument, first made in 1981, has gained even greater urgency after the Palestinian uprising that began in December 1987. "Everyone in Israel knows that *de facto* the land has already been redivided," he wrote in October 1988, referring to the effect of the strikes, the demonstrations, and the many forms of civil disobedience. The situation, following King Hussein's withdrawal in July, was in Hertzberg's view the "turning point," forcing both the Israelis and the Palestinians to focus on the steps needed to move to a resolution. "The moderates on both sides have . . . gone remarkably far during the last few months. . . . The partition of Palestine now seems conceivable for the first time in over forty years."[30]

While sources of Israeli objections to ceding territories and allowing the creation of an independent Palestinian state have been examined, it is also important to examine serious objections by the Palestinians and the Arab states. It is clear that movement toward a resolution of the Israeli–Palestinian impasse that does not deal with Syria's outstanding conflict with Israel over the occupied Golan Heights will be sharply attacked and probably undermined by the Syrians. Syria, for its part, has been in no hurry to reach agreements with the Israelis, contending instead that real negotiations can succeed only when Syria has achieved military parity with Israel and thus negated the strategic asymmetry. The Syrians have also been reluctant to see a PLO led by Yasir Arafat and the Fatah faction take the lead in a settlement with Israel. They have supported breakaway Palestinian groups and factions loyal to Syria in a number of intra-Palestinian disputes. But it should also be noted that Syria is a signatory to UN Security Council Resolutions 242 and 338 and, while not happy with Israel and its policies and actions, Syria is reconciled to Israel's permanence in the Middle East. Syria must be dealt with seriously in any pre-negotiation planning and in the negotiations that follow if a failure like that in Lebanon in May 1983 is not to be repeated. An attempt to negotiate an issue of direct interest to Syria without direct or at least tacit Syrian involvement is destined to fail. While Syria in principle has supported the call for an international peace conference, it shares no sense of urgency with most of the other parties; it is currently in no rush.

A formula for a negotiated creation of a Palestinian state would be welcomed in important sectors of the Arab world since it recognizes the Palestinian right to self-determination and includes the PLO as a negotiating partner. What about Palestinian rejectionists or maximalists? While recent sessions of the Palestine National Council and statements by the major Palestinian leaders have made clear the commitment to a two-state solution by all major factions of the PLO, including the Popular Front for the Liberation of Palestine (PFLP) and the Democratic Front for the Liberation of Palestine (DFLP), smaller factions, primarily allied to Syria, have objected. While they cannot block acceptance of the basic policy, they can create turmoil and sow confusion and increase Israeli fears and anxieties. The longtime unwillingness of the rejectionist Palestinian groups to drop their "maximalist" claims—a democratic secular state in all of Palestine—stems from at least three sources. One is the centuries-old tie to the land. A second reflects an ideological position that supports broader revolutionary goals for the whole Arab world. The third and perhaps controlling factor is the ties that several of the rejectionist groups have to other Arab states, namely Syria and Libya, which do not consider a settlement with Israel to be in their national interests at this time. Nor do the rejectionists believe that an acceptable Palestinian state can be achieved through negotiation; therefore, they advocate continued armed struggle. The rejectionists, however, though vocal, represent a very small minority of the Palestinian movement. Palestinian moderates claim that if a state were about to be formed, many of the rejectionists would not want to be left out.[31] Since the reunification of the PLO at the April 1987 PNC meeting in Algiers, the inclusion in the majority of the Popular Front for the Liberation of Palestine (PFLP), the Democratic Front for the Liberation of Palestine (DFLP), and the Palestine Communist Party has strengthened the leadership and more fully isolated the Syrian-linked rejectionist factions. The role of the Soviet Union in helping to reestablish unity between the moderate and more radical factions of the PLO gives added stability to the PLO's decision-making processes.[32] The strong mandate given at the 19th PNC meeting in November 1988 to pursue the formation of an independent Palestinian state alongside Israel has strengthened the moderates' hand. The overwhelming vote in favor and the subsequent recognition of the new Palestinian state by most Arab countries strengthens the hands of the PLO majority and further isolates the few rejectionist groups. The clear statement by the voting minority of the PNC meeting that they would accept the majority decision and not walk out gave an added sense of the current political unity of the PLO.

But there is, in fact, some uncertainty about the limits of Palestinian goals. Some recent Palestinian statements, while accepting the formulation of a state in the West Bank and Gaza, also regard the establishment of this state as the first step in the reunification of all of Palestine. This fires Israeli fears that an independent Palestine would serve as a military base against Israel. Some Israeli critics claim further that a Palestinian state might provide an opening for Soviet interference in the region, particularly since the U.S.S.R. has supported Palestinian efforts and supplied a significant amount of arms. Changing Soviet policies in the region, especially Soviet and Eastern bloc moves to reestablish diplomatic ties with Israel, have ameliorated this fear. Others point to the Saudi Arabian role as the major financial supporter of the PLO and argue that the Saudis would exert a moderating and stabilizing influence. In addition, the extent to which a Palestinian state, located between Israel and Jordan, would have to depend heavily on Jordan for political and economic assistance and support augurs were for a further integrating influence. Continued reference to some form of confederation with Jordan is aimed at allaying fears in Israel (and the United States) and at providing greater stability for the Palestinian state. Further, the Palestinian state in the view expressed by Walid Khalidi would be precluded from entering into military alliances with any other country.[33] In any case, a Palestinian state would be militarily weaker than Israel. The increasing willingness with which the mainstream of the Palestinian nationalist movement accepts the two-state solution with its obvious limitations is an important element in overcoming the fear of rejectionism. The clear voice with which the leadership of the uprising in the West Bank and Gaza seeks the formation of a Palestinian state alongside Israel adds a serious note to the pragmatic intent of Palestinians. Just as it is important for the Israelis to recognize the contradiction between the desire to hold on to all Eretz Yisrael and the wish to achieve peace with the Palestinians, so too it is critical for the Palestinians to separate the dreams of old homes in Haifa and Ramle from the political realities of establishing an independent state in the West Bank and Gaza. As one Palestinian journalist put it: "I don't think we have to deal with people's dreams. We only have to settle the question of what people are willing to live with. By supporting the PLO and the statements of the Unified Command, Palestinians have made it very clear that they are for an independent Palestinian state in the West Bank and Gaza, and not a secular, democratic state in all of Palestine. They are calling for an end to the occupation, not an end to the state of Israel."[34]

Considerations of this sort are of great importance to the process through which Palestinian independence would be achieved and the use to which a transition period would be put. They weigh against unilateral Israeli withdrawal and support the importance of Israel's positive involvement in finding a genuinely acceptable resolution for all parties. The importance of demilitarized zones and internationally guaranteed and supervised borders during the transition period is highlighted by these security considerations. Also important is the need to generate confidence among peoples who have been locked in conflict for generations. People on both sides of the divide will have to be brought to understand what the other side is really after. They will have to communicate to each other in unambiguous fashion; they must share a willingness to reach accommodation, to achieve independence and a secure national existence; and, as Harvard psychologist Herbert Kelman put it, each side must be "prepared to negotiate a historic compromise that assures the *other's* independent and secure existence."[35]

The issues of Palestinian refugees from the 1948 war and Israeli settlers in the occupied territories should be confronted directly. There should be an agreed-upon limited right of return of Palestinians to Israel itself to reunite families and planned but unlimited right of return to the Palestinian state. Most Israeli settlers would probably be expected to leave the territories, with special agreements for some of the settlements to remain but under Palestinian law.

Transition Toward a Palestinian State

To facilitate the peace initiatives we have discussed, there are several important steps that can be taken.

1. Israel, if it chooses the path of peacemaking and enters into negotiations to trade land for peace, must accept full Palestinian involvement and recognize that it cannot dictate to the Palestinians who their representatives should be. Settlement building and further integration of the occupied territories into the political economy of Israel should be halted during the period of negotiations

and transition. A modus vivendi between the military authorities and the civilian population should be in place allowing for appropriate civil and political life, probably including withdrawal of Israeli troops from population centers and refraining from the use of the military in maintaining civil order.

2. The Palestinians, if they are to successfully enter negotiations for their independent state, will need great clarity in their political positions and clear understanding of the barriers of mistrust among Israelis that must be overcome. The PLO has taken an important step by renouncing terrorism against Israel. The Arab nations can speed the process by indicating their own interest in achieving peace with Israel as part of the resolution of the Palestine question.

3. To move this process forward and to demonstrate its commitment, the United States should take seriously its dialogue with the PLO and adopt the explicit aim of encouraging the PLO's full involvement in the peace process. Washington must indicate its acceptance of the role the PLO must play if the Palestinian question is to be resolved.

4. A special role for the United Nations should be carefully examined. Would a limited UN trusteeship during a transition period provide a basis for security and justice for both Israelis and Palestinians?

Designs of a Transition[36]

Discussions with Palestinians, including civic and political leaders in the West Bank and the Gaza Strip, have indicated that an interim period or transition is acceptable before establishment of an independent state. The late Fahd Qawasmi, deported mayor of Hebron, set the tone: "If Israel says this is the land of the Palestinians, then we can discuss security, future relations between us, how to arrive at peace, a hundred times. But the aim of negotiations must be clear from the start."[37] This same theme emerged in many interviews with Palestinians in the territories during the *intifadah*.[38] While Secretary of State Shultz, in his efforts in the spring of 1988, pointed to the need to speed up the transition process, serious attention must be paid to the plans for the period of transition so that it does not become an obstacle to ultimate separation. West Bank Palestinians stress that it is necessary that they have assurances that the interim regime is not a step toward Israeli annexation. Instead, the transition period should prepare Palestinians and Israelis to live apart. Most plans call for some form of interim Palestinian governing authority or council. The council to be established in the West Bank and the Gaza Strip should have adequate and secure financing; it should have powers of taxation and the ability to receive loans and grants from abroad, from Arab countries and European and American sources. In addition, the council should have authority over administrative affairs such as agriculture, commerce, customs, education, health, industry, police, postal services, social welfare, and tourism. Relationships between the council and the municipality and village bodies would need to be clarified.

On questions of transport and movement, the Palestinians believe the movement of goods and people between Gaza and the West Bank on designated roads across Israel and across the Jordan River bridges should be guaranteed. The proximity of the two regions seems to make this realistic. The council should develop the Gaza port facility and have full use of Kalandia Airport north of Jerusalem. The security arrangements necessary at border crossing points should be negotiated.

Other important issues have been addressed by Palestinians considering a transition period. Security, a point of critical importance for Israelis, brings a realistic response from some Palestinian analysts. Israeli military presence limited to specific strategic sites along the Jordan River at observation posts in the central mountain ridge is probably acceptable during a transition period. Internal security should, however, be handled by a Palestinian police force, and Israeli troops should not be permitted to patrol city streets, enter houses, and arrest residents. Responsibility for the military court and prison system should be assumed by the Palestinian council. Further, Palestinians would welcome United Nations or other international neutral forces in the territories to help assure the security of both Israelis and Palestinians.

Refugees, from the Arab–Israeli wars of 1948 and 1967, also pose problems for an interim governing authority. Their right to move to the West Bank and the Gaza Strip must be established through negotiations. Their return would probably have to be phased in carefully to fit with a broad plan for economic and social development. While identity cards for all residents and returning

Palestinians would be required during transition, the issuance of passports to Palestinians remaining abroad could be deferred until later in the negotiations. Negotiations on behalf of the Palestinians would have to be carried out by the PLO. Virtually all leaders in the West Bank and the Gaza Strip are unanimous in this view.

It is not reasonable to assume that all Palestinians living in the Arab states, whether in refugee camps or integrated into their host society, could or would want to return to a Palestinian state. As part of a realistic transition, the Arab states should indicate their willingness fully to accept some Palestinians as permanent residents and thus make refugee camps unnecessary and relieve continued Palestinian resentment. Special arrangements will have to be made for the Palestinians living in the refugee camps and elsewhere in Lebanon. The instability of that country and the severe pressures Palestinians have been under demand rapid, humane action.

There are advantages for both Israel and the Palestinians in accepting current proposals for mutual recognition, negotiation, and transition to the creation of an independent Palestinian state. Israel should take advantage of the increased willingness of important Arab states to exchange recognition and peaceful relations for a solution to the Palestinian question. The Arab states and the PLO should press ahead with these realistic and just peace proposals. The international community, especially the United States, should be prepared to aid the Israelis, Palestinians, and Arabs to take steps which they may not be able to accomplish alone.

It is not only Israeli doves who disagree with those who insist that Israel maintain sovereignty over the occupied West Bank. General Yehoshafat Harkabi, former chief of Israeli Intelligence and a man with a hawkish reputation, believes it is in Israel's interests to leave the territories. "I am for finalizing the conflict, and you cannot do that without recognizing that the Palestinians, like any other human group, deserve self-determination. The British had to get out of India and Israel will have to get out of the West Bank." It is Harkabi's view that in spite of the former extremism of the Palestinians and lingering doubts about the PLO's readiness for peacemaking, realism requires "seeing that the other side are human beings, too, with needs" that must be recognized. "We have to understand the fate of the West Bank will be decided by its people, and they are overwhelmingly Arab." But he insisted:

"They must also recognize that we deserve political self-determination. What I want is the final account—not leaving the door open, which is the PLO position."[39] As Harkabi added in his most recent statement: "Israel faces a moment of truth, in the full sense of the word . . . we must develop a vision of the 'Zionism of quality'—and we have the prerequisites for that in the vast talent in this country—instead of a 'Zionism of acreage' and populism."[40]

NOTES ON JERUSALEM

In our many conversations with Arabs, Israelis, and Palestinians, AFSC has found that the deepest and most anguishing problems are centered on Jerusalem. We have also found, however, a virtually unanimous agreement that these problems should not be dealt with at the outset of negotiations. Their solution, it is held, will come as part of an agreement reached on other central issues. When Israeli security and Palestinian statehood are assured, Jerusalem may be discussed with new confidence and mutual trust. We, therefore, have chosen to discuss Jerusalem briefly in this separate note.

To Israelis and Palestinians, Jerusalem is of profound significance; it involves historical, religious, nationalist, security, and economic considerations. It is unnecessary to belabor their attachment to the city. What is important is to try to identify where the attitudes of the two sides could conceivably permit some accommodation and where the bedrock imperatives lie.

The Jerusalem issue involves almost solely the dispostion of the areas occupied by Israel in 1967. Israel's possession of West Jerusalem (the part under Israeli control prior to 1967) in the context of a final settlement is not seriously questioned. The earlier concept of an internationalized city including both Arab and Israeli Jerusalem, set forth in the 1947 UN General Assembly resolution that contained a partition plan and established the State of Israel, is no longer thought to be realistic by the major parties. The areas in dispute are: the walled Old City, about one square mile, in which are located the major Christian, Jewish, and Muslim shrines and in which communities of Israelis, Palestinians, and non-Palestinian Christians live; the modern Palestinian business and residential districts, largely north and east of the Old City, into which Israel has introduced sizable Jewish housing projects and where some pre-1948 Jewish institutions have been much expanded; and outlying Palestinian communities, beyond the pre-1967 boundaries of Jerusalem, which Israel incorporated into the city in late 1967 and which are considered by Israelis to be an integral part of Jerusalem as annexed by them on July 30, 1980.

On major issues, the stated positions of Israel and the Arabs seem far apart and irreconcilable. Israel insists that the city remain undivided under Israeli rule, having declared its incorporation into Israel in 1967 and formally annexed it in 1980. The extensive urban housing neighborhoods built by Israel on Arab lands in a ring around Jerusalem provide additional "facts on the ground." The aim was to make the city indivisible. The Arabs demand essentially a return to the pre-1967 status, though there is some evidence they might accept the concept of a physically united city. Publicly at least, neither side has spelled out a position in detail, and probably will not, pending serious negotiations, but each no doubt has priorities which will guide its proposals.

Israeli Position

In any negotiations Israel would insist on continued free movement in Jerusalem. Israelis must have access to their holy sites, particularly the Western Wall in the Old City, and to the university and related institutions on Mount Scopus, north and east of the Old City. They would also have a much higher degree of security for their own populated areas in the city than would be the case if immediately adjacent Arab areas were closed to them. They would certainly insist that the Jewish community continue to live in its reconstructed quarter of the walled city. Moreover, Israelis would also insist that freedom of movement and residence not be at the sufferance of any outside authority, whether Arab or international. Their experience of the divided city during the period of Jordanian rule (1948–67) in East Jerusalem, when they were barred from access to the Western Wall and saw their holy sites abused, is still fresh in their minds.

If any Arab administration were to have or share authority (assuming Israel would agree to this as part of a peace agreement), it will be essential to Israel that it represent an Arab state that in itself is not threatening. Since Palestinian authority in Jerusalem under any conceivable peace settlement would be exercised by the administration of the Arab areas contiguous to the city—the West Bank—the identity and acceptability of that administration would have to be established before Israel would accept an agreement involving Jerusalem, which would ultimately have to be negotiated in the context of the West Bank solution, since the two are inter-related in so many ways. This became evident during the autonomy negotiations that stemmed from the Camp David agreements when questions arose at an early stage whether Arab Jerusalem as a geographic area was to be considered part of the autonomous area, or even if the population of Arab Jerusalem was to have some relationship to the process of establishing an autonomous authority on the West Bank. Even should it be possible to obtain Israeli agreement to some Jerusalem settlement involving the West Bank Arab authority, however, it is not conceivable that Israel would agree to the presence of Arab military forces in any part of the city.

Israel might be more flexible on the modalities of governing Jerusalem so long as any administrative arrangement satisfied the basic requirements outlined above. The Israeli authorities have gone to great pains to make it difficult to divide Jerusalem again politically. The Jewish housing projects strategically planted among and around the Arab districts now have a population of over 100,000, compared with an Arab population for the enlarged post-1967 city of about 130,000. Some of these projects, and a major settlement to the east between Jerusalem and Jericho, were designed to interrupt the contiguity of the Arab areas of Jerusalem to the adjacent West Bank. In addition to these physical barriers, Israel has taken legislative steps intended to put Israeli sovereignty over the entire city beyond question in the future. In response to nationalist pressures following the Camp David accords, the Knesset enacted the Basic Law on Jerusalem of July 30, 1980, in effect formally annexing the expanded city to Israel. Nonetheless, if a satisfactory settlement of the entire Palestinian question depended on it, and if major Israeli priorities were provided for, the current Israeli insistence on full sovereign control over the entire city might be negotiable.

Arab Position

The Arabs, for their part, have varied sets of priorities depending on who and where they are, but some priorities seem likely to be irreducible. The Palestinian population of East Jerusalem, whether Christian or Muslim, wants to be free of Israeli control and to live under Arab rule. They, and other Palestinians, believe that Jerusalem must be the seat of government of the Palestinian state that will be established in the West Bank and Gaza in a peace settlement and that Arab Jerusalem, therefore, not only must be under Arab rule but must be linked to this wider Arab entity. Such linkage is important not only for historical and political reasons but also because Jerusalem is the logical and traditional economic and transport center for a good deal of the West Bank. Now, as in biblical times, it is Jerusalem that holds the northern and southern regions together. For Arabs other than Palestinians concerned with Jerusalem as a religious center, the paramount consideration would be the ability to visit Muslim holy sites without being subject to Israeli authority.

Arab flexibility could be hoped for with respect to the precise arrangements for governing East Jerusalem (particularly the walled city), the continued residence there of Jewish communities, freedom of movement about the city, and the exact nature of the relationship between Arab Jerusalem and the adjacent Arab entity of which it would presumably be the capital. Might there also be some flexibility in defining the area of Jerusalem that would be the Arab capital? For the Arabs, and in particular the Palestinians, a general solution of the Palestinian question would have to be in sight in order to expect compromise on agreements on the specific and knotty aspects of Jerusalem.

Potential Solutions[41]

Our suggestions about higher and lower priorities do not reflect the stated official positions of either side. However, the ability to deal successfully with a few key issues will determine the success or failure of any Jerusalem negotiation:

Nature of the administration of Arab Jerusalem. It will require a unique and imaginative form of administration if:

- There is free movement about the entire city
- For the Israelis, this freedom is not at the sufferance of an Arab authority
- Palestinian residents of East Jerusalem are under Palestinian, not Israeli, rule
- Jerusalem becomes the capital of both Israel and the West Bank–Gaza Palestinian state

We do not know of a well-constructed proposal to satisfy these difficult administrative needs. But to illustrate some elements that might be considered, we offer the following thoughts: A solution seems to become more practicable when fewer general principles, such as national sovereignty, are applied and more local considerations are used to fashion the administrative system. The "borough system" proposed by some Israelis falls short of Palestinian requirements but might point the way to a solution. Under it, Jerusalem would be divided into sections, or boroughs, some Palestinian and some Israeli: each would be administered by an authority of its own nationality. Such an arrangement in itself begs the question of who would ultimately control the entire city, especially its security (the Israeli borough idea assumed Israel would), which cannot be avoided entirely though it can perhaps be deemphasized by joint Palestinian–Israeli performance of some functions and by the form of linkage between Jerusalem and the contiguous Israeli and Palestinian areas.

In pursuing local solutions, special treatment might be accorded to the walled city, which is of such great importance to communities throughout the world that it might be the one part of the city that could have an international hand in its administration along with Palestinian and Israeli.

Relationship with surrounding areas. A settlement that provided that there would be free movement throughout Jerusalem and that the city would be the capital of the respective contiguous national areas would pose the problem of establishing an effective border control between Israel and the West Bank–Gaza Palestinian entity. Unless special steps were taken, anyone entering Jerusalem from either country would be free to cross Jerusalem into the other country. Again, inventive solutions would be required, the most obvious of which would involve special treatment of all traffic into and out of Jerusalem. For example, a form of such control, based on license plates, has been applied to vehicular traffic by Israeli authorities since 1967.

The relationship between both countries and Jerusalem might be affected in other ways as well. Israel, for example, might well insist that military forces of a Palestinian West Bank entity (limited though they might be) should not be brought into Jerusalem. To secure such a limitation, Israel might have to accept a similar restriction on its forces, with the effect of achieving a form of demilitarization of the city in many ways appropriate to its world-wide religious significance.

At some early stage in a period of transition, it could be valuable to convene a meeting of Israeli and Palestinian experts and scholars familiar with Jerusalem to create a list of reasonable options that could serve as a basis for effective negotiations.

6

The Tragedy of Lebanon

Lebanon must wait for a solution to its searing domestic conflicts and civil war; it has little choice. Lebanon's problems are its own, but they are also the problems that have kept the broader Middle East conflicts alive for more than four decades.

By the time the major battles of the Lebanese civil war came to an end in 1976, the human toll was high. More than 65,000 men, women, and children were killed during the first nineteen months of that war. This number takes on stark significance when compared with the 39,900 people killed in all four Arab–Israeli wars. Some 1.5 million people were uprooted from homes in cities and villages of Lebanon, and almost half of them remain displaced. One family in ten fled Lebanon during the fighting. More than 400,000 children were victims of the warfare—wounded, displaced, abandoned, and orphaned—all in a country of 3.5 million people.[1]

The guns of the civil war never really fell silent. The Green Line (really barricades and a burnt-out no-man's-land separating the Christian and Muslim parts of Beirut) that was created during the war became "sniper land." Lebanese and Palestinian militias have fought continuing large and small skirmishes in many parts of the country; Syrian forces intervened in 1976 and have been involved in large- and small-scale military actions ever since; and on two occasions Israeli forces invaded Lebanon, first in the limited Operation Litani in March 1978 and then in the full-scale invasion four years later in June 1982—Operation Peace for Galilee. Israeli forces remained involved in skirmishes in southern Lebanon until the spring of 1985, when they withdrew to an enclave more than five miles wide on the Lebanese side of the border; there, with the mercenary South Lebanese Army, they have engaged in periodic small-scale battles with Lebanese and Palestinian militias. For the more than thirteen years since 1975, Lebanon has known no peace; over 100,000 people have been killed and twice as many wounded or disabled. Its social and physical fabric has been rent asunder; almost half the population has been forced from their homes and communities; the political entity that was a single state is now in reality a series of armed enclaves—a nation in name only.[2][3]

Historically, Lebanon was a place of refuge for Christian and Muslim heretics who came to hide in its rugged mountains. In the past, Lebanon's doors were open to Christian Armenians and Assyrians and Muslim Kurds and Palestinians fleeing oppression and war. Now refugees from war and civil disorder in Lebanon have spread to many other parts of the globe.

INTERNAL ROOTS AND EXTERNAL PRESSURE

All outside observers, as well as the Lebanese, agree that the fundamental problems in Lebanon are Lebanese—a deep internal division along religious and socioeconomic lines. These divisions are made greater by a mixture of confessional rivalry, nationalism, enthnocentrism, and class conflict. Lebanon has lived with the fiction of the existence of a small Christian majority and this advantage had been translated into political authority and power. In addition to these Lebanese issues there are intense inter-Arab rivalries, pressures generated by the Israeli–Palestinian struggle, and the presence of armed Palestinian guerrillas in substantial numbers.[4]

The problems of political representation date from the National Pact of 1943, put in place as the French withdrew after twenty-three years of mandate control. They left behind a political system dominated by the Francophile Maronite Christians, who had, under French rule, become a privileged class. The political arrangements of the 1943 independence divided political power by sects; the President was to be Maronite Christian, the Prime Minister Sunni Muslim, and the Speaker of the Parliament Shiite Muslim. Christians were to enjoy an artificially established six-to-five advantage in legislative representation. It was inevitable that the 1943 sociopolitical status quo would collapse as the demographic reality changed. While no census has been taken since 1932, Lebanese Muslims almost certainly constitute a majority of the population, with Shiite Muslims probably the largest subgroup. The rise of Muslim political movements, seeking greater political power and representation, challenged Christian predominance in important government and commercial sectors. The left-leaning Muslim groups have often urged reform or abandonment of the confessional politics and governance, which gives such preeminence to the role of religious groups in the nation's politics.

The confessional system from even before the civil war, led to a weak central government that either encouraged or tolerated factionalism and reliance on private militias. Economically, the central government has had little power, with a limited right to tax, and consequently it has offered limited social services and little aid for development. With growing inflation, economic inequalities became an even more serious problem.

Confessional divisions blocked the establishment of a national identity that might have helped knit together the fragments assembled by France in the period of the 1920s to the 1940s. One Lebanese Christian scholar summed up the situation:

> The Christian predominance discouraged formation of a distinctive Lebanese identity among Muslims. The Muslim mainstream was weak in both fact and perception and so many sought outside support, first from Nasser's Arab nationalism and later from the Palestinian movement. Lebanese Muslims are now disenchanted with both, but they are left without an effective identity. Lebanese Maronites, for their part, also sought outside patrons, from France to Israel, and for many of them Lebanon meant nothing more than their Christian identity.[5]

Any long-term solution of Lebanon's problems will have to include some form of a recast sociopolitical contract which more nearly represents the demographic realities of the confessional groups and addresses the needs of group identity and equity.

LEBANON, ISRAEL, AND THE PALESTINIANS

Tens of thousands of Palestinians fleeing Haifa on the coast and villages in the Galilee in northern Palestine in 1948 made their way across the border into southern Lebanon. By 1952 they numbered at least 100,000 and, since they were largely Muslim, posed a special problem for Lebanon's delicate confessional balance. They were refused integration into the Lebanese political system, and since most of them were peasants, it was difficult for them to enter Lebanon's economic system.

The 1967 war brought a new influx of Palestinian refugees from the West Bank into Lebanon and the Arab defeat stimulated militant Palestinian nationalism. A guerrilla campaign was launched against Israel from both Lebanon and Jordan, leading to strong Israeli reprisals to disrupt Palestinian operations and to force Lebanon and Jordan to crack down on the Palestinians. Jordan's King Hussein, with the support of a strong army, succeeded during 1970 and 1971 in halting guerrilla actions from his country and in driving the Palestinian guerrilla leadership and forces out of Jordan following the battles of "Black September" in 1970, when Palestinian groups tried to overthrow the King. Most went to Lebanon. The weak Lebanese government and army could not suppress the Palestinian forces, which had significant support from sectors of the Lebanese public and also had strong Arab backing for their attempts to persevere in Lebanon—their only political and military base.

By the mid-1970s, the Palestinian population had grown to well over 200,000, or 8 percent of Lebanon's population, and it could not be assimilated. Indeed, neither the Palestinians nor the Lebanese Christians wanted Palestinian assimilation. The Palestinian movement was initially supported by most Muslim and many liberal and leftist Christian Lebanese but was resented and feared by the Christian right. Palestinian attacks against Israel caused Israel to intervene in Lebanon with great force, thus exacerbating sectarian and political tensions. The Palestinians, living together in organized communities with a quasi-governing structure of their own, numerous local industries and social services, and a substantial armed force, created a "state within a state." Indeed, in Lebanon in the late 1970s the Palestinians developed the closest thing they ever had to a state and government of their own. They had what was probably the best-organized and best-armed fighting force in Lebanon and they became allied with the Muslim political movements attempting to redraw the political map of Lebanon and achieve greater social influence. In the south of Lebanon, where the PLO had established major military camps after its ouster from Jordan, there was continuing and growing friction with the local Shiite population. In Beirut, whole sections of the western sector of the city, from Fakahani through Sabra and Shatila to Burj el-Barajneh, resembled a Palestinian city, with hospitals, schools, and "government" offices. The Palestinians had become a major force in Lebanon, but they were not of Lebanon.

LEBANON: THE SURROGATE BATTLEFIELD

Neither side could have won the civil war by itself. The Maronite-dominated Lebanese Front, which had already established a working liaison with Israel, was being pushed hard by the Muslim militias, which had finally enlisted the direct involvement of a reluctant PLO. The Lebanese army was as badly split as the nation itself, and by April 1976 it disintegrated and elements of it joined the several independent militias. Syrians, watching nervously from across the border, were fully ready to heed the call by the new Lebanese President, Elias Sarkis, and they intervened militarily in April 1976. The Syrians, who initially were against the radical-Palestinian forces and later against the Christians, were determined to maintain the status quo. They feared that if the radical-Palestinian alliance triumphed, the Israelis would intervene, thereby challenging what Syria believed to be a critical part of its own sphere of influence. After the fact, the Arab League voted to give Syria a legitimate role as the leading group in an Arab peace-keeping force. Thus a tense truce brought the main fighting of the civil war to an end and left Syrian forces in the middle of a standoff between the Maronite Lebanese forces and the alliance of the National Movement and Palestinians.[6]

Lebanon had suffered during the civil war; it was further violated when it became the surrogate battlefield for the intractable conflict that has kept the Middle East in turmoil for more than four decades. As the civil war wound down in late 1976, Israel stepped up attacks against Palestinian refugee camps, villages, and military installations in southern Lebanon that Palestinian groups used as staging grounds for attacks on Israel. But more than Palestinian forces were hurt by the fighting; Palestinian and Lebanese civilians and their property bore the brunt of the attacks; for example, a major Israeli assault in July 1981 killed 300 civilians and wounded an additional 800 when bombs were dropped in the heavily populated Fakahani section of West Beirut, which served also as headquarters for many Palestinian organizations.

The largest and most damaging Israeli assault in Lebanon prior to 1982 was its invasion of the south in March 1978. It came in reprisal for a terrorist attack by the PLO on the coastal highway near Tel Aviv that resulted in the killing of innocent Israeli civilians. Israel responded by sending 25,000 troops into Lebanon as far north as the Litani River, which raised local fears about Israel's long-term intentions in Lebanon. An intensive air and artillery bombardment that preceded the use of Israeli ground forces damaged 80 percent of southern Lebanon's villages and destroyed some completely. Approximately 200,000 Lebanese and 65,000 Palestinian refugees fled the area, and the press reported that between 1,000 and 2,000 Arab civilians were killed. The March 1978 invasion confirmed, one Lebanese observer claimed, that "Israel is the most powerful actor on the Lebanese stage. Syria can do nothing against it and certainly the Palestinians can't. Israel can control the Christian forces in the south and has a lot of influence on the Christian forces in the rest of the country."[7]

As Israel withdrew its forces southward after passage of UN Security Council Resolution 425 (March 19, 1978), it left behind an Israeli-supported Lebanese militia led by a breakaway Lebanese army major, Saad Haddad. The forces of Major Haddad controlled an area about five miles deep along most of the sixty-mile Lebanese–Israeli border from the slopes of Mount Hermon in the east to the Mediterranean coast in the west. The militia, supplied and paid by the Israelis, often engaged in joint operations with Israeli troops, who entered the zone on a regular basis.[8] This zone, in southern Lebanon near the border, was to have been turned over to the control of the newly created United Nations Interim Force in Lebanon (UNIFIL). Instead, Israel, when it withdrew three

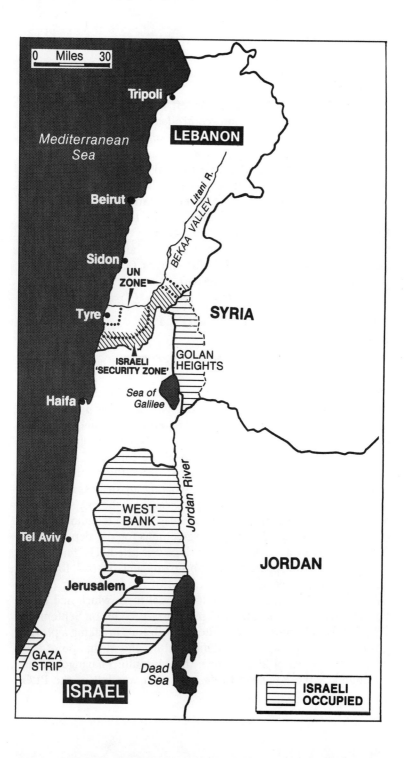

months after the March invasion, turned the region over to Major Haddad.

The remainder of Lebanon was left badly divided (virtually a de facto partition) into regions controlled by different forces: (1) the Syrian army (three-fifths of the country in the central and northern regions, especially along the Syrian border); (2) the right-wing Christian Phalange (East Beirut and the traditionally Christian Mount Lebanon highlands); (3) a smaller Christian faction led by former Lebanese President Suleiman Franjieh (confined to the north, the base of Franjieh's political and clan support); (4) the Lebanese leftists and the PLO (West Beirut; the southern coastal region from Damour to Tyre and eastward between the Zahrani and Litani rivers); and (5) UNIFIL forces (south of the Litani River to the Haddad–Israeli enclave).

ISRAEL'S INVASION OF LEBANON, 1982

It was into this stalemated situation that Israel launched its Operation Peace for Galilee, on June 6, 1982. The attack followed a year of an uneasy truce negotiated in July 1981 by Philip Habib, special U.S. envoy, with help from the Saudi Foreign Minister. During the first stage of the invasion, Israeli troops pounded the cities, villages, and refugee camps of southern Lebanon and advanced rapidly north to Beirut, encircling the city by June 13, and then engaged in a two-week battle to secure control of the mountains overlooking the city. The next stage of the battle was the seven-week siege of West Beirut, involving air strikes, naval and artillery bombardment, and direct pressure on the city's inhabitants—when food supplies, water, electricity, and telephones were cut off. On August 12, when an agreement for the departure of the PLO forces was agreed on, the siege was lifted. The final stage of the invasion, and probably the most damaging to Israel, followed quickly on the heels of the withdrawal of the four-power (U.S., British, French, and Italian) multinational force which had been brought in to supervise the PLO pullout. At 5 p.m. on September 16, 1982, Israeli troops moved into West Beirut, breaking a pledge given to the U.S. negotiator, Philip Habib, and at that point Defense Minister Ariel Sharon gave the Maronite Phalange militia commanders the go-ahead to destroy what was left of the PLO infrastructure in the refugee camps. "I don't want a single one of the terrorists left," he is quoted as saying. Two days earlier, the Phalange leader and newly elected Lebanese President Bashir Gemayel had been assassinated by pro-Syrian Phalangist dissidents and revenge seemed to motivate the militia. While Israeli troops surrounded the two Palestinian refugee districts, Phalangist militiamen entered two Palestinian refugee camps, Sabra and Shatila, and for two days carried out a massacre that left more than 1,000 dead, mainly women, children, and the elderly.[9] A report subsequently issued by a commission headed by Israeli Supreme Court president Yitzhak Kahan was sharply critical of Israeli leadership, civilian and military, and forced the removal from office of Minister of Defense Sharon and several senior military staff. Israeli public reaction was strong, and much of the support for the invasion disappeared. The largest demonstration in Israel's history— 400,000 people, or almost one-seventh of the entire Jewish population—gathered in Tel Aviv's Municipality Square to condemn the massacres and the war. The number killed in the two refugee camps was only a fraction of the estimated 19,000 dead in the war itself or of the 600,000 displaced as the army rolled north and then shelled Beirut. But the massacre became a symbol of Israel's moral failure, which overshadowed any successful aspects of the invasion.

The final phase of Israel's longest war was fought out with Lebanese militia groups for almost three years until Israel's pullback into the so-called Security Zone on Lebanon's southern border in June 1985. It became a war of attrition, with a large number of Israeli casualties, amounting to over 600 in all; the alienation of the population of southern Lebanon continued. By early 1984 Israeli troops faced an average of four armed attacks each day.[10] During this period of occupation, the Shiites of southern Lebanon, who had been among those who welcomed Israel's role in removing the unwelcome PLO forces, turned against the Israelis and developed important new militias and political groups. The Amal or mainstream Shiite militia was joined by an Iranian-inspired Muslim militia, the Hizballah, and together they drove up the cost of the Israeli occupation and drove out (not quite all the way) the Israeli forces. Among Arabs and especially among the Palestinians, this was widely perceived as a military victory over the powerful Israeli army. Even some Israelis shared this assessment.

Why did Israel invade Lebanon in June 1982 in spite of the fairly successful cease-fire that had been worked out between Israel and the PLO in the summer of 1981? Ze'ev Schiff and Ehud Ya'ari, Israel's leading military affairs correspondents, quoted Defense Minister Sharon (1981) directly:

> I am talking about an action that will mean destroying the terrorist organizations in Lebanon in such a way that they will not be able to rebuild their military and political base. It is impossible to do this without running into the Syrians. . . . It is possible to achieve [a long-lasting change] on condition that a legitimate regime emerges in Lebanon, not just a puppet government; that it signs a peace treaty with Israel and that it becomes part of the free world. In order to establish a government of this kind, you need sixty-six out of the ninety deputies to the Lebanese Parliament, and a list of deputies will be prepared.[11]

Sharon reasoned that with the PLO thus weakened, and its legitimacy gone, its influence over the West Bank and Gaza would wither. A conciliatory Palestinian leadership could then emerge, and could conduct negotiations for autonomy with Israel, thereby forcing any independent political aspirations the Palestinians might have to be focused on Jordan (the old Sharon plan). All this, in Sharon's view, would assure unchallenged Israeli supremacy for several decades.[12] In addition, a security zone in southern Lebanon would be permanently established along Israel's northern border and the Syrians would be expelled from Lebanon.[13]

At the cost of leaving Lebanon close to political, economic, and physical ruin, Israeli policy has failed on almost every count. After six years of an almost nonstop low-intensity (sometimes high-intensity on a local level) conflict, Lebanon was left in September 1988 with two governments—one Christian, one Muslim—after the parties failed to agree upon a mutually acceptable presidential candidate. Syrian forces, far from being excluded from Lebanon, now number approximately 30,000; they control much of the area from Sidon north and east through the Bekaa Valley, patrol the streets of West Beirut, and remain the dominant external influence. Even so, Syria has been unable to reconstruct a unified Lebanon. The Maronite-led Christian community, with its substantial militia and continued aid from Israel, remains in control of East Beirut, many of the northern coastal cities (not as far as Tripoli), and their traditional stronghold in the Metn, the mountainous region to the northeast of Beirut. The Shiites, who have emerged as the major Muslim political force, control much of southern Lebanon and parts of the Bekaa and themselves have been split, with a radical wing that has plagued Western interests by taking hostages and embarking on (often self-destructive) military actions. The Druze maintain their independence (and an alliance with Syria) in their Shouf mountain stronghold. The PLO, initially dispersed among a number of Arab states and weakened by factional disputes (some Syrian-supported), have made a significant political comeback and remain the dominant voice in Palestinian political life. The *intifadah* in the West Bank and Gaza is just the type of revolt that Sharon's grand design was aimed at preventing. While by no means a major military force in Lebanon, PLO militia groups have infiltrated back into the country and remain strong in areas near the large Palestinian camps and settlements. The border Security Zone still exists, but at constant cost of death and injury to Israeli troops and to their surrogates in the Christian-led South Lebanon Army.

The United States played a role at several key junctures in recent Lebanese history that has left American policy and reputation in shambles. From a high point of President Jimmy Carter's important effort to convince Israel to rapidly withdraw its forces after the March 1978 invasion, the United States seemed to allow itself to become ensnared in supporting one group or party against another and found its personnel, diplomatic and military, targets of disastrous attacks. Several Israeli analysts concluded that Secretary of State Alexander Haig gave what Israeli Defense Minister Sharon interpreted as a "green light" just before the June 1982 invasion.[14] Although the United States did vote for UN Security Council Resolution 509, during the first days of the war, calling for Israel to "withdraw all its military forces forthwith and unconditionally withdraw to the internationally recognized boundaries of Lebanon," the resolution had no effect. The Reagan administration was unwilling to take the next step and demand Israeli compliance and threaten sanctions, and on June 8 the United States vetoed a UN draft resolution to that effect although it was supported by all the other Security Council members.[15]

The United States, acting through its special ambassador, Philip Habib, was instrumental in negotiating the PLO withdrawal from Beirut and the establishment of a special multinational force to oversee the evacuation. A series of confidential agreements about protecting Palestinian civilians and providing security for the refugee camps were also made. The rapidity with which the United States withdrew its Marine force immediately after the PLO units were evacuated left considerable confusion about the nature of the U.S. commitment and seemed to provide the space into which Israeli troops moved as they entered Beirut on September 12, violating what the United States believed was its agreement with Israel prohibiting the Beirut move. It was in this context that the massacres in Sabra and Shatila took place, leaving the United States partially to blame for not fulfilling its part of the agreement by protecting the Palestinian camps from long-feared Phalangist revenge.[16] The United States and other members of the four-nation force rapidly returned their troops to Lebanon following the massacres and slowly the United States entered a new phase of the civil war on the Christian–Phalangist side. Agreements were reached to rearm and retrain the Lebanese army; other forms of help were offered to the new, relatively weak government of Amin Gemayel, the brother of the slain President. This involvement did not sit well with other groups in Lebanon, particularly those aligned with Syria, most pointedly the Shiite and Druze political communities. The U.S. embassy was destroyed by a massive car bomb in April 1983, killing sixty-three people, including seventeen Americans. U.S. forces shelled Druze and Syrian positions in the mountains east of Beirut during a mountain battle in which U.S. Marine forces fought alongside the Lebanese army to hold a crucial site. Two U.S. naval vessels were active off the Lebanese coast and shelled Druze mountain villages. On October 24, 1983, a suicide attack using a truck loaded with explosives demolished a U.S. barracks, killing 241 Marines. The same day a similar attack destroyed a French military headquarters.[17] By mid-February 1984, under continuous attack by Shiite militia forces, the Lebanese army broke up along sectarian community lines and the United States withdrew all its military forces. While the withdrawal was essential, the nature of the military engagement had been ill-conceived.

The major American diplomatic effort in Lebanon also ended in failure. A treaty, negotiated with strong U.S. backing (including personal involvement by Secretary of State Shultz), between the Lebanese government of Amin Gemayel and Israel set conditions for Israeli and Syrian withdrawal and terms for Lebanese domestic and international behavior. The opposition within Lebanon was highly critical. Syria, which had not been consulted during the drafting of the treaty and whose position in Lebanon would be severely compromised by its terms, flatly rejected it. The Syrians saw the treaty as designed in defiance of their country since it granted Israel excessive privileges and rewards for its 1982 invasion. In addition, Syria viewed the treaty as a repetition of the Camp David accords and a further attempt to break up the Arab bloc.[18] An unlikely and temporary coalition in the Lebanese Parliament blocked ratification of the treaty; Israel withdrew unilaterally, without winning concessions, and Syrian forces (some 30,000) remained in Lebanon. A standoff between Syria and Israel (with U.S. backing) has continued ever since.

IS A SOLUTION POSSIBLE IN LEBANON?

The social and political fabric of Lebanon has not been reconstructed, and the government does not successfully govern. Indeed, with the failure of the Parliament to elect a new President in September 1988, when Amin Gemayel's term expired, two governments emerged: one, appointed by Gemayel as his final act, was led by General Michel Aoun, the Maronite head of the Lebanese army; the second was led by Selim Hoss, the Prime Minister in the caretaker Cabinet that had been in place prior to the presidential "crisis." The country remains an armed camp with no national political authority; armed local militias of the many parties maintain control over sections of Beirut and most other sectors of the country. Syria maintains significant armed forces in many regions of the country, and Israel maintains 1,000–2,000 troops and supports a Lebanese force in the border enclave in the south. As one observer put it: "There are now more guns than people in Lebanon."

Although Syria has emerged as the dominant external force in Lebanese affairs, it has also failed in its goal to re-create a unified (even weakly united) Lebanon in spite of several major efforts. Syrian influence is vigorously opposed by the Maronite political leadership and its supporters in Israel. There are also segments of the Muslim community unhappy with Syria's close alliance with the Shiite Amal militia and the Druze forces.

All parties seem agreed on one critical issue—no full solution in Lebanon will be possible until the Israeli–Palestinian conflict is resolved. An interim solution may be within reach. It will, however, demand cooperation by parties who have long been at odds—Syria, the United States, and Israel. Help or at least acquiescence would be needed from others—the Soviet Union, Iraq, and Iran.

Elements that might help bring about an interim settlement include:

- The major powers agreeing to steps to insulate Lebanon from the influences of external conflicts, particularly by working with their own allies and surrogates in the region: the United States with Israel, the Soviet Union with Syria.
- The UN Security Council, through the Secretary-General, calling the relevant parties together to establish basic terms to protect Lebanon's independence, sovereignty, and territorial integrity.[19] The recent UN successes in mediating conflicts—Iran–Iraq, Afghanistan, Southeast Asia—give added strength and legitimacy to a renewed, active role for the UN. This becomes more likely as the United States and the Soviet Union find the means to resolve regional conflicts where they have often supported opposing sides.
- The United States and Syria vigorously pursuing joint efforts to identify and act on matters of common interest. Recent signs of new U.S.–Syrian efforts to agree upon a broad set of principles for maintaining a unified Lebanon are hopeful. Attempts in recent years to freeze Syria out of serious diplomatic efforts in the Middle East will have to be given up. An effort in which the United States works jointly with divided Lebanese communities and Syria to find a modus vivendi could be valuable.
- International efforts dealing directly with the conflict between Iraq and Syria to prevent its spilling over once again into Lebanon.
- Special attempts by the Palestinian nationalist leadership—the PLO—to reassess its role in Lebanese politics and conflicts and relieve Lebanon, as much as possible, of the burdens of Palestinian conflicts with Israel and Syria.

It is difficult to be optimistic about solutions for the endless crisis in Lebanon. But it is essential not to become callous about the continued conflict and violence in Lebanon, not to put the problem out of sight or to assume that dealing with the Lebanese crisis can be delayed until other, more visible conflicts are resolved. The people of Lebanon deserve better from the international community.

7

The Arms Race

The Middle East today is the largest importer of arms in the world, buying well over one-third of all the world's arms exports at a rate approaching $12 billion a year; it accounts for 50 percent of weapons imported by all Third World nations. During the early part of the decade the sale of arms was the fastest-growing sector of the economies of most states in the region. By the mid-1980s this remained true only for those countries directly or indirectly involved in actual combat. The Middle East is spending more than $35 billion per year on its armed forces, has the highest per capita military expenditure and the highest rate of arms growth, more than 350 percent since the 1967 war. Six of the ten leading arms-importing countries are in the Middle East.[1] In the decade 1973–83, annual military expenditures in the region rose almost 300 percent in constant dollars, corrected for inflation. While the growth has slowed slightly in the past five years, it is still high. The increase is proportionately larger than in any other sector of the world; the Middle East's share of world military expenditures (1973–83) rose from 4.2 percent to 7.8 percent. The rate of increased expenditure is more than double that of NATO or the Warsaw Pact. Arms are no longer a symptom; they have become an important part of the problem.

The Middle East arms race has taken on a life of its own, spurred by a variety of causes: local rivalries and the desire to obtain ever more sophisticated weaponry; the brutal Iran–Iraq war; the long-standing unresolved Arab–Israeli conflict; the desire of the super-powers to "play out" their conflict in the Middle East by securing allies through arms-transfer agreements; the desire of the Western industrial nations to recycle through arms sales the petrodollars created by their reliance on expensive imported oil; and, ironically enough, the Egyptian–Israeli peace treaty, which called for the United States to supply the two countries with massive new arms and continued military aid.

The leading arms exporters are the United States, the Soviet Union, France, Great Britain, and the People's Republic of China (in that order). The United States and the Soviet Union together account for over half the arms supplies to the Middle East. One reason for this predominance has been the willingness of both countries to share some of their most sophisticated weapons with their customers in the Middle East. This practice is not common in arms sales to other Third World countries. China's ascendancy to fifth place was based largely on the arms it sold to Iran and Iraq.[2]

If investments in armaments and armies are any indicator, it would be hard to conclude that any state in the Middle East is really interested in peacemaking. The only constraints on a constant increase in acquisitions have been falling oil revenues in the Arab world and a period of crippling inflation followed by stringent budget limits in Israel. During the past twenty years the region has seen the creation of permanent warfare states. Social and economic modernization has given way in many societies to militarization.

In the Middle East plowshares are being beaten into swords. The military has the largest work force and is the predominant employer of those with education; it is the leading employer in urban areas. For the region as a whole, approximately 16 percent of the gross national product (GNP) is spent on the military; the figure is considerably higher in Syria, Israel, Iran, and Iraq, where an average of about 26 percent of all government expenditures is for the military.[3]

The pattern of supplying arms to the Middle East has undergone some clear changes in the past few years. The increasing reluctance of the U.S. Congress, under strong prodding from the pro-Israel lobby, to approve arms sales to the so-called moderate Arab states has both reduced the U.S. share of sales to the region (with the exception of Israel) and encouraged the Arab states to purchase from other sources. For example, after the U.S. Congress rejected the sale of 48 F-15 fighter planes to the Saudis in 1986, they turned to the British to buy an estimated $17 billion package consisting of 72 Tornado combat aircraft, 48 strike aircraft, and 24 interceptors, plus training craft, parts, and munitions.[4] In 1986–87 Jordan concluded substantial arms deals with Britain, France, and the Soviet Union for a wide range of equipment.[5]

On their side, the Soviets, following the implementation of an important new policy for relations with the nonsocialist Third World, abandoned most ideological tests for weapons customers and sold arms to states that previously would not have been eligible (or often willing) to receive Soviet and Eastern bloc military equipment; nonetheless, the amounts supplied to new customers are small in comparison with the amounts sent to long-standing customers Syria and Iraq, who between them account for more than 40 percent of all Soviet arms transfers to the Third World.[6]

Another factor in the changing patterns arises from the great increase in the number of suppliers of arms to the Middle East, particularly to Iran and Iraq. Their wartime acquisition policies made sales very lucrative and their need for rapid delivery led them to many new suppliers, governments, private brokers, and semi-legal middlemen. Almost all the European suppliers, East and West, willingly shipped arms to both Iran and Iraq. The Soviets and the United States fit the same pattern.[7] One of the anomalies of the Iran–Iraq war is the fact that Israel was joined by Syria and Libya in supplying arms to Iran, while all the other Arab states shipped arms to Iraq.

The desire for greater independence in choosing and acquiring weapons has led Israel to develop a substantial arms industry of its own, manufacturing not only small arms but tanks, planes, and missiles as well; Israel, however, was forced to abandon building the Lavi fighter/attack aircraft in 1987 when the development costs became too great and the United States, which had paid 90 percent of these expenses, objected to continuing the project.[8]

The economies of a number of the key countries in the region have been severely strained and subjected to inflationary pressure by their military budgets and arms imports; Israel in the early 1980s annually suffered inflation rates over 100 percent, with other countries trailing but still sharply affected. Major problems for the Shah of Iran in his final few years arose directly from his massive and expensive arms-acquisition program. Weapons are purchased largely at the expense of social and economic development. Huge military expenditures take other tolls on social structure and balance. The creation of military sectors of the society, the growth of elite officers' groups (often sent to other countries for training by superpower sponsors), and the extensive spread of training in the use of arms have had destabilizing effects on societies in the Middle East as elsewhere. There is no single pattern, but it would be irresponsible to ignore the extent to which military regimes, or regimes where the military have the ultimate power, have emerged in the Middle East.

The arms race there involves a number of critically important factors. The magnitude and the rate of increase already noted have until recently been the most obvious. In both operational jet combat aircraft and main battle tanks, the numbers in the Middle East are almost equal to those of the total NATO forces in Europe.[9] In addition to their numbers, there is the matter of sophistication. Middle Eastern countries have obtained new conventional weapons just as rapidly as they have been developed. The latest Soviet MiG-23 fighter planes and the newest U.S. F-15 fighters are already in use, and agreements are in place for delivery of the new-generation Soviet MiG-29s and C and D type U.S. F-16s. The 1981 U.S. decision to sell to Saudi Arabia five AWAC highly sophisticated advance-warning radar and control planes previously used only by U.S. forces is a further indication of the trend. The situation is the same with other conventional weapons systems, such as tanks, TV and laser-guided missiles, electronic countermeasure systems, helicopters, and aerial tankers for refueling of combat aircraft. Recent battles between Iran and Iraq, for example, where such weapons were used, have proven significantly more devastating to combatants and civilian populations as well as more destructive of both civilian and military physical facilities.

With economically forced reductions in military spending in many of the countries of the Middle East (Iran and Iraq remain exceptions) there has been a shift in focus of acquisitions from increased quantity to qualitative weapons improvements. The new weapons of choice in the region are ballistic missiles; Iran, Iraq, Israel, Syria, and Saudi Arabia have all recently acquired or are in the process of acquiring missiles capable of reaching significant targets of present and potential enemies. Iran and Iraq demonstrated their capabilities with attacks on each other's capital cities and other military/civilian targets. In each case the range of their missiles was enhanced by technological adjustments. Both are probably in the process of acquiring new missiles which will give them a reliable range of at least 300–500 miles.[10] Perhaps the most striking addition of missiles to a Middle East arsenal was the People's Republic of China's sale of intermediate-range (1,600+ miles) CSS-2 missiles to Saudi Arabia. This delivery system, developed by China, probably with the help of Israeli technicians, can reach every part of the region with a heavy payload and a fair degree of accuracy.[11] Israel has had missiles deployed since 1968; first the Jericho I, with a range just under 300 miles, and more recently, but not publicly acknowledged, the Jericho II, with a range of more than 400 miles; the Jericho "IIB" now being tested, with an extended range of 900 miles, can reach not only distant Arab capitals—Baghdad (700 miles) and Riyadh (770 miles)—but also southern sectors of the Soviet Union. It is viewed by strategic analysts as having a deterrent intent.[12] Syria, which has been engaged in an ongoing attempt to achieve "strategic parity" with Israel, has deployed, since 1973, the Soviet-supplied Scud-B, a liquid-fueled, relatively inaccurate missile with a 190-mile range. It is said to have acquired in 1983 Soviet SS-21s, solid-fueled, more accurate but with a limited 120-mile range; it is rumored, largely from Israeli sources, that the Syrians are trying to acquire SS-23s, with a range of 300 miles, which would put Israeli air and military bases within reach.[13] An additional concern with the proliferation of advanced missile-delivery systems is the fact that almost all of them, with slight technical adjustments, are capable of carrying nuclear warheads. Although an international Missile Technology Control Regime was completed on April 16, 1987, and agreed to by the major Western technology suppliers (including Japan), the treaty came just too late, as several countries (Saudi Arabia, Israel, and Iraq) were well advanced in bolstering their missile capabilities.[14]

But if nuclear capability is one reason to fear missile proliferation (at the moment only Israel among Middle East nations has nuclear warheads), chemical weapons are of a much more immediate concern. The repeated use of chemical weapons during the Iran–Iraq war, Libya's employment of chemical weapons in its conflict with Chad, the probable use by Iraq against its Kurdish minorities, all suggest that the threshold against chemical warfare might have been significantly lowered. Egypt, Israel, and Syria are all known to have stockpiles of chemical weapons. The nations that have these chemical agents also have ballistic missiles. The need for the international community to move rapidly and decisively to reinforce the ban against chemical weapons and sharply to curtail ballistic missile proliferation is obvious. But there can be little expectation that smaller nations will take these problems seriously while the major powers and their allies develop their own capabilities and all too readily market technologies and materials.[15]

The pattern of weapons distribution is also changing. There is an ever-spreading arena of conflict. In the 1950s, the flow of arms to the region was more or less confined to Israel and the Arab states confronting it; almost forty years later, the Middle East arms race has widened to include both the Persian Gulf region and North Africa. In the 1980s, conflicts in the Horn of Africa (Ethiopia and Somalia) and Southwest Asia (Afghanistan and Pakistan) have become interlinked with those in the Middle East. Conflicts are piled one on top of another, with the result that local crises and confrontations often assume international stature out of proportion to their importance.

One striking feature of arms-transfer agreements has been their fluidity. With the exception of the long-term relationship between Israel and the United States, arrangements have shifted during the past three decades (initially back and forth between the United States and the Soviet Union), with some countries receiving weapons simultaneously from both superpowers. Until 1975 Egypt received the bulk of its military equipment from the Soviet Union, but since then the United States has supplied upward of $1 billion per year in weaponry and associated military supplies. Until 1979

Iran was the largest importer of arms in the Middle East. The major Middle East arms importer now is Saudi Arabia and in actual purchases it has been the leading world customer for U.S. arms since 1975.[16] Somalia, on the Horn of Africa directly across from the Arabian peninsula, has been a recipient of Soviet arms aid and allowed the Soviets to construct a deep-water harbor and airstrip for the use of Soviet military forces. Today it receives its arms aid largely from the United States and has negotiated with the United States for the use of the harbor and airstrip built by the Soviets. Ethiopia, its enemy, now receives Soviet arms. Almost any war now fought in the region, and especially any future Arab–Israeli war, will find U.S.-supplied weapons and technologies available to both sides. This pattern of shifting and insecure alliances will continue because it reflects local and regional interests in spite of superpower attempts to impose bipolar East-West divisions.

Production of arms in the Middle East itself is growing. Israel is the leader not only in the region but among all small producers and Third World nations, currently accounting for the production of almost one-quarter of this group's arms. It is the largest Third World exporter of arms as well, with the major portion of exports going to Taiwan, Singapore, and Latin America. Israel has come under criticism for its sale of arms to South Africa, estimated by a UN report to be in the range of $300 million per year.[17] Arms are now Israel's largest single export (about $1.5 billion) and account for over 30 percent of all Israeli industrial exports. Although originally established to supply their own needs, the Israeli arms industry has become a critical element of the economy, earning much-needed foreign exchange.[18] The industry currently produces all but the most sophisticated armaments and heavy weapons for its own armed forces and now exports an advanced fighter-bomber and a tactical missile system as well as a wide variety of small arms.

Although far behind Israel, other Middle East and Southwest Asian countries, notably Egypt and Pakistan, are also acquiring the capability to manufacture major armaments. For example, part of the far-reaching agreement between the United States and Egypt in the wake of the Camp David treaty calls for U.S. assistance to develop Egypt's arms industry, and several co-production agreements have been negotiated.

The decision by a number of Middle East countries to create

military capabilities is further evident in their large-scale projects to build military infrastructure. Israel obviously undertook such an effort early in its national existence. More recently, Iran and now Saudi Arabia have been spending large sums of money on air, land, and sea bases, on training centers, communications networks, headquarters and command centers. In Saudi Arabia, for example, the U.S. Army Corps of Engineers has been under contract for approximately $30 billion in a multi-year project.

An analysis of arms transfers shows some important trends. From 1950 to 1966, the countries directly involved in the Arab–Israeli conflict and the Persian Gulf countries (including Iran) imported arms at approximately the same rate. In the period 1966 to 1972, the nations directly involved in the 1967 Arab–Israeli war accelerated their arms procurements, and the Persian Gulf states lagged behind, reaccelerating their rate of imports in 1973. The cumulative value of arms imported by the nations involved in the Arab–Israeli conflict still remains greater, but it is worth noting that significant arms acquisitions by the Persian Gulf states predate the 1973 oil embargo and price increases, though expenditures since 1973 have risen. Iran and Iraq have been substantial importers of arms during the eight years of their conflict and in spite of the truce of the summer of 1988 there is every indication they will go on procuring weapons at a substantial if somewhat less than the wartime rate. The Arab–Israeli confrontation, therefore, while certainly one major cause for the Middle East arms race, is not the only one. Other factors, other fears, sometimes related but often separate from the focal conflict between the Arab states and Israel, have also fueled the process of massive arms acquisitions in the region.

ARMS EXPORT AND ACQUISITION POLICIES

The Soviet Union

Soviet policy through the Stalin period accepted a rigid division of the world into capitalist and socialist camps, and ideology dictated that only socialist countries could be given tangible assistance. After Stalin, the Soviet leadership began to reassess its foreign policy, deemphasized ideological criteria, and became more pragmatic.

With respect to the Third World, the Soviets recognized the existence of a group of nations motivated by nationalist forces "uncommitted" to either the capitalist or the socialist camp. By cooperating with these nations, many of which had only recently won their independence from colonial rule, the Soviet Union hoped to enlist them in the Soviet orbit. More recently Soviet policy in the Third World has undergone thorough reanalysis, even in many areas where the Soviets had established alliances or given economic/military aid to counter U.S. influence. Today the Soviets have drawn back and seek to reach settlements or deescalate the conflict.

The initial change in Soviet policy was motivated by the perceptions of the policies being pursued by the United States in Europe and in the Third World. The post–World War II U.S. doctrine of containment led to the construction of a series of regional alliances along the periphery of the Soviet Union explicitly to stem the expansion of Soviet influence. Using economic and military aid, successive U.S. administrations built NATO in Europe, SEATO in Southeast Asia, and the short-lived Baghdad Pact (CENTO) in the Middle East. Thwarting these encircling alliances became a major Soviet preoccupation.

The Middle East was an obvious region for the new Soviet policy to focus on. First, its proximity to Soviet borders made it important. Domination of the region by an adversary was considered to be a threat to Soviet security, a perception which, it should be pointed out, was shared by the Soviets' Czarist predecessors. Second, there was the Western world's growing dependence on oil from the Middle East. Any weakening of the pro-Western alliance in the region was thought to diminish the West's access to a vital resource. Third, the region presented the Soviet Union with an opportunity because of local resentment against the traditional Western colonial powers, France and Great Britain.

These three reasons led to the 1955 Soviet decision to extend military aid, for the first time, to a Third World country, Egypt. For its part, Egypt turned to the Soviet Union out of anger at Western support for the new State of Israel and the failure of the West to provide similar support for Egypt's economic and military development.[19] Similar motives underlay subsequent Syrian and Iraqi ties with the Soviets. All three states had only recently thrown off traditional monarchies and established forms of "Arab socialism." Eventually the Soviet Union extended military aid to liberation movements in the region, including the PLO.[20] The Soviet Union, like the United States, adopted a policy of selling and transferring arms as a means of buying and winning political friends.

Also, as is true for the United States, Soviet arms exports to this region constitute the largest segment of Soviet arms transfers to the Third World. They account for 50 to 60 percent of total Soviet arms exports in any year. In another parallel to U.S. arms-transfer policies, Soviet exports increased greatly after the 1973 Arab–Israeli war. CIA estimates show that Soviet arms exports were five times as great in the 1974–79 period as they were in the interwar years of 1967–73.[21]

After 1974, the Soviet Union adopted a policy of supplying up-to-date versions of its fighters, tanks, and missiles and no longer selling outmoded, reconditioned equipment. At the same time it considerably tightened the financial terms on which such exports were negotiated. Sales of the new MiG-25 and MiG-27 jet fighters, IL-76 transports, SA-9 surface-to-air missile systems, and T-72 tanks were made for hard Western currencies. Demanding economic gain for its arms arose from economic pressures similar to those that have clearly spurred the West to try to recoup petrodollars. In addition, the Soviets have earned Western currencies for purchasing technologies from Europe and the United States.

Four Arab countries account for more than 70 percent of Soviet arms exports to the region, with Iraq and Syria far in the lead. The Soviet Union has provided jet aircraft, light and medium tanks, armored personnel carriers, naval craft, and ballistic missiles to Iraq.

Syria, the other recipient of Soviet arms, predates Iraq as a Soviet client and, now that Egypt has dropped its Soviet ties, is the oldest Middle East recipient of Soviet military supplies. Syria signed a "Treaty of Friendship and Cooperation" with the Kremlin in late 1980 to remove the last obstacle to the receipt by Syria of the Soviet Union's latest and best weaponry. Unlike Iraq and Libya, however, Syria has no oil wealth with which to purchase

Soviet arms. It is ironic that Syria's funds have come largely as annual allotments from the oil-rich Gulf states. Some strains in this latter arrangement arose during the Iran–Iraq war since Syria was supporting Iran while the Gulf states saw Iran as menacing their security.

In addition to receiving arms from the Soviet Union, a large number of Middle East personnel have been given military training in the Soviet Union, and sizable Soviet military units help operate and maintain Soviet equipment. In addition, the Soviets built and use a large naval facility in the People's Democratic Republic of Yemen (South) and a more modest naval base in Syria.

It is not fully clear what changes are to be expected in the coming years, although we know that the Soviets have strongly urged Syria to be more forthcoming in its diplomatic and economic relations with Israel, to give fuller support to an international peace conference, and also to work toward bettering relations with Iraq and Yasir Arafat's PLO. Nonetheless, Soviet military supplies have kept flowing to their Middle East customers and as yet they have not initiated any significant effort to control this dangerous situation. Nor for that matter has the United States.

Western Europe

The European rationale for arms exports to the Middle East has been less ideological than that of the Americans or the Soviets. Rather than being tied to rigid strategic policies, European exports have been motivated principally by economic considerations. Because arms supplies have not been linked to a grand strategy, European suppliers have found themselves simultaneously selling to both sides of a conflict, the most recent example being the war between Iraq and Iran.

During the 1950s and 1960s, the three main European suppliers (Britain, France, and West Germany) played a small role. Germany, as a defeated Axis power, was not yet a significant arms exporter. While Britain and France were important suppliers of armaments to their former colonies (for example, Great Britain to Jordan and Iraq), an all-out conventional arms race was prevented by a 1950 arms-limitation agreement negotiated by the Foreign Ministers of Britain, France, and the United States.[22] This tripartite commitment, growing out of the truce which followed the 1948 war, stipulated that supplier countries would not stimulate an arms race between Israel and the Arab countries.

Arms exports from Europe were further limited by contemporary political disputes. Egypt's support for the Algerian revolution and Nasser's overthrow of King Farouk, for example, made France and Britain loath to supply the Nasser regime. Of even greater significance was the ill-fated seizure of the Suez Canal by Britain and France in 1956, which chilled bilateral relations between the Europeans and nearly every Arab country. As a consequence, Israel, which had cooperated in the canal seizure and the invasion of Egypt, became the leading recipient of European weapons—a situation that lasted until the June 1967 war.

Between 1969 and 1971, Britain's policy shifted and it withdrew all its troops from east of the Suez. The United States, which wanted to fill the vacuum left by the British, was already stretched to the limit by its commitments in Vietnam and to NATO. The consequent search for a regional power to protect Western interests focused on Iran. Iran then sought arms from all manufacturers of modern military weapons, including Britain, France, and, for the first time, Germany. Iran's increased oil wealth made this possible, and the Shah came to value modern weapons as a symbol of power.

The European countries entered this growing Middle Eastern market in the 1970s. As the research, development, and production costs of their arms industries grew, a major justification for such extravagant industries was the profit to be realized by selling sophisticated weapons to the Third World and the consequent reduction in unit costs of production. The oil-rich nations were prime customers.

The oil embargo imposed by the Arab producers in 1973 affected European arms sales to the Middle East. Oil was costlier, and the stability of its supply was in doubt. Arms exports were needed to help pay the bill for costly imported oil and often were inducements, "sweeteners," to reach oil-supply agreements.

In 1988, fifteen years later, the economic motivations still predominate, but new elements have emerged. Arab oil producers have become wary of depending too heavily on the United States and have shown their dissatisfaction at continuing U.S. support for Israel. They have negotiated agreements with European suppliers that virtually barter sophisticated armaments in return for guaranteed oil supplies, access to Arab markets, and Arab investment in European industry. European governments are willing to negotiate on these terms because they fear that the continuing stalemate over the Palestinian issue may have a negative effect on the availability of oil. In addition, handsome profits can be made.

The United States

The twofold justification for U.S. arms exports to the Middle East has been remarkably consistent since 1950. The prime objective has been to strengthen any government in the region that is friendly to U.S. political, strategic, and economic interests, because the Middle East is, in the words of the State Department, "the greatest strategic prize." A parallel objective has been to deny influence in the region to the Soviet Union, the one power deemed capable of supplanting American hegemony. In addition to this strategic rationale, a pattern of special aid to Israel developed as a permanent part of U.S. Middle East policy. In recent years, with the increased strength of the pro-Israel lobby, this pattern has often conflicted with the aim of supporting and supplying moderate or conservative Arab states.

Forty years ago, the U.S. government, recognizing the volatility of the region, opted for arms restraint. Harry Truman persuaded Britain and France to go along with the 1950 tripartite declaration to prevent an arms race between the Israelis and the Arab states. But this policy was undercut during the Eisenhower years because the United States refused to treat the Soviet Union as a country whose interests in the Middle East had to be taken seriously. Egypt's anger at the West's refusal to support its army against Israel, however, led the new Egyptian leader, Gamal Abdel Nasser, to turn to the Soviet Union for military aid in the late 1950s, thus dooming attempts to control the sales of arms in the region.

Early in the 1950s the United States began actively pushing the same formula that had worked in Europe and the Far East— namely, establishment of a regional alliance among pro-Western countries, held together by U.S. economic and military aid. The Baghdad Pact of 1955 stretched from Turkey across the Middle East as far as Pakistan, but in contrast to NATO or SEATO, it was essentially a theoretical alliance. The complex and constantly shifting alignments within the region obviated its unity and stability. But it is fair to say that U.S. arms sales to the region increased in almost direct proportion to fears of instability; the 1967 and 1973 Arab–Israeli wars, the fall of the Shah in 1979, and the Soviet invasion of Afghanistan in the same year were precipitating events, and arrangements for U.S. arms transfers shot up.[23]

Early U.S. arms exports to the Middle East were actually modest and limited. The presence of British troops stationed at critical points throughout the region made them less essential for U.S. policy. There were American bases as well, including Wheelus Air Force Base in Libya, which in the early post–World War II years was the largest foreign air base operated by the United States. Until 1965 the United States refrained from supplying Israel with significant amounts of weaponry, and Britain and France served as the Israelis' chief suppliers. This arrangement was preferred by the United States since it did not want to disturb its relations with the oil-producing Arab states. Lastly, of course, throughout the 1950s and 1960s the United States focused its military strength on the Korean and Indochinese wars.

But the pace of U.S. exports accelerated dramatically when Britain announced its intention to withdraw all its troops from bases east of the Suez Canal by the early 1970s. It was in these circumstances that the Nixon administration sought in Iran a reliable policeman for Western interests in the region. This represented a departure from the regional arrangements previously sought by U.S. policymakers.

In an unprecedented step, Henry Kissinger and the White House told the State and Defense Departments to accede to any weapons request the Shah might make, regardless of anything their own analysts might say. This decision marked the beginning of one of the most rapid and massive militarizations of a region the world has ever seen.

In the 1970s economic factors such as cost overruns plagued U.S. arms exports. U.S. arms manufacturers and the Pentagon, like their European counterparts, saw spiraling research and development costs and inflated production costs. The Vietnam War had created a war economy that, even as that war wound down, had little incentive to retool and shift to civilian production. The result was a built-in lobby for conventional arms sales in key congressional districts throughout the country. The sale of arms protected jobs, maintained the Pentagon budget, redistributed overhead and research and development costs, and assured corporate profits. And arms sales helped recoup dollars being spent on petroleum. The 1973 embargo and OPEC price increase, as we have seen, increased the pressure to sell arms. The Middle East arms race was fueled by both "push" and "pull" factors.

The fall of the Shah in January–February 1979 brought about an immediate American reassessment of the wisdom of relying on a Third World country to protect Western interests. Direct U.S. military involvement in the region was renewed, and at the same time the amount of U.S. arms being exported to the region remained high. Indeed, under the Reagan administration, the United States accelerated its efforts to forge a regional strategic alliance, however unnatural and unreliable; the United States attempted to prevent threatening revolts and secure the region against Soviet influence. Current U.S. strategic concerns stretch from Morocco in the west to Pakistan in the east and include Egypt, Israel, Jordan, and Saudi Arabia.

In addition, the United States has moved to secure major bases in Egypt, Kenya, Somalia, Oman, and the island of Diego Garcia in the Indian Ocean. As part of its new military involvement in the region, the United States developed a mobile force (Central Command) which could be dispatched to deal with perceived internal or external threats to the stability of countries in the region. This 325,000-troop force (originally called the Rapid Deployment Force, reorganized in 1983 as the Central Command) represents a significant escalation of U.S. military commitment to the region. In addition, when the Iran–Iraq war spread into the Gulf with sustained attacks on shipping, the United States in 1987 became directly involved by reflagging Kuwaiti oil tankers and dispatching a sizable naval force to the Gulf.

The most significant transfers of U.S. arms and military assistance to the Middle East have occurred since the 1973 Arab–Israeli war. Among the three countries receiving the most—Israel, Saudi Arabia, and Egypt—there are some differences. Saudi Arabia's total is extraordinarily large because of the $30 billion construction program conducted by the U.S. Army Corps of Engineers. The United States, in serving as the contract coordinator, is building the entire Saudi military infrastructure, including army, air force, and naval bases, providing training for personnel, as well as ship-ping large amounts of late-model, highly sophisticated weaponry.[24] Israel, which ranks as the third-largest recipient of U.S. arms, contrasts with the Saudis in the nature of the materials bought. Virtually every Israeli purchase is hardware, the most up-to-date weaponry, while substantial portions of the Saudi expenditures are for infrastructure. This means that in a genuine sense the imme-diate military value of Israel's purchases is greater than the larger amount spent by Saudi Arabia. Further, Israel's purchases are largely financed by Foreign Military Sales (FMS) credits, unlike the Saudis', which are direct sales. For example, Israel to date has received more than $11 billion in credits from the United States to finance its military purchases from government and private sup-pliers. A further important indication of Israel's special relation-ship with the United States is that it alone among all the recipients of FMS credits has been forgiven payment on about 50 percent of these credits each years and has had all loans forgiven.[25] By the end of 1987 total U.S. military aid to Israel reached $22.5 billion, of which only $12.2 billion is to be repaid.[26]

Egypt, one of the three or four largest (the actual position changes from year to year) buyers of U.S. arms sold to the Third World, is also a large recipient of FMS credits. As the Shah was being overthrown in Iran, Egypt was signing the Camp David accords, making it eligible to receive more than $4.6 billion in arms in just over four years. Some observers estimate that Egypt will get as much as $10 billion in arms within a decade as it strives to replace Iran as the guarantor of U.S. and Western interests in the region.

The U.S. pattern of ever-enlarging military involvement in the Middle East includes elements of conflict and contradiction. First, as noted, the United States is now a significant supplier to both the Arab states and Israel. Jordan, next to Egypt as a recipient of U.S. arms exports (albeit considerably fewer), has a long common border with Israel and has fought alongside the other Arab states in wars against Israel. It is ironic that Jordan has aided the transport of Soviet-supplied weapons across its territory from the port of Aqaba to Iraq during its war with Iran. Saudi Arabia considers itself closely tied to the other Arab states in their ongoing con-frontation with Israel and has been a major financial supporter of

Arab efforts, including direct grants to the PLO. Egypt, until it concluded its peace agreement with Israel in 1978, was a major belligerent power on the Arab side and had supplied the largest contingent of forces in each Arab–Israeli war. It is surely one of the weaknesses of the peace treaty that it has triggered a massive rearmament of Egypt, comparable in scale and rate to the arming of Iran begun in 1969.

Israel's arms-acquisition policy has flowed from its judgment that it must maintain an undisputed military superiority in the region. Each U.S. sale of arms to Arab states (or their acquisition of arms from the Soviet Union) has been matched by new supplies for Israel. This direct linkage was evident during the U.S. negotiations with Saudi Arabia for F-15 fighters (and improvements for them) and AWAC aerial reconnaissance aircraft. Even arms sales to Egypt following the peace treaty were interpreted by Israel as threatening, requiring additional American assurances and supplies for Israel. Thus U.S. policy has not been able to achieve even its stated goals. As we have seen, U.S. attempts to gain security and stability have fueled insecurity and instability. Each addition to Israel's arsenal has given the country a greater sense of independence from the United States and has tempted Israel to strike out alone in dealing with its Arab neighbors.

It is hard to see the interests of any party or nation being truly served by the current arms race in the Middle East. Insecurity remains high; for the wealthy states in the region, military expenditures represent a diversion of resources from social and economic development; in the poorer states, arms purchases stimulate cruelly high inflation and distort economies; the superpowers pursue increased military involvement and commitment in a volatile area only to experience continued uncertainty as to how long allies will remain allied; for the people of the region, the arms race means that each new conflict—or continuing conflict—exacts a heavier toll in devastation and destruction.

The arms race in the Middle East is out of control. The policy of avoiding conflict by maintaining a dynamic military balance between conflicting parties has failed. This failure is demonstrated by repeated Arab–Israeli wars, the fall of the Shah, the Lebanese civil war, Syrian and Israeli intervention in Lebanon, the Libyan conflict with Chad, and the Iran–Iraq war. The arms race itself has become an increasing source of tension and provocation. Even peace agreements have led to new levels of armament. The one slim chance for slowing and limiting the deadly spiral lies with the major arms-supplying countries—the United States, the Soviet Union, France, Britain, and West Germany.

NUCLEAR WEAPONS IN THE MIDDLE EAST

In June 1981, Israel used a preemptive air attack to destroy an experimental nuclear reactor in Baghdad, Iraq. This dramatic show of force instantly brought the danger of nuclear weapons in the Middle East to world attention. Revelations by an Israeli nuclear technician, Mordechai Vanunu, confirming the existence of an extensive Israeli nuclear bomb project created a storm of controversy when published in the London *Sunday Times* in October 1986. Although there are many unanswered questions about nuclear capabilities in the region, some things are known. Several Middle East nations have active nuclear reactor programs. Not all those countries with advanced nuclear development have committed themselves to refrain from building nuclear weapons by signing the Nuclear Nonproliferation Treaty and permitting regular inspection by the International Atomic Energy Agency.[27] Europe and the United States, as suppliers of reactor components, fuels, and technical advice, have not always insisted on full acceptance by the recipients of nonproliferation and effective inspections.[28]

Israel is the Middle East country with the most advanced nuclear program and is widely believed to possess a stockpile conservatively estimated to consist of fifty to sixty nuclear weapons and the capacity to construct additional bombs on short notice. While the Israeli government has maintained silence on its nuclear weapons capacity and has said it would not be the first nation to introduce nuclear weapons in the Middle East, it has also declared that it will not be the last; Israel has refused to sign the Nuclear Nonproliferation Treaty and has not allowed international inspection of its nuclear facilities.[29] Israel's nuclear delivery systems include ballistic missiles and fighter-bombers that can be refueled in the air. The Central Intelligence Agency issued a five-page memorandum as early as September 1974 asserting its strong suspicion that Israel already had produced nuclear weapons. It based its assessment on the belief that Israel had been involved in clandestine acquisition of large amounts of uranium. There has been continuing discussion in Israel concerning the need for a nuclear weapons strategy to deal with the shifting military balance in the Middle East.[30] But Israel faces a problem in that nuclear discussion does not occur in public; part of Israel's strategy has been to keep its nuclear potential shrouded in ambiguity, allowing just enough to be known to serve as a deterrent, but not enough to serve as a stimulus for the Arabs to actively acquire nuclear weapons of their own. Some Israeli analysts have called Israel's strategy "opaque proliferation."[31]

The earliest confirmation of Israel's nuclear capacity came from the late General Moshe Dayan, who served as both Minister of Defense and Foreign Minister in recent Israeli governments. Just after Israel's raid on the Baghdad reactor, Dayan announced that although Israel did not have an atomic bomb, it had the capacity to construct one rapidly should the Arabs make one of their own.[32] Of all the nations in the Middle East, Israel certainly possesses the most advanced technological capacity and the most significant pool of trained scientists. In addition, its overall nuclear facilities are the most developed.

Three other countries in the region—Iran, Iraq, and Libya— have on occasion demonstrated interest in acquiring nuclear weapons; yet all three are signatories of the Nonproliferation Treaty.[33] Iraq is the only other country in the region with a serious nuclear reactor program but it is far behind Israel's, and its pool of technical skills is considerably lower; the destruction of its Osirak reactor represented a significant setback. Was Iraq building nuclear weapons or developing the capacity to build nuclear weapons? Iraq, unlike Israel, was an early signer of the Nonproliferation Treaty and had regularly permitted its facilities to be inspected by the IAEA. In January 1981, not long before the Israeli attack on the Baghdad reactor, the inspectors were satisfied that Iraq was not diverting materials to make bombs and that Iraq was abiding by the terms of the treaty. But it is also possible that the technologies of the reactor program undertaken by Iraq could have been altered in order to make weapons. The type of reactor under construction and the nature of fuels Iraq had received has raised such doubts in the minds of some international nuclear experts.

Egypt and Libya, the two other Middle East states with announced nuclear programs, are at such early stages of their development that there seems to be no threat that either country will have nuclear weapons in the near future. Egypt has not yet started building its first nuclear power plant.[34] It ratified the Nonproliferation Treaty in 1980 and at the same time called for creating a nuclear-free zone in the Middle East.

Pakistan is not a signatory to the Nonproliferation Treaty and is widely believed to be eager to match the nuclear weapons capacity of India, its longtime rival. In the past Pakistan has received its nuclear technologies and fuels from Europe and the United States. Recently it negotiated with the Reagan administration for the United States to resume fuel shipments that had been stopped because of American fears that Pakistan was building nuclear weapons.

Syria, considered by many to be the Arab country most belligerent in its relations with Israel, possesses too small a nuclear infrastructure to be considered a direct threat. Yet on several occasions in 1984 and 1985 the Syrian Minister of Defense claimed that the Soviets had promised to provide nuclear weapons should the Israelis use nuclear weapons against Syria. The Soviets have repeatedly denied this claim and certainly their record elsewhere leaves it highly unlikely that they would ever place nuclear arms under Syrian control. While this position is reinforced by the new Gorbachev policies, there are nonetheless several thousand Soviet advisers in Syria, a sign of their serious concern for Syria's security.[35]

One additional fear is that the Saudis, who have purchased conventionally armed intermediate-range missiles from the Chinese, might join with Pakistan to develop a nuclear warhead, especially since Pakistan is believed to have received Saudi funding for its nuclear weapons project; this, of course, would be the often rumored "Islamic bomb." (There were also reports of some Libyan funding of the Pakistani efforts.) But in late April 1988 the Saudis considerably lessened this fear by agreeing to the Nonproliferation Treaty, including the formal pledge to refrain from developing a bomb and to accept international inspections.[36]

Is the Middle East poised on the edge of a full-scale nuclear arms race? Will the Vanunu revelations of the extensive Israeli nuclear arsenal unleash increased Arab efforts to make nuclear arms? Does the failure to resolve the Israeli–Palestinian/Arab conflict enhance the likelihood that another war will erupt and with it the increased threat of the use of nuclear weapons? We would like to answer each of these questions in the negative, but even though nuclear war in the region seems highly improbable, the situation contains too many uncertainties. The introduction of new "threshold-crossing" weapons—ballistic missiles and chemical weapons—suggests that the situation is not static and that under certain conditions could explode. The Middle East, therefore, poses a critical test of the Nonproliferation Treaty, the International Atomic Energy Agency, civilian nuclear development, and the depth of international commitment to the treaty. The addition of nuclear weapons to the massive conventional arsenals in the volatile and war-prone Middle East is frightening.

It is extremely urgent that efforts be made to halt the proliferation of conventional and nuclear weapons in the Middle East. A nuclear arms race there will indeed contribute to further destabilization and insecurity in the region and to superpower confrontation. Therefore, we offer the following recommendations.

RECOMMENDATIONS ON CONVENTIONAL WEAPONS

The key to breaking the cycle of the Middle East arms race lies to a large extent with the supplier nations, the United States, the U.S.S.R., France, the United Kingdom, and West Germany. First, we call upon the conscience of these nations and urge them to take strong and immediate actions to stop and, ultimately, reverse the staggering buildup of arms in the Middle East. Additional international agreements such as the Missile Technology Control Regime of April 1987 need to be strengthened and implemented in order to slow the transfer of new missile technologies. But this regime, which represents an agreement largely among Western nations, has as yet no international agency able to monitor compliance and no means to enforce restraints.[37] Beyond this agreement there is need for additional steps to block or restrain exports of ballistic missiles and to prevent acquisitions of new missiles. Second, with the recent use of chemical weapons in the Middle East, the Geneva Protocol (1928) must be vigorously supported and strengthened. The new Chemical Weapons Convention, with its ban on all means of offensive chemical warfare and production of chemical weapons, has reached a hopeful but critical stage of negotiations and requires significant effort before it is signed and ratified. But it is amply clear that as long as the major powers and their allies continue developing increasingly sophisticated missiles and create and add to chemical weapons arsenals, the nations of the Middle East will pay little attention to the strictures of the major powers.

A comprehensive peace will provide the basis for long-term arms reductions, but since large numbers of sophisticated arms have become part of the problem, reductions in arms cannot wait for peace. It is essential, however, that an arms-transfer limitation agreement be achieved. In the current situation, it is unrealistic to expect the Middle East states to negotiate an arms agreement by themselves. A serious moratorium on the shipment of new weapons to the Middle East is an achievable lifesaving step which the suppliers can undertake. We call upon the leaders of our nation to take the initiative in arranging an arms-transfer moratorium and call for the full involvement of the other major suppliers. Such a moratorium could stimulate longer-term, comprehensive agreements on arms limitations and significant arms reductions.

To start the process, a standing committee on arms control might be established by supplying nations and involve the buyers. Their first task might be to set restrictions both on arms sales to each of the states and on transfers of arms between them. As an interim step an arms-limitation treaty might first reduce the armed forces of all nations in the Middle East to purely defensive low-firepower weapons and ban all high-firepower arms, particularly those destructive of civilian populations. This might mean that interim security control will be organized, in part at least, by United Nations or other international forces. The savings in lives could be monumental, if the losses in recent conflicts—Lebanon, Iran–Iraq—are any guide.

Agreements among the suppliers to restrict the types of arms transferred could be entered into and enforced by the suppliers. In the past, both the United States and the Soviet Union have been reluctant to supply the most advanced weapons systems. The United States, for example, refused Israel's requests for Pershing l ballistic missiles armed with conventional warheads. The Soviet Union refrained in the past from supplying its most advanced fighters and surface-to-air missiles. As we have seen, both countries have recently reversed this policy of restraint and have been responsible for agreements transferring the most sophisticated new weapons systems. If arms limitations and reductions are to be pursued, this policy must be reversed. An immediate joint American–Soviet effort at agreement could set the pace for others.

The recipient nations have in the past accepted restrictions on the use of sophisticated weaponry. During the 1973 war both Egypt and Israel were deterred from using surface-to-surface missiles against each other's cities and entered into a tacit agreement toward this end negotiated by the International Committee of the Red Cross. The United States has included use restrictions on weapons it has sold to Israel and Saudi Arabia. Each restriction, even if not adequately enforced, is a limited form of arms control. Multinational agreements, particularly initiated by the suppliers, not only are possible but could be an important constraining element. These should cover not only weapons themselves but also components and technologies essential to weapons development and production. Beginning at once, new restrictions to limit arms sales should be enacted. But all these efforts sound hypocritical if not linked to substantial arms reductions and severe limits on arms development on the part of the supplying nations themselves.

CREATING A NUCLEAR-WEAPONS-FREE MIDDLE EAST

Although nuclear reactor technologies are widespread in the region and one state, Israel, has a small arsenal of nuclear weapons, it is not too late to create a nuclear-weapons-free zone in the Middle East. None of the Middle East nations has adopted a strategy reliant on nuclear weapons, and leaders in several key countries, including Egypt, Kuwait, and Israel, have in the past indicated interest in a nonnuclear Middle East. The signing of the Treaty of Rarotonga in December 1986, which established a South Pacific nuclear-weapons-free zone, might be a workable model.[38]

Extraordinary steps must be taken. Included in our concern regarding the proliferation of nuclear weapons is the role of civilian nuclear power. We question the short-term gains—economic or political—to be had through the export and development of nuclear reactor technologies. We believe that any gains are thoroughly outweighed by the possibility that these technologies will be used to proliferate nuclear weapons in the region. The history of the diversion of materials from the civilian to the military sector and the misuse or misappropriation of technologies is now too clear to allow anyone to be sanguine about civilian nuclear power reactors.

There are immediate steps that can be taken to make the region free of nuclear weapons:

1. All nations in the region not already signatories to the Nuclear Nonproliferation Treaty and safeguard agreement should sign and ratify the treaty. Egypt, Iran, Iraq, Saudi Arabia, and Libya are signatories. Israel, India, and Pakistan are not.

Middle East nations, as required by the treaty, should open their nuclear facilities fully to regular inspection by the International Atomic Energy Agency (IAEA).

IAEA safeguards should be improved to enhance confidence in them. This is especially important for dealing with sensitive materials, such as highly enriched uranium and plutonium and the facilities for handling them. It may be necessary, for example, to increase the number of inspections and to permit IAEA inspectors to make "surprise" visits.

The supplier nations should also make stronger commitments to the Nuclear Nonproliferation Treaty and to IAEA requirements, through their bilateral agreements and by broadening the enforcement powers of the IAEA or other international agencies.

2. Israel, as the only Middle East nation with nuclear weapons, should, to build confidence, rapidly accept, sign, and ratify the Nuclear Nonproliferation Treaty and work within the community of nonnuclear-weapons states to increase the credibility of the IAEA and to strengthen its safeguards.

Israel should open its own nuclear facilities to inspections by the IAEA. As part of this step, Israel should demonstrate its commitment to a nonnuclear Middle East by dismantling the components, or weapons, that currently exist.

The Arab states, as a confidence-building and reciprocal step, should sign the Nuclear Nonproliferation Treaty if they are not already signatories. Or they should reinforce their commitment to the treaty and make explicit their desire for a nuclear-weapons-free Middle East.

3. The United States and other nations supplying nuclear fuel and technology should immediately announce their refusal to export nuclear fuels or technologies to nonsignatories of the Nuclear Nonproliferation Treaty. Further, they should tighten their own safeguards as part of bilateral nuclear export agreements.

The United States can immediately take the lead by rigorously following these suggestions in relations with Pakistan and Israel.

4. To indicate their serious commitment to halting the spread of nuclear weapons, the United States and the U.S.S.R. should take immediate steps to achieve control and reduction of their own nuclear weapons as actually required by the Nonproliferation Treaty. While the Intermediate Nuclear Forces agreement abolishing U.S. and Soviet intermediate-range missiles was a welcome addition to a decade devoid of serious arms-control agreement, the failure to make progress on the reduction of strategic weapons is disappointing. So too is the U.S. threat to withdraw from the ABM Treaty (1972) in order to develop the Strategic Defense Initiative—"Star Wars."

5. The United States, the U.S.S.R., and other states possessing nuclear weapons should agree to make the Middle East a nuclear-weapons-free zone and join the nations there to achieve this end. The Tlatelolco Treaty covering Latin America and the Treaty of Rarotonga for the South Pacific exist as models for the Middle East. The nuclear club should pledge to keep nuclear weapons out of the region.

8

Iran

Events in Iran during the past decade have cast a pall over the Middle East. On February 11, 1979, Shahpour Bakhtiar, the last Prime Minister appointed by the Shah, fled the country. The collapse of his government came only twenty-six days after the Shah, Mohammed Reza Pahlavi, had left Teheran for an "extended vacation." He never returned to Iran and died in a Cairo hospital in exile. The fall of the Shah was precipitated mostly by peaceful means; general strikes and massive street demonstrations rendered Iran's sophisticated 400,000-person army—the fifth-largest military force in the world—ineffective.

It is useful to consider the background and the important developments leading to the Iranian revolution, in order to understand the role of the Shah and Iran in U.S. foreign policy, to comprehend the implications of the Iranian revolution for the Middle East, and to analyze the war between Iran and Iraq and its meaning for stability and peace in the region.

Iran's first serious attempt at government reform occurred at the turn of the century. The Constitutional Movement (1905–11) reflected a growing discontent with corruption in government and with foreign (primarily British and Russian) economic control. The reform movement, like the goverment itself, was weak and ineffectual. This period of constitutional experimentation ended when

Reza Khan (father of the late Shah), then the leader of the Cossack brigade, seized power in a British-assisted coup d'état in 1921.

Initially, Reza Khan, founder of the Pahlavi dynasty, sought the support of the clergy. However, his accommodationist policies soon became secondary to his far-reaching program of Westernization, modernization, and centralization of governmental power. His policies produced a major upheaval in the traditional social order, and during his reign Reza Khan became increasingly despotic; he suppressed political parties, trade unions, and the press.

In 1941, Britain and the U.S.S.R. demanded that Reza Khan (believed to be pro-Nazi) expel the large number of Germans in Iran. When he refused, Soviet and British troops entered Iran and forced him to abdicate. His son, Mohammed Reza Pahlavi, became the new Shah. Britain, the Soviet Union, and later the United States stationed troops in Iran for the duration of World War II.

In 1945, the communist Tudeh Party, working closely with the Soviet Union, overthrew the central government in the Azerbaijan and Kurdistan regions of Iran. In 1946, the young Shah's gendarmerie, assisted by U.S. military advisers, effectively crushed this leftist uprising. This was the beginning of a long and intimate relationship between the Shah and the United States.

On February 4, 1949, a lone gunman tried to assassinate the Shah. Although no evidence ever linked him to a political party, the Shah responded by outlawing the Tudeh Party and proclaiming martial law. The monarch also banned newspapers deemed too critical of his policies or his family and ordered the arrest of many opposition politicians, including Mohammed Mossadegh.

Responding to this show of force, a group of prominent liberal politicians headed by Mossadegh, a circle of religious leaders (most notably representing the middle-class bazaar merchants), and various secular and nationalistic parties all allied to form the National Front. Their demands included free elections, a free press, an end to martial law, and nationalization of the British-owned oil industry. Within months, support for the National Front was made evident in the many mass rallies and a general strike in the oil industry organized by the outlawed Tudeh Party. The much-shaken Shah appointed Mossadegh Prime Minister in May 1951. Mossadegh immediately nationalized the oil industry and appropriated the Anglo-Iranian oil company installations, a move that prompted the British government to impose sanctions on Iran.

In July 1952, in an effort to make the reforms permanent, Mossadegh called for civilian control of the military. The Shah refused, later changed his mind in the face of public demonstrations, and eventually left Iran. Mossadegh continued his policies of reform. But the National Front began to disintegrate. The nationalization of oil and the victories over the Shah had removed the focal points around which the National Front had been united.[1]

Iranian army officers, heartened by the National Front's fragmentation and directly supported financially and logistically by the CIA, took the offensive. The military occupied government offices and arrested Mossadegh while crowds of CIA-paid demonstrators marched through Teheran to create the image of popular support for the Shah and against Mossadegh. The Shah returned to Iran, accompanied by Allen Dulles, the director of the CIA, and Kermit Roosevelt, the agent who masterminded the successful coup d'état which returned him to the throne.[2] The Shah moved quickly to consolidate his power. He outlawed the National Front, arrested most of its leaders, and dismantled the Tudeh Party.

The 1953 CIA-assisted coup was something of a watershed. It effectively ended Iran's second attempt at constitutional politics. It also marked the beginning of close cooperation between the Shah and the United States in intelligence, economic, and military matters. In 1952 Gamal Abdel Nasser had overthrown King Farouk in Egypt and started the chain of events that led to revolts in Syria and Iraq and ushered in a period of radicalization of politics in the Arab world. Iran and important segments of the Arab world were headed in opposite directions. Bolstered by rapidly increasing oil revenues, the monarch began to build a massive military establishment. The Iranian army grew slowly from 1953 to 1968 and then more rapidly, eventually rising from 120,000 troops in 1953 to more than 400,000 in 1976.

In 1957, with the aid of the CIA and the Israeli intelligence agency, Mossad, Iran's National Security Organization (SAVAK) was formed. Much has been written about its brutal tactics, especially during the 1970s. Torture victims, former agents, and periodic reports by Amnesty International and the International

Committee of the Red Cross paint a grim picture of SAVAK's efforts to assure Iran's "security" against its domestic opponents. The Shah's political repression was central in pushing the Iranian people toward revolution. In the popular perception (as well as in reality), the CIA was working hand in glove with SAVAK.[3] Despite SAVAK's tactics, in the period between 1957 and 1963 opposition to the Shah continued to mount. Bricklayers, teachers, cabdrivers, and oil-field workers went out on strike. Responding to the pressure, and with the encouragement of the United States, which feared instability, the Shah launched the so-called White Revolution, or "revolution from above," in the early 1960s with the stated purpose of improving the lot of the Iranian citizenry. Some critics assailed the program for having as its real goals increasing the power of the Shah and enhancing his role as gendarme of the Middle East.

The Shah's White Revolution did generate improvements in health services, education, literacy, and the standard of living. Also, the program broke up large landholdings and redistributed some of the arable land. But for the majority of Iranians the Shah's policies failed. While many families in Teheran found modern apartments and were able to buy consumer goods, shantytowns proliferated, and urban crowding and inflation worsened. By the late 1970s, over 40 percent of the 4 million residents of Teheran lived in inadequate housing, there was still no sewer system, and public transportation was minimal. The Shah's government produced uneven results in the countryside. Certain poor families received land in the redistribution, but it was almost impossible for them to make a living without adequate credit, which was not available. Many of them sold their farms and moved to Teheran. In some sectors of Iran large farms were established for mechanized cash crops; however, many of them ran into financial and organizational difficulties. With tempting urban salaries drawing people from rural Iran, and a lack of appropriate government interest, agricultural production began to decline. When Mohammed Reza Pahlavi assumed the throne in 1941, Iran could feed itself. By 1976, it imported 76 percent of the food products it consumed.

One aspect of the Shah's approach to agriculture is reflected in his autobiography, *Mission for My Country*, in which he boasts about the tobacco monopoly:

The government operates a very lucrative tobacco industry, practically doubled in capacity through a big plant expansion completed in 1960. Every working day we now turn out about 50 million cigarettes—enough to keep even quite a few chain-smokers busy—plus about 10 tons of pipe tobacco. In any Persian village you can see farmers smoking inexpensive cigarettes from our government factories. Lately we have followed the Western trend by starting the manufacture of filter-tip cigarettes, and now we are opening up a new market by embellishing the boxes with lavish Arabian scenes and sending them to the Persian Gulf sheikdoms.[4]

While the Shah's government was engaged in expanding cigarette sales, 87 percent of Iran's roughly 50,000 villages had no schools, only 1 percent had medical facilities, and the national literacy rate of 15 percent was seldom approached outside the large towns.

The failures in the implementation of the White Revolution served to broaden the ranks of the opposition. There were mass demonstrations by teachers, clergy, students, and bazaar merchants. In early June 1963, the Ayatollah Khomeini, an already prominent Shiite religious leader, raised the banner of revolt by openly denouncing the Shah and his policies. Bazaars throughout the country closed in support of this leading cleric. Then, in a swift move, the armed forces struck at peaceful demonstrations in Qum, Teheran, Tabriz, and Isfahan. Thousands were killed, and Khomeini was arrested and exiled to Iraq. In 1978 he moved to France. In putting down the successive rebellions in 1946, 1953, and 1963, the Shah alienated ever larger numbers of people. From 1963 to 1979, public resentment smoldered under the surface. Many individuals, like Mehdi Bazargan[5] and Ali Shariati,[6] and influential groups, like the Marxist Fedayeen and the Islamic leftist Mujahideen al-Khalq, emerged as leaders of the opposition. Both these groups were brutally suppressed after Khomeini came to power.

While inflation crippled most of Iran, the Shah continued to enlarge and modernize the army, aggravating inflation even further by diverting large sums to the military. This was spurred by the Nixon doctrine which designated Iran as the West's surrogate "policeman" for the Gulf region. Between 1973 and 1978 the Shah spent some $18 billion on armaments in the United States, making him at that time the single largest customer for U.S. arms sales abroad. During the halcyon days of the Iranian–U.S. liaison it was widely known that no Iranian arms request would be denied. Thus began the policy of supplying "state of the art" weapons to a Middle East power.

By 1978 some 500 U.S. firms were operating in Iran. In addition to a large contingent of military advisers, between 40,000 and 50,000 American expatriates were living and working in Iran, many of them enjoying privileges usually reserved for diplomats. For the most part, they were paid salaries of $40,000 to $80,000 a year because Iran was considered a "hardship post" and the local cost of living was high. At the time, the average Iranian's annual income was between $2,500 and $3,000.

Mohammed Reza Pahlavi had no substantial fortune when he became the Shah, although he had inherited certain lands from his father, some of which he donated to the state. He later reconfiscated this land and sold it for a very high price, and began to amass his vast family fortune. Within two decades the Shah and his family were among the wealthiest people in the world; his twin sister, Ashraf, had twelve palaces in different parts of the world, while his brother-in-law was found guilty of accepting multimillion-dollar payoffs for helping with contracts from the Textron Corporation. Devout Muslims as well as many of Iran's poor were angered by the lavish parties given by the Pahlavi family, by their "jet set" image, and by the drug trafficking of the Shah's sister Shams, who in 1976 was apprehended in Switzerland with $20 million worth of heroin in her car.[7]

The Shah attacked many aspects of Iranian culture, restricted freedom of speech, and censored the press. The Iranian calendar, traditionally based on Islamic events, was changed to the monarchical calendar. Religious activities were limited and in some instances prohibited. University students were monitored by SAVAK agents in the classroom, at home, and even on campuses in the United States. During the 1970s, SAVAK repression was intensified. Accurate figures are hard to obtain. However, Amnesty International charged the Shah with one of the worst records of human rights violations in the world. While the 1976 Amnesty International annual report said the number of political prisoners in Iran was uncertain and gave an estimate of several thousand, other estimates ranged as high as 50,000. In the same year, the International Commission of Jurists reported that "there can be no doubt that torture has been systematically practiced over a number of years against recalcitrant suspects under interrogation by the SAVAK."[8]

The precise number of people who died under torture or who disappeared is not known. Estimates range as high as 100,000. During the last two years of the revolution, 60,000 to 80,000 died.

An acute economic crisis between 1975 and 1977 touched off large-scale strikes and demonstrations which characterized the final years of the Shah's rule. By this time, most segments of society— from the intelligentsia and the educated middle class to the powerful religious establishment and the bazaar merchants who feared the damaging expansion of multinational corporations—were determined to limit and finally to end the monarchy.

In view of widespread resentment simmering beneath the surface in Iran, the words of President Carter's 1978 New Year's toast, as he and Mrs. Carter at the White House celebrated the holiday with the Shah and his wife, are poignant in their irony:

> Iran under the great leadership of the Shah is an island of stability in one of the most troubled areas in the world. This is a great tribute to you, Your Majesty, and to your leadership and to the respect, admiration and love which your people give to you.

These words suggest how out of touch with Iranian reality Washington had become; within a year the Shah was deposed from his throne. (It should be noted that the Soviets were equally out of touch with Iranian political changes and were also thoroughly surprised by the Khomeini-led revolution.)

THE ROLE OF ISLAM IN THE IRANIAN REVOLUTION

Although much of the anger of the Iranian people against the Shah stemmed from specific complaints against him or his family's cruelty, profiteering, and corruption, the forms in which the anger was expressed reflected certain Islamic components which have remained incomprehensible to most Western observers. Because the prophet Muhammad was both secular and spiritual ruler of Medina and Mecca, orthodox Muslims have expected their secular leaders to maintain high standards of ethical and spiritual behavior, to live austerely and incorruptibly, and to observe behavior appropriate for a Muslim, one who "submits" to the will of God.

Furthermore, from the days of the Qur'an (Koran)[9] Muslims have been enjoined to view the lands of the world as divided into two categories: (1) The lands of Islam (*dar al-Islam*), where the name Allah is invoked in public, the call to worship is heard five times a day, Friday is a holy day, Ramadan (the annual month of fasting) is observed, and imams, mullahs, and other religious leaders are respected. (2) The lands of struggle (*dar al-harb*), in which unbelievers predominate, where Muslim observances must be followed privately or, perhaps, even clandestinely, and where Muslims must struggle to establish a *dar al-Islam*.

By the 1970s the Shah and his family were seen by more and more Iranians to have abandoned the austere and incorruptible model of a Muslim leader in a *dar al-Islam* and to have adopted the decadence and luxury of the *dar al-harb*, the non-Islamic West. As public demonstrations against the Shah escalated, Islamic elements emerged. The struggle was called a jihad (sometimes translated as "holy war")—a term used throughout the Muslim world to connote a holy struggle to achieve an ideal. Citizens who were imprisoned, tortured, or killed were identified as martyrs. The tradition of martyrdom is strong among Muslims. In the Qur'an, martyrs are promised a direct path to paradise, or heaven. The tradition of martyrdom has played a particularly important role among the Shiites, the branch of Islam which comprises the bulk of Iran's population. Every year on the tenth day of the month of Muharram, Shiites commemorate the death of Hussein, the prophet Muhammad's martyred grandson, and accompanied by such memorabilia as bloodstained banners and arrow-pierced water bags, processions of Shiites cut themselves with knives and other sharp instruments to the accompaniment of chants and prayer. The bloodstained clothes of mourners symbolize the blood-soaked clothes of the martyred Hussein.[10] During the months of anti-Shah demonstrations, when police and helicopters fired into crowds, the victims' bloodstained clothes were held aloft by the crowd in a manner reminiscent of the Muharram Shiite processions, and during this period visitors to Iran were regularly shown the graves of the martyrs who died in the holy struggle against the Shah.[11]

When the Shah finally yielded to public pressure and left Iran, his appointed Prime Minister, Shahpour Bakhtiar, remained. Few people were surprised that the Iranian public rejected Bakhtiar. What puzzled the world was the person the public chose to replace him—the Ayatollah Ruhollah Khomeini, an elderly Muslim theologian who had once dominated the religious life in Qum (Iran's most holy city), whom the Shah had exiled in 1963, and who from his base in Paris had issued continuing public denunciations of the Shah and appeals for the establishment of an Islamic state. Large pictures of the Ayatollah Khomeini had been carried in countless street demonstrations, and his name became a household word throughout Iran. His voice and his message became well known as cassette tape recordings smuggled into Iran were copied and replayed in mosques throughout the country. Revolution by tape recorder was possible in Iran because of the central role played in Shiite Iran by the mullahs, the local religious leaders.

The concept of an Islamic state dates to the time of the prophet Muhammad. Under his leadership and that of the first four caliphs, the precedent for Islamic government was set in Mecca and Medina during the eighth century. Since then, there have been numerous attempts to use that government as a model. Following World War II, several predominantly Muslim countries, upon achieving independence from colonial powers, declared themselves to be Islamic states, Pakistan being the best known.

What *is* an Islamic state? The answer varies as widely as the answer to the questions: "What is a Christian state?" and "What is a Jewish state?" In Pakistan, which declared itself an Islamic state in 1947, the question remains unanswered, as one constitution replaces another, a woman becomes Prime Minister, and as orthodox mullahs vie with socialist intellectuals and internationally trained lawyers to provide a "correct" explanation of what an Islamic state should be. For some, an Islamic state requires the establishment of an elected legislative assembly committed to public service and the general welfare. For others, an Islamic state requires the socialization of the means of production and the distribution of goods and services to all people on the basis of their needs.

In post-1979 Iran, the definition was provided by the Ayatollah Khomeini. Within the Shiite tradition, a complex hierarchical system among the clergy has developed over the centuries, with the highest rank that of Ayatollah. A cleric emerges as an Ayatollah when it is the consensus of his fellow Muslims that he possesses vast knowledge of the Qur'an and Islamic jurisprudence. To these qualifications the Ayatollah Khomeini added his sixteen years of exile by the Shah and his participation both in Iran and from France in the popular struggle to rid his country of the Shah. The Ayatollah Khomeini, upon his return from exile, became the de facto political authority for the country, and all decisions affecting elections, presidents, budgets, petroleum production, inflation, and foreign policy had little force until they had been approved by the Ayatollah himself.

The state apparatus that emerged in Iran in the decade since the revolution has become thoroughly controlled by a vigorous, traditionalist Muslim leadership. Elements of the political left and secular political movements have been completely suppressed. The Marxist Fedayeen, the communist Tudeh Party, the leftist Islamic Mujahideen, each of which had been an ally of the Islamic movement during the revolution against the Shah, have been wiped out. Their leaders and members either fled the country or were killed or imprisoned. The centrist, bourgeois groups that emerged from the bazaars led by figures like former Prime Minister Mehdi Bazargan have been suppressed, although not all of their key figures have been imprisoned. Others among the centrist leadership of the revolution, such as former President Abolhassan Bani-Sadr, escaped from the country and live in political exile. There is little doubt that the eight-year-long Iraq–Iran war, involving as it did the total mobilization of the society, exerted a second strong influence on the shape of the society created by the revolution.

The revolution that swept the Shah from power and established an Islamic state in Iran was a clear manifestation of a resurgent, militant Islam. The question asked by many in 1979—is this the harbinger of Islamic militancy throughout the Middle East?—cannot be given a definitive answer. First, the immediate caution: Shiite Islam in Iran is not the same as the majority Sunni Islam in the Arab world, and of course the immediate and real political/economic crises of 1970s Iran are not duplicated in other areas. However, the early successes of an Islamic revolution did embolden and encourage Islamic movements in many disparate societies, but in each case—Egypt, Syria, Gaza, Tunisia—the political elite and social structures were able to contain them. Only in Lebanon, where the sizable Shiite community was in social revolt, was a direct Iranian impact felt. This was especially true in the more militant sectors of the Shiite community. In addition, several thousand Iranian Revolutionary Guard volunteers went to Lebanon to take a direct part in the fighting. But a notable example of the failure of the Shiite Islamic revolution to influence action outside Iran was the almost total rejection by the Shiite majority in Iraq of the Ayatollah Khomeini's call for revolt against the secular, Ba'athist government of Iraq.

U.S. RESPONSE TO THE IRANIAN REVOLUTION

The United States had a lot to lose with the fall of the Shah, and the U.S. government has been consistently critical of the Iranian revolution. Former Secretary of State Henry Kissinger called the "loss" of Iran "the greatest single blow to U.S. foreign policy interests since World War II," and Jimmy Carter's national security adviser, Zbigniew Brzezinski, discussed with his military advisers the possibility of dislodging the Khomeini-led government by military force.

The crisis came in October 1979, eight months after the Shah fled Iran, when President Carter allowed the exiled monarch to enter the United States—ostensibly for medical care at a New York City hospital. Carter's decision, combined with the fact that the U.S. government had not formally recognized the new government in Teheran, brought sharp reaction throughout Iran, and for two weeks there were large but peaceful demonstrations and protests demanding that the Shah be forced to leave the United States and returned to Iran for trial. Iranians knew well the history of CIA involvement in the 1953 coup d'état, and there was widespread fear that another coup was being planned.

On November 4, 1979, a well-organized group of some four hundred militant Iranian students stormed the U.S. embassy compound and seized the Americans there, beginning the drama which dominated the attention of the U.S. media for 444 days. The behavior of both governments during the hostage stalemate removed any chance for improving relations between the two.

Initially, the seizure of the embassy received widespread support among Iranians. Symbolically, tiny Iran had brought the hated

American giant to its knees. Soon, however, the whole affair became hopelessly enmeshed in domestic Iranian political struggles, and as the standoff continued, Iran became increasingly crippled by intense dissension and the political and economic costs of continuing to hold the Americans became quite high.

Throughout the ordeal, the U.S. media selectively described the Iranian government's vacillations, "feudal" policies, and executions. Political cartoonists and commentators were harsh in their portrayal of the Ayatollah Khomeini. At times, resentment against Iran and the Ayatollah spilled over into acts of retaliation against Iranians in America and remarks of general hostility against Muslims elsewhere in the world.

Declarations from the government in Washington reflected an inability to see Iran as anything but a source of oil and a strategically located military base. This limited view continued under the Reagan administration, and on October 1, 1981, the President stated: "We will not allow Saudi Arabia to become another Iran . . . as long as Saudi Arabia and the OPEC nations—and Saudi Arabia's the most important—provide the bulk of the energy that is needed to turn the wheels of industry in the Western world, there is no way we could stand by and see that taken over by anyone that would shut off that oil."[12] It is this perspective which led ultimately to the decision by Reagan in 1987 to reflag Kuwaiti oil tankers and to send U.S. naval forces to the Persian Gulf.

But one of the anomalies of U.S.–Iranian relations was the secret decision by the Reagan White House to initiate the sale of arms to the Iranians. What we do know of the "Iran-Contra Scandal" has been told at length and will not be repeated here, but the series of mixed motives which seemed to lie behind the arms sales tell much about the conflicting attitudes held by each government toward the other. That the Iranians would engage in an arms deal with the United States ("the Great Satan") was probably due largely to their desperate need for sophisticated armaments and spare parts. That the United States would sell weapons to the country it had labeled "terrorist" certainly reflected deep confusions in U.S. policy, not to mention the failure brought on by indecision among policymakers. Some believe the policy was based on the desire to ransom U.S. hostages held in Lebanon by groups close to Iran. But the record also suggests the continuing interest, especially prevalent in U.S. security agencies such as the CIA, in reestablishing links with Iran, a country that in spite of its ruthless government still occupies a strategic position between the Soviet Union and the oil-rich Gulf.

The Iranian revolution has had other repercussions. Iran's neighbors (including Iraq, Saudi Arabia, and other Gulf countries) have become anxious lest the model of a successful Islamic uprising against an unpopular ruler be followed in their own countries. This fear has been reflected in sharp increases in the purchase of arms, which are defended as providing security against Iran, the Soviet Union, and Israel but which may also be used against their own people should they demand change.

In Afghanistan, the possibility of one or several indigenous mullahs patterning themselves after the Ayatollah Khomeini and becoming politically powerful at the expense of Afghanistan's indigenous Marxists was among the factors in the Soviet Union's decision to invade Afghanistan. The war in Afghanistan, called a jihad by the anti-Soviet Afghans, attracted support from Iran and other Muslim states. The desire to restore Islam to a position of prominence is one of the common goals binding together the disparate bands of Afghan guerrillas.

THE IRAN–IRAQ WAR

Iraq's President, Saddam Hussein, ordered his troops across the Shatt-al-Arab waterway into the Khuzistan section of Iran on September 11, 1980. He did so for several reasons. First, he was emboldened to take this step because of the disarray in revolutionary Iran and the expectation that effective military resistance would be impossible. Second, Saddam was irritated at the Ayatollah Khomeini's call to the Shiites of Iraq to join the Islamic revolution and he also hoped that the Arab minority in Khuzistan might abandon Iran and support Arab Iraq. Third, and perhaps at the core, was the border that had been forced on Iraq by the Shah in 1975 when he pushed the international boundary from the Iranian shore to the middle of the Shatt-al-Arab waterway. President Saddam Hussein's expectations of an easy victory were not fulfilled; although Iraqi forces were able to capture several miles of Iranian territory and in early November even seized the cities of Khorramshahr and Abadan, by January 1981 Iranian counter-offensives began to prove successful and in September the Iranians recaptured Abadan. The eight years of ensuing war were largely indecisive, exacting a heavy toll, not only in human life but also on the material resources of both Iran and Iraq.

By the time the UN-mediated cease-fire came into effect, on August 20, 1988, estimates of losses ranged up to 800,000 dead and as many as 3 million wounded on both sides.[13] The economic and financial costs were devastating. Iran's own Ministry of Planning and Budget put the costs for the first five years (1980–85) at $309 billion, half of which was lost in the oil sector. Iraq's losses have been comparably high; it began the war with very large foreign-exchange reserves, but by the end of 1986 this surplus had been turned into a foreign debt of $45–$50 billion; by 1985–86 Iraqi military spending was above 50 percent of its GNP.[14]

The war, which certainly had territorial disputes as one cause, also was being fought (and possibly more importantly as time passed) to determine which of the two nations would become the dominant economic, political, religious, and cultural influence in the region. While initially Saddam Hussein seemed in position to realize his aims to reshape the boundaries between the two states and demonstrate Iraq's superior power in the face of a weakened and internally fractious Iran, the conflict became a battle which increasingly involved other Gulf states, spilled over into serious attacks on Gulf shipping, and in its last stages brought naval units of both the United States and the Soviet Union into the Gulf.[15]

By March 1981 the Iraqi forces, which had expected a short war, began to weaken and the battle turned in Iran's favor. Baghdad, then willing to negotiate, was rebuffed by Iran, which had turned the conflict into a "holy war" and set a high price for ending it: the overthrow of Saddam Hussein, an acknowledgment of Iraqi war guilt, substantial reparations, restoration of the 1975 boundaries, complete withdrawal of Iraqi troops, and repatriation of 100,000 Shiite Muslims expelled from Iraq.[16]

During the 1982 Iranian offensives, huge numbers of regular troops, augmented by partially trained but highly motivated Revolutionary Guards, began to use the tactic of "human-wave assaults." After a series of campaigns over a period of almost two years, Iran succeeded in capturing some key strips of Iraqi territory near the city of Basra, Iraq's main oil port. Iraq's retaliation involved an expansion of the war. A maritime exclusion zone was declared in August 1982 in the northern Gulf, and Iraq began bombing Iranian ports, oil installations, neutral ships, and tankers entering or leaving Iran. By 1984, after an indecisive war of attrition on the ground, Iraq adopted two new tactics: First, attacks on merchant shipping escalated from a total of 28 in the first three years to 72 in 1984 alone and spread farther into the Gulf. At the same time, reports of Iraqi use of chemical weapons became more persistent (Iran had made charges as early as May 1981), and an international team in March 1984 concluded that mustard and nerve gas had been used during battles in February 1984.[17] By March 1986, UN Secretary-General Pérez de Cuéllar directly accused Iraq of using chemical weapons.

Iran's retaliation in the Gulf included attacks on oil tankers serving Kuwait and Saudi Arabia and ultimately involved firing on freighters as well. The attacks, which Iran hoped would cut support from Iraq's allies, had the effect of increasing the Arab countries' fears of a possible Iranian victory, the effects of which might spill over into their own societies. The toll on Gulf shipping was substantial: between March 1984 and March 1987 the International Association of Independent Tankers reported 173 ships attacked, with 41 destroyed. It was in light of these escalating attacks on shipping that Kuwait appealed to both the United States and the Soviet Union late in 1986 to protect its ships. The Soviets rapidly deployed three warship escorts; by May 1987 the United States acted, reflagging eleven Kuwaiti tankers and dispatching a naval force in July which at one point numbered forty vessels deployed in the Gulf and the northern Arabian Sea. The incidents which followed, including Iranian mining of shipping channels (several vessels were hit), direct U.S. engagements with small Iranian boats, and attacks on land installations, threatened to escalate the "tanker war" into a confrontation between the United States and Iran. At the time, the United States rejected suggestions for the creation of a UN-sponsored naval unit to keep the waterways open for navigation. In part at least, the United States seemed intent on playing a highly visible role in order to offset the adverse reaction of even the moderate Arab nations to its involvement in selling arms to Iran in the complicated Iran-Contra scheme.

By many standards, mediation efforts should have been able to resolve the Iran–Iraq conflict, particularly in its early stages, when neither side proved able to achieve real military advantage. Between November 1980 and February 1981, Olof Palme, the Swedish Prime Minister, acting on behalf of the UN Secretary-General, made three attempts to find a formula to settle the territorial dispute, which on the surface seemed at the time to be focused on control of the Shatt-al-Arab waterway.[18] He failed, finding the differences irreconcilable. As Palme's efforts ended, the Islamic Conference Organization in February 1981 dispatched a high-level mediation team to Teheran and Baghdad advancing a formula for withdrawal and arbitration by the Islamic group. They were rebuffed by both governments. By May 1981, the Movement of Non-Aligned Nations attempted to bring the disputants to arbitration. Both sides insisted on their original demands and even began escalating them. Subsequent efforts by those who had tried earlier and a new initiative by the Algerian Foreign Minister early in 1982 all failed. A behind-the-scenes effort by the six-nation Gulf Cooperation Council in July 1982 involved an offer by the six to pay war reparations to Iran (as had been demanded as a condition for ending the war) and to contribute substantial funds to Iraq to help defray the costs of reconstruction. The secret proposal was never accepted.[19] Mediation efforts continued sporadically and with added urgency, but without success, as the "tanker war" took an increasing toll.

Failures on the diplomatic front were matched by a lack of success in preventing the flow of arms to the two combatants. After a decline in global arms sales, the Iran–Iraq war took up the slack with arms merchants, and new supplier nations emerged to take full advantage of the expanded market. Initially, the United States and the Soviet Union declared their neutrality and refused arms shipments.[20] Others were not so reluctant; China, Vietnam, North and South Korea, Israel, and Syria all supplied arms to Iran, proving a great willingness to ignore their strong antagonisms and share in the arms sales. By 1982, as the tide of battle shifted against Iraq, the Soviet Union reversed its policy and became Iraq's largest arms supplier, joined by Egypt, China, and France. By 1983 the United States initiated Operation Staunch, the much-touted attempt to enforce an arms embargo against Iran, but was caught violating its own ban in the arms-for-hostages deal.

The military balance in the war shifted in late 1986, in part because Iraq proved able to acquire more sophisticated weapons, aircraft and missiles, as a means of offsetting Iran's advantage in ground forces. The expansion of the war to attacks on Gulf shipping and the ultimate involvement of significant foreign naval forces to protect shipping also seemed to weigh in Iraq's favor, but was by no means enough to win the war. One knowledgeable military analyst of the war wrote in the early summer of 1988: "The eighth year of the Iran-Iraq War is nearly over, but the conflict shows little sign of ending anytime soon. . . . 1988 appears destined to be just another year of bloody stalemate in a seemingly endless war."[21] But by July 19, 1988, Iran had accepted the UN cease-fire plan (Security Council Resolution 598) voted just a year earlier, and the long, contentious process of turning a truce into peace began. The Ayatollah Khomeini reluctantly gave the plan his blessing and called off his holy war, although he commented at the time that it was "like taking poison."[22] Iran, having suffered setbacks on the ground—the loss of the Fao peninsula in April 1988 and a retreat to the international border—had shifted responsibility for command of its war effort to Parliament Speaker Ali Akbar Hashemi Rafsanjani. Early in July 1988, a U.S. naval vessel, carrying the most sophisticated radar equipment, shot down a civilian Iranian Airbus, killing all 290 passengers and crew; some speculated that the loss of the plane gave Iran a minor moral triumph, thereby allowing rapid moves to end the fighting.[23] But for whatever reasons, the Iran–Iraq war, which had seemed interminable, ended as abruptly as it had begun. Historians will in time extract many lessons from the very costly conflict, but some immediate observations are pertinent: it was much easier to start the war than to stop it or even contain it; large-scale military buildups of the sort that both Iran and Iraq engaged in during the 1970s, before their war, can be significantly destabilizing; arms-exporting nations do not have much control over the uses to which their weapons will be put; the UN mediation effort was finally successful only because both the Soviets and the Americans favored it. The legitimacy and importance of the UN as an agency for peacemaking has been reaffirmed.[24]

ASSESSMENT OF THE IRANIAN REVOLUTION

The Iranian revolution stands as one of the more remarkable political events of recent history. Millions of Iranians, using primarily nonviolent collective action, rendered ineffective the most powerful and best-armed military force in the Middle East. A broad-based coalition peacefully deposed the Shah while he still enjoyed the full support of his secret-police apparatus and army as well as the backing of the United States.

After the Shah's departure, elements of this coalition fragmented into groups struggling for power. Censorship, arrests, and firing squads reemerged as ways to settle old scores, eliminate political alternatives, and suppress such minorities as Jews, Christians, Bahais, Kurds, Turks, Baluchis, and small tribal groups. The revolution, and indeed much of the Iranian war effort, demonstrated the ability to mobilize people by the millions. But as the analyst Fred Halliday pointed out, "this mobilization has been misled and deceived."[25] Democracy has not been achieved and the religious leaders of the state are as contemptuous of the people as the Shah had been. The Shah's centralized control has been replaced by a Shiite dictatorship. Social and economic reforms have largely been put aside, including efforts to introduce the ethics of "Islamic economics"; the economy is still dependent on oil exports; unemployment is high; illiteracy has not been tackled; and for women there has been a retreat from the limited gains toward equality achieved during the Pahlavi years.

For those who were sympathetic to the courage and commitment of the Iranian people and to their largely nonviolent overthrow of the Shah's regime, the continued severe violations of human rights and the resort to repressive measures to maintain power are deeply depressing. We can all hope that with the end of active fighting Iran can be successfully reintegrated into the community of nations and that the hostilities from outside mirrored so fiercely inside can be replaced by real improvements at the social, economic, and political levels.

The war and the Iranian revolution have left unfinished business which needs international attention and effort:

- The fragile cease-fire must be strengthened and expanded into a peace treaty if the threat of war is to be permanently overcome.
- International efforts to reverse the arms race between Iran and Iraq (and the other Gulf states) must be made, with special attention to two new classes of weapons introduced in this war—chemical weapons and missiles. The nations of the Middle East must be brought into the current chemical weapons talks and become parties to the emerging Chemical Weapons Convention. The development of effective sanctions against the use of chemical weapons is essential if the international "benign neglect" of their use in the Iran–Iraq war is not to be repeated. A similar attempt to halt the introduction of missiles into the Middle East is urgently needed.
- The need to address the marked violations of human rights within both Iran and Iraq requires strong international attention. In the wake of the war, the temptation to settle old scores in both countries has wreaked havoc on ethnic and religious minorities as well as dissident political groups.
- Iraq has emerged from the war with renewed confidence and a battle-hardened military force; it is arguably the strongest force in the Arab world. The need to create the appropriate international climate for curbing the use of that military force is important. Iraq can become a significant factor in an emerging peace in the region or slip into the role of a threat to that peace. One particular front where third-party efforts might prove valuable is the growing confrontation between Syria and Iraq in its surrogate location—Lebanon.

9

Afghanistan

The Soviet invasion of Afghanistan in December 1979 and the immediate and strong U.S. military response in the Indian Ocean, the Persian Gulf, and the Arabian peninsula thrust Afghanistan into the politics of the Middle East.

The overwhelming majority of Afghanistan's population are Sunni Muslims; its two major languages, Dari (Afghan Farsi) and Pashto, are written with a modified Arabic script; and Muslim pilgrims make the *hajj* to Mecca every year. But except for these cultural links, for the past 150 years Afghanistan has appeared to have few ties to the Middle East. During that period the Mohammedzai dynasty dominated Afghan politics; its major wars were with Russia (to the north) and Britain (in British India to the southeast). During the past thirty years, Afghanistan's most persistent international problem has concerned the political loyalties of the Pashto-speaking tribes which occupy the rugged terrain along Afghanistan's southeastern border with Pakistan.

In 1964, under the direction of King Mohammed Zahir, an Afghanistan constitution was drawn up; national elections were held in 1965 and again in 1969. But the "partyless democracy" envisioned in the constitution failed to take root. In 1973, Daud Khan, first cousin and brother-in-law of the King and Prime Minister of Afghanistan from 1953 to 1963, staged a coup while the King was abroad, declared Afghanistan a republic, and presented himsclf as the new President and Prime Minister. In 1978 another specially convened *Loya Jirgah* (gathering of leaders) approved a second constitution and elected Daud Khan the first President.

The constitutional and personnel changes in Afghanistan's political hierarchy had little effect on the nation's domestic and international policies. Afghanistan chose a nonaligned stance, which left it free to accept aid from any source, and the two superpowers were quick to provide aid in the form of special development projects, advisers, and loans. U.S. assistance produced such benefits as the Hilmand Valley project and Ariana Afghan Airlines, while Soviet assistance produced the Darunta hydroelectric project and the improved north-south road to Kabul, including the three-kilometer-long Salang Tunnel.

Afghanistan pursued a domestic policy of modified, centralized economic planning based on a series of five-year plans. These were carried out with assistance from the United Nations, China, West Germany, Yugoslavia, Czechoslovakia, France, Japan, and India—although most aid came from the U.S.S.R. and the United States. Afghanistan's leaders followed a social policy of cautious reform, including voluntary removal of women's veils and the establishment of more women's facilities for higher education. The emphasis on constitutional government during the 1960s and 1970s accompanied the development of political parties. Frequently, however, political organizers were imprisoned, and newspapers publishing critical stories were closed down.

On January 1, 1965, a leftist party known as Khalq (Masses) was formed under the leadership of, among others, Noor Mohammed Taraki. In June 1967 a second leftist party, known as Parcham (Banner or Flag), was formed under the leadership of Babrak Karmal, at least in part as a result of personality and policy clashes between Karmal and Taraki. The Khalq Party tended to be more oriented toward Pashto-speaking Afghans and to concentrate its organizing efforts on members of the military and civil services, while the Parcham Party was more oriented to the Dari-speaking Afghans and concentrated its efforts on the intellectuals and urban middle classes.[1] On April 27, 1978, leaders of the combined Khalq and Parcham parties launched a coup, and to the surprise of many, it succeeded. President Daud Khan and a group of his close supporters were killed, and the combined Khalq-Parcham leadership announced the establishment of the Democratic Republic of Afghanistan (DRA). In their first public statement, the leaders of the "Saur Revolution" (it occurred during the month of Saur) declared that they were not communists and that their policies would be based on Afghan nationalism, respect for Islam, a continuing commitment to a nonaligned foreign policy, and economic and social justice.

Between the end of April and November 1978, the DRA, under the leadership of Taraki and a revolutionary council initially composed about equally of Khalqis and Parchamis, issued eight decrees. The council abolished usury, granted equal rights to women, and prohibited forced marriages; dowry and marriage expenses were regularized, and land reforms were introduced. Lofty in principle, these decrees were largely the work of urban-based intellectuals, with little appreciation for the rural resistance such decrees would generate.

As the urban intellectuals began to try to enforce their decrees, they triggered two responses: armed resistance in the countryside and the flight of Afghan refugees, primarily across the border into Pakistan but also across the western border into Iran. Armed resistance in the countryside met armed enforcement by the DRA authorities, and within a few months Afghanistan was embroiled in a running civil war.

The complexities of the civil war were aggravated by an increasingly open rift between the Khalqis and the Parchamis. Prime Minister Taraki and his Khalqi supporters arrested an increasing number of Parchamis, charging them with plotting to overthrow the government, extorted "confessions" from them, and broadcast their "confessions" over Radio Afghanistan. Parcham leaders such as Babrak Karmal went into hiding or fled the country, and their supporters, and those afraid of being denounced as their supporters, added to the flow of refugees leaving Afghanistan. With the domestic situation deteriorating, Taraki went to Moscow, where he and Leonid Brezhnev, on December 5, 1978, signed a Treaty of Friendship and Cooperation, which stipulated that Afghanistan and the Soviet Union would consult each other on all major issues affecting both parties.

By the spring of 1979, armed revolts, largely uncoordinated and under the direction of local landlords and mullahs, had erupted in all the provinces. Soviet military advisers played a role in directing DRA military units in their warfare against the rebelling country-side. The DRA military units, composed largely of conscripts, faced problems of morale and desertion. By mid-August 1979, approximately 165,000 refugees had fled from Afghanistan into Pakistan, and Radio Afghanistan had begun accusing Pakistan and Iran (and eventually China, the United States, Israel, and Egypt) of arming and training the men in the refugee camps and assisting them in their guerrilla raids back into Afghanistan. All these countries denied the accusations.

Troubles within the DRA high command continued. In September 1979, a shoot-out between DRA President Taraki and DRA Prime Minister Hafizullah Amin resulted in Taraki's death and a takeover by Amin.[2] But under Amin's direction, the instabilities in the countryside continued, as did the threats of arrests in those locations under Kabul's control. By December 1979 the DRA controlled only the major cities and their link roads—and those only by day. By night, virtually the entire countryside, as well as sections of the major cities, reverted to the control of the opposition. That opposition also was plagued by internal dissension and lack of coordination. It was united only in its deep sense of Afghan nationalism and its commitment to carry out a jihad, a holy struggle against the DRA leadership in Kabul.

THE 1979 SOVIET INVASION OF AFGHANISTAN

The full details of the Soviet invasion may never be known. The U.S.S.R. maintains that the Afghanistan Revolutionary Council, without the knowledge of Amin, invited the Soviet troops to help restore order in the country and thereby allow the formation of a new government committed to the welfare of all Afghans. The Revolutionary Council, with its loyal troops, then overwhelmed and killed Amin and replaced him with Babrak Karmal, longtime leader of the Parchamis, who had been living outside the country since 1978. According to Moscow, Soviet troops arrived in Kabul with a clear and limited objective—to protect order; they would return to the Soviet Union as soon as they had achieved it.

Critics of the Soviet Union maintain that the Soviet invasion was initiated by Moscow, and the death of Amin immediately following the troop arrivals casts doubt that the Soviet troops were requested. Critics claim also that the arrival of Babrak Karmal as Afghanistan's new ruler reflects all too clearly the imposition of a Soviet-backed puppet government on Afghanistan.

Regardless of which interpretation is closer to the truth, on the night of December 27, 1979, after hearing the constant drone of military planes for several days and nights followed by outbursts of shooting in various sectors of Kabul, Afghans heard a broadcast by Babrak Karmal announcing that Hafizullah Amin, "that treacherous foe of God . . . the CIA agent and scheming spy of American imperialism," was dead.[3] Karmal's only reference to the Soviet troops was to mention the "observation of the Treaty of Friendship and Cooperation of December 5, 1978, with the Soviet Union." Karmal announced that his policies would include the release of political prisoners, the abolition of arbitrary arrests, respect for Islam, a nonaligned foreign policy, and loyalty to the United Nations.

Within a few weeks, Soviet troop levels in Afghanistan reached between 85,000 and 90,000; another 30,000 troops were in the Soviet Union just north of the Afghanistan border.[4] Soviet forces in Afghanistan reached a "steady state" level of some 120,000 soldiers and remained at that number into 1988. The strength of the DRA army, despite calls for more rigorous conscription, declined from about 70,000 at the time of the Soviet invasion to about 25,000–30,000, with an additional hard-core group of about 10,000.[5] The Mujahideen, as opponents of the DRA call themselves, have waged ongoing guerrilla warfare, moving around the countryside with relative freedom. They developed a total fighting force estimated at 50,000–80,000, operating in as many as 1,500 separate, conflicting guerrilla units.[6] The DRA and Soviet military units have typically fought from within armored vehicles and helicopter gunships. At night they returned to well-guarded military bases adjoining airfields.

The war settled into a continuing battle, with Soviet troops doing much of the fighting, and became the longest, largest, and most expensive Soviet military operation since World War II.[7]

REFUGEES AND MUJAHIDEEN

Civilian casualties reached several hundred thousand during the more than eight years of fighting, and an estimated 4 to 5 million Afghanis (out of a population of 15 million) fled the country as refugees, largely to northwestern Pakistan. An undetermined number of men among these refugees used the refugee camps as bases from which to stage raids across the border into Afghanistan. Their weapons in the early days of the war consisted largely of traditional handmade mountaineer rifles, captured Soviet weapons (or weapons brought over by defectors), and an assortment of more modern weapons, such as Egyptian-made Kalashnikov rifles and Chinese recoilless rifles. Their supply has since been augmented by a well-funded program, largely directed from Washington, which by 1986 included the highly effective Blowpipe and Stinger ground-to-air missiles, which have sharply reduced the Soviets' use of helicopters. The leaders of various Mujahideen groups concentrated in the region of Peshawar (Pakistan) constantly squabbled among themselves. No single leader or group of leaders was able to unite the disparate tribal, regional, political, or sectarian groups into a unified military or political force. The periodic announcement of a new unified effort generally preceded the next round of requests to the U.S. Congress for funding. Support for the refugees came from the government of Pakistan and the UN High Commission for Refugees, as well as from numerous church relief agencies and the Red Crescent agency. The Mujahideen guerrillas, while hard pressed for support at first, fairly quickly found that one problem they did not have was a shortage of funds. By 1985 they had received $250 million from the United States, supplemented by that much again from Saudi Arabia, Israel, and China.[8] In 1987 *The Washington Post* reported they received a total of $660 million in aid from the United States alone, and the total reached nearly a billion dollars by 1988.[9]

WORLD RESPONSE

The world's response to the Soviet invasion of Afghanistan was consistent. On January 15, 1980, the UN General Assembly condemned the invasion and called for the immediate withdrawal of

Soviet troops. Each year since, the UN General Assembly adopted a toughly worded resolution condemning the Soviet invasion. In 1987, 123 nations voted in favor of condemnation.[10] In late January 1980, the Conference of Islamic States, which included representation from the PLO and Iraq, condemned the U.S.S.R. for its invasion of Afghanistan, suspended Afghanistan as a member of the Conference, and called for the immediate withdrawal of Soviet troops. At a subsequent meeting in May 1980, the Conference of Islamic States again condemned the invasion and appointed a special committee, composed of the Foreign Ministers of Pakistan and Iran and the secretary-general of the Conference, to seek a political solution to the problem. In Iran the Ayatollah Khomeini publicly condemned the Soviet intervention. In September 1980, the sixteen-nation Asian and Pacific Commonwealth Nations conference in New Delhi also called on the Soviets to withdraw their troops from Afghanistan.

In the face of strong international criticism, the Soviet Union and the government of Afghanistan maintained that the Soviet Union did not "invade" Afghanistan but, instead, responded to a legitimate request from Afghanistan based on the December 5, 1978, Treaty of Friendship and Cooperation. Furthermore, they stated that a precondition for Soviet troops leaving Afghanistan would be political stability in Afghanistan and the end of outside assistance to the rebels fighting the Kabul government.

As early as 1982 the UN undertook negotiations aimed at a Soviet withdrawal from Afghanistan. From the very beginning a three-part agreement was proposed: first, Pakistan and Afghanistan would stop military supplies going to the Mujahideen through Pakistan; second, the same parties agreed to the return of the refugees to Afghanistan (the large numbers were already becoming a major burden for Pakistan); third, the Soviet Union and Afghanistan would set terms for Soviet withdrawal; guarantees of these arrangements would be undertaken by both the United States and the Soviet Union.[11] The UN effort continued through the next six years, finally achieving success in March 1988.

UNITED STATES RESPONSE

The American response to the presence of Soviet troops in Afghanistan has been more severe than that of most of the rest of the world. On January 4, 1980, President Carter announced a grain embargo against the Soviet Union, banned exports to the U.S.S.R. of certain sophisticated technology, limited certain Soviet fishing privileges in U.S. waters, and urged an international boycott of the 1980 Olympic Games to be held in Moscow. In his State of the Union message later in January, President Carter declared that the implications of the Soviet invasion of Afghanistan "pose a serious threat to peace," marking the first time since World War II that the U.S.S.R. had moved its forces into a nation outside its direct sphere of influence.[12] In a smiliar vein he enunciated the Carter Doctrine—that threats to the Gulf region challenged vital American interests and the United States would be prepared to meet them with force. He requested congressional authority to reinstate registration for the draft, increase the U.S. military budget by at least 5 percent above the rate of inflation during each of the next five years, loosen controls over the CIA to permit covert operations, offer increased military aid to Pakistan, and expand the U.S. military presence in northeastern Africa, the Persian Gulf, and the Indian Ocean. In May 1980, a special meeting of NATO Foreign and Defense Ministers declared they were bolstering their strike capabilities in response to the Soviet Union's continued occupation of Afghanistan. In August 1980, the United States, Canada, Japan, and West Germany were among the nations boycotting the XXII Summer Olympic Games in Moscow to protest the continued Soviet presence in Afghanistan, and in November 1980, the Western delegates to the Madrid conference reviewing the Helsinki human rights accords again criticized the Soviet Union's refusal to withdraw its troops from Afghanistan.

The Reagan administration continued many of the Carter policies aimed at strengthening U.S. capabilities in the Gulf area. These have included:

1. Developing a Rapid Deployment Force of combat troops able to move quickly into the world's trouble spots to protect U.S. interests, with primary focus on the Middle East.

2. Acquiring access to ports and airfields throughout the greater

Gulf area for logistical support for the Rapid Deployment Force. The Reagan administration's interest in including U.S. troops in the Sinai peacekeeping force between Egypt and Israel has also been linked to the increase of U.S. military personnel in the Gulf area.

3. Providing Pakistan with substantial new military support, beginning in September 1981, with a six-year $3.2 billion economic aid and military sales package. The package included forty F-16 fighter aircraft. Pakistan had also requested a Pakistan–U.S. security treaty that would assure U.S. assistance if the country were involved in combat, whether with the Soviet Union, India, or any other of its neighbors.[13]

4. Developing a "security consensus" with countries extending from Egypt to Pakistan that would make *local* troops available initially to block any Soviet moves or local revolts until the United States could bring in its Rapid Deployment Force.

5. Upgrading the 200,000-member Rapid Deployment Force in 1983 to a full-scale Central Command, with about 325,000 troops and a substantial naval and air component, including three aircraft carrier battle groups and more than 400 fighter and attack aircraft. In addition there are arrangements for prepositioned supplies and basing rights in Qatar, Saudi Arabia, Oman, Somalia, Egypt, Morocco, Kenya, and Diego Garcia.

6. Adopting a policy of sharply increased "covert" aid to the Mujahideen that reached close to a total of $1 billion by fiscal 1988. The Afghan guerrillas became by far the largest recipients of U.S. covert military assistance without any controversy in Congress; the guerrillas received more aid in a single year than the total of all the support that had gone to the Contras fighting the Sandinistas in Nicaragua. Afghanistan is the only country where U.S. covert aid is used directly against Soviet troops. One interpretation suggested that the United States was attempting to "bleed the Soviet Union into a military defeat or at least [to ensure] that the occupation is costly."[14]

The Reagan Doctrine, of which the Afghanistan effort is only one example, represented a commitment to a global war against communism; the United States gave "covert" military support to guerrillas who challenged Soviet-sponsored governments. The doctrine was seen as the mirror image of the much-criticized Soviet support for liberation movements in the 1960s.

There is irony in the vigorous support the United States has given to the guerrilla groups in Afghanistan—called "freedom fighters" by some U.S. political figures; the most favored leaders, men like Gulbudding Hekmatyar, are radical Muslim fundamentalists similar in many ways to the very forces the United States has opposed in Iran.

SOVIET RESPONSE

On May 15, 1988, Soviet troops began their withdrawal from Afghanistan, to be completed in ten months; the lengthy UN-sponsored negotiations finally worked. Even though they fought for eight years, the Soviets' goals in Afghanistan were never extensive.[15] They made no claim of sovereignty over any part of Afghanistan and never increased their military commitment to a magnitude that could bring victory; within weeks of the December 1979 invasion they agreed in principle to withdraw (a long time in fulfillment), which is in sharp contrast to their position in Eastern Europe; in retrospect, their actions and diplomacy did not bear out the early U.S. fears that the Soviets were engaged in a program of significant territorial expansion, possibly reaching south for a warm-water port. The Soviet military actions were destructive of both civilian and military targets and brought a great deal of human suffering; between 10,000 and 15,000 Soviet soldiers were killed and the war became increasingly unpopular at home. The initial Soviet aim, to rescue a regime in trouble and to stabilize it and then rebuild the country's infrastructure, was never more than partially successful—most of Afghanistan remained under the control of local leaders and local guerrilla groups. As the Soviets undertook their withdrawal, they were surely aware that the government they had supported in Kabul could not survive intact without their military support.

The Soviet decision to withdraw their troops was probably made in 1983 by Yuri Andropov during the brief period he led the Politburo. It clearly went "on hold" during the short period when Konstantin Chernenko was the Party's General Secretary. Implementation of the decision had to wait until Mikhail Gorbachev assumed leadership in the spring of 1985; he began referring to the situation as a "bleeding wound" and initiated a series of political and diplomatic efforts which led in February 1988 to the announcement that Soviet troops would withdraw without any prior agreements on the formation of a coalition government to replace the Soviet-backed regime.

The leadership of the People's Democratic Party of Afghanistan (the communist-led party that absorbed the two factions) was changed on May 4, 1986, when Dr. Najibullah replaced Babrak Karmal as General Secretary. Then in July, Gorbachev announced a symbolic withdrawal of 8,000 troops; in November, during a visit to India, he made new overtures to Pakistan and then initiated high-level talks in Islamabad; prodded by Gorbachev to seek political compromise, Najibullah on January 1, 1987, called for "national reconciliation" and a cease-fire—it was largely rejected by the Mujahideen.[16]

Beginning in 1983, UN Under Secretary Diego Cordovez pursued negotiations among the critical parties—the Afghanis, the Pakistanis, the United States, and the Soviets. The basic terms of an agreement fell into place in 1985 and 1986—these included a mutual pledge of noninterference; international guarantees of the agreement; voluntary and safe return of refugees; a specific timetable of Soviet withdrawal; and UN monitoring of the accord.[17] On February 8, 1988, Gorbachev broke a stalemate on the touchy fourth point and announced that Soviet troops would begin withdrawing in three months, on May 15, 1988, and complete the withdrawal in ten more months. On April 14, at UN headquarters in Geneva, Cordovez secured the signatures of Pakistan and Afghanistan and the guarantees of the United States and the Soviet Union. An important stage in a long and bitter war was brought to a close. A new leadership determined to end the Soviet military role in Afghanistan made deep compromises. But the end of conflict in Afghanistan is by no means assured; civil war is all too likely.

CONCLUSIONS

It is unclear what form the political structures of Afghanistan will take once Soviet troops leave. In the first instance, armed conflict seems sure to continue. The Soviets will provide arms aid to their former client government and the Americans insist on supplying weapons to the various Mujahideen factions. Finding a coalition government that can govern seems highly unlikely; the guerrillas insist that they will continue their jihad against the parties that the Soviets had backed. It is quite possible that unless the United States and the Soviets deal with the problem successfully, proxy war will result. In addition, the leadership of the guerrilla alliance of seven factions is all Sunni and unlikely to be trusted to form a government by the Shiites, who make up some 15 percent of the population. The idea of a neutral government headed by Afghani leaders now in exile, such as former King Mohammed Zahir, had been suggested but not agreed to prior to Soviet troop withdrawal; such a government might be supported by a UN peacekeeping force.[18]

The United States and the Soviet Union have an opportunity at this stage in Afghanistan's strife to work together to avoid the almost certain bloodshed that will occur if a compromise government jointly supported by both major powers is not helped into place and given essential support. Too many commentators, knowing the fractured nature of the society and the deep competition that exists among the Mujahideen, point to the tragic alternative to Soviet–U.S. cooperation—Afghanistan becoming another Lebanon armed and manipulated by outside parties.[19]

AFGHANISTAN AND THE MIDDLE EAST

There are important ways in which recent events in the Middle East and events in Afghanistan have impinged upon each other.

1. Events in the Middle East (as well as in Western Europe and the United States) may have contributed to the international climate in which the Soviet Union decided to send troops into Afghanistan. The steady deterioration of détente, beginning in the summer of 1979, and political events in Iran may have weighed significantly in the minds of the Soviet leaders as they decided how to respond to the worsening situation in Afghanistan. To them, a

"worst possible scenario" would have been the collapse of the Democratic Republic of Afghanistan, with numerous feuding leaders emerging, and an anti-Soviet foreign policy that might have brought U.S. missiles into northern Afghanistan on the Soviet border and might strengthen the hands of the hawks in the Kremlin (who initially sent Soviet troops into Afghanistan).

2. Soviet troop movements into Afghanistan suggested to the United States the possibility of further Soviet military expansion into the Middle East and South Asia. After all, if Soviet troops invaded Afghanistan in 1979, what would prevent their invading Iran or Pakistan later? Soviet actions in Afghanistan strengthened the arguments of American hawks that the U.S.S.R. was bent on territorial expansion. The Reagan doctrine of intervening in support of anti-communist guerrilla groups was welcomed when applied to Afghanistan and never drew the opposition that the doctrine faced when applied to Nicaragua or Angola.

3. The eight-year presence of Soviet troops in Afghanistan and their involvement in military operations up to the border of Pakistan have provided the United States with reasons for significantly escalating its arms supplies to Pakistan, despite Pakistan's violations of U.S. rules on nuclear proliferation and its poor record on human rights.

4. The continued presence of Soviet troops in Afghanistan has provided the United States with the major reason for increasing its own military presence in the Middle East. In later years, escalation of the Gulf war provided further grounds for these American actions.

5. The Soviet Union's maintenance and rotation of military personnel in Afghanistan may have inhibited its willingness to assign troops to military duty elsewhere in the world. Analysts have speculated that the Soviet Union's decision not to invade Poland in the spring and summer of 1981 was related in part to Moscow's military activities in Afghanistan.

6. The invasion of Afghanistan cost the Soviet Union considerable goodwill in the Arab world as well as in much of the rest of the Third World. In the past, the Third World has frequently condemned U.S. economic and military interventions in Third World affairs. But Afghanistan gave what was seen to be an equally

clear illustration of Soviet willingness to intervene militarily in a Third World country when it served Soviet purposes.

7. Gorbachev's changes in foreign policy suggest the extent to which Soviet–U.S. relations in regional conflicts might be radically altered. However, the failure to achieve a political compromise on Afghani government structure and on limiting arms to both sides shows that much more than the pullback of major powers must be achieved if regional conflicts are to end in a workable peace.

10

The Soviet Union

The interpretation of events in the Middle East often becomes more important than the events themselves. Washington has long viewed them largely in the context of an "arc of crisis." According to this view, the Soviet Union has been actively encouraging, or actually precipitating, crises in an "arc" of nations stretching from Ethiopia and Yemen in the west to Afghanistan and Bangladesh in the east. The Soviets, according to this view, manipulate indigenous problems for their own political ends. OPEC price increases, the fall of the Shah, the invasion of Afghanistan, the continuing crisis between Arabs and Israelis, the Somali–Ethiopian war, and the Iraq–Iran war were all seen as fitting the Kremlin's master plan with the ultimate goal of winning territory or support for the Soviet Union. Successive U.S. administrations have developed policy reflecting this interpretation of events. The Carter Doctrine was enunciated in this context and a large-scale arms buildup in the region was launched; the Reagan administration kept up the armaments and in addition enunciated a Reagan doctrine of providing direct support to armed insurgencies against Soviet-backed or anti-U.S. governments. This represents, however, a significant distortion and oversimplification of the realities of Soviet Middle East relations.

Soviet policy in the Middle East has been marked by continuity and recently by some important changes. This policy has reflected two levels, one applicable to the Third World as a whole and the other related directly to the Middle East.

Significant Soviet activism in the Third World began about 1954 and was designed largely by Nikita Khrushchev. Many of the recently decolonized states saw in the Soviet Union a noncolonial power that had itself achieved rapid economic and social development and thus could serve as a model.[1] The Soviet Union was also believed to serve as a balance to Western (former colonial) influence both economically and militarily. The Soviets, from their point of view, were anxious to support both socialism and nonalignment in order to offset Western strength. But the Soviets, through most of the Khrushchev years, were militarily weak and could not aid their friends and allies; they watched the defeat of Gamal Abdel Nasser by Britain, France, and Israel during the Suez war of 1956 and were unable in 1967 to prevent the defeat of the Arabs in the war with Israel.

By 1970 a second phase of Soviet–Third World relations developed; military elements of Soviet policy were activated, involving direct intervention in regional conflicts, as when Soviet forces operated Egypt's air defense systems (in Nasser's War of Attrition in 1969–70) and large-scale arms transfers became common; the Soviets supported proxy armies in Angola and Ethiopia; the 1979 invasion of Afghanistan represented still another form of direct Soviet involvement in the Third World, albeit on their own border. The Soviets signed treaties of friendship and cooperation (involving various levels of support) with Egypt (1971), Iraq (1972), Somalia (1974), South Yemen (1974), Ethiopia (1978), Afghanistan (1978), Syria (1980), and North Yemen (1984).[2] Even during the years of détente, the Soviets maintained the right to support movements for national liberation, although under the terms of the Brezhnev Doctrine they eschewed direct military intervention in cases not involving the socialist-bloc nations. But the basic objective of Soviet Third World policy remained in place, to limit the military and political influence of the United States while keeping intact their own opportunities for political outreach. Washington and Moscow in many ways had developed "mirror image" policies toward each other and the Third World.

Geography and the Soviet concept of security have been important elements in their policies. The Soviet Union and the Middle East share a common border of over 1,200 miles. This is the only region, except for Scandinavia, where the Soviet Union has major land borders with the noncommunist world. The Soviet southern border is close to the Arab world, only 135 miles from Iraq, fewer than 250 miles from Syria; Yerevan, the capital of Soviet Armenia, is about an hour's flight from Beirut, Baghdad, and Damascus; Cairo is nearer to Moscow than to either London or Paris.[3] The Soviet Union shares borders with Afghanistan, Iran, and Turkey. Various religious and ethnic groups straddle the Soviet–Middle East border: Muslims, Jews, Christians, Armenians, Turkomans, Uzbeks, Tajiks, and Kirgiz. The Middle East impinges on the Soviet economy more than does any other Third World area. Of ten major noncommunist countries that have received Soviet aid since 1954, seven are in the Middle East and North Africa.[4]

Soviet policy in the Middle East has been a mixture of success and failure. As one knowledgeable analyst recently noted: "The Middle East . . . has been the most unstable and unpredictable of the main areas bordering the Soviet Union."[5] From 1956 to 1974, Egypt was the cornerstone of Soviet Middle East policy. President Sadat abruptly canceled the Treaty of Friendship and Cooperation between the two countries and instead sought political, economic, and military ties with the West and entered into the U.S.-sponsored Camp David peace treaty with Israel. The invasion of Afghanistan and the subsequent war were unmitigated failures. The Iranian revolution replaced the stable, if cautious relations that the Soviets had developed with the Shah with a rhetorically hostile Islamic government with whom the Soviets maintain only partially satisfactory relations. The Iran–Iraq war created great instability on the Soviets' southern border and pitted Iran against a Soviet ally, Iraq; and Iraq itself, in an attempt to gain Western military and political support, reestablished relations with the United States and adopted a moderate policy in its relations with both the conservative and the moderate Arab states. There are three socialist Arab states with whom the Soviets have maintained strong relations: Libya, South Yemen, and Syria. Libya, because of its highly unstable foreign policy and its support for Iran in the war, has been largely marginalized by other Arab states; South Yemen, the Soviets' most loyal ally in the region, has been badly compromised by the internecine strife that tore the country apart in January 1986; Syria, the strongest of the Soviets' allies, also supported Iran, because it had a long-standing ideological fight with Iraq. Syria has also been instrumental in encouraging a deep fissure in the PLO, has taken positions contrary to those of the Soviet Union on Israeli–Arab peacemaking, and has remained deeply involved in the seemingly irreconcilable Lebanese civil war. But it is clear, because of long-running conflicts in the Middle East, that there has been a continuing role for the Soviet Union both as arms supplier and as political advocate. These conflicts, however, have also served to bog the Soviets down and at times to limit their freedom of action because of their ties to a local client.[6] These troubles, in the Soviet view, brought about an increasing U.S. role in the region that ran counter to the Soviet Union's broader strategic interests.

GORBACHEV AND FOREIGN POLICY

Although a new and fully articulated Soviet Middle East policy has not yet emerged, important elements of it are clear and they are closely linked with new Soviet thinking about the Third World as a whole. A commanding feature of all their policies is their subordination to the domestic demands of *perestroika*, the restructuring of Soviet economic and political life. The Soviets want to avoid or minimize direct confrontation with the United States. Their desire to achieve substantial arms agreements with the United States has taken precedence over most regional conflicts. They fear being drawn into confrontation with the Americans as a result of risks taken by their Third World allies.[7]

The Soviets have come to insist that their allies rely much more on their own resources; they have pushed hard to end a number of long-standing conflicts, such as the war in Angola, which they have supported financially and through arms transfers. They have also been reevaluating each commitment to determine if it has direct relevance to their own interests; they have substantially downgraded conflicts that were largely pursued as part of a zero-sum game with the United States, in which they would continue as long as they seemed to be hurting American interests.

Further, they have adopted a policy, of which there were hints during the Andropov years in the early 1980s, of developing positive political and economic relations "with all countries large and small," including, of course, nonsocialist and capitalist-oriented nations.[8] In the Middle East this has led to improved relations with Oman, Qatar, the United Arab Emirates, Bahrain, Kuwait, North Yemen, Egypt, and Saudi Arabia. The Soviets reached an agreement with OPEC on oil production and prices. They have given up unsuccessful efforts to create a radical Arab bloc of supporters. American and other Western diplomats in the region have expressed envy of their Soviet counterparts during the past three years as the latter have emerged with flexible and often imaginative diplomatic initiatives.

The Arab–Israeli confrontation first engaged the Soviets in the 1950s, and since then they have never been far removed from the dispute, although they have seldom been able significantly to influence its course. When the UN partition of Palestine was approved in 1947, the Soviet Union supported it and rushed to recognize the newly formed State of Israel. These moves were denounced by the Palestinian Arabs and the neighboring Arab states. Even though the Soviet Union broke diplomatic relations with Israel following the 1967 Arab–Israeli war, it has continually and explicitly supported Israel's right to exist. Furthermore, the Soviet Union has never wavered in its support for UN Security Council Resolution 242 (calling on Israel to withdraw to its pre-1967 borders and guaranteeing secure borders for all states in the region) and Resolution 338 (establishing the 1973 cease-fire and calling for a peace conference under appropriate auspices). Egypt signed the Camp David peace treaty in September 1978, after the rupture of relations with the Soviets. Partly as a result of the Soviet stance, conservative Arab nations have periodically charged the Soviet Union with participating in a Zionist-communist conspiracy. On the other hand, when the United States supplied arms to Israel, the Soviet Union became the major supplier of arms to the Arabs, including the PLO. The Soviet Union and most Arab states have been hostile to the Camp David agreements. This has been interpreted by many in Washington as a sign of the Soviets' desire to keep the Middle East in turmoil, but the Soviet position is more complicated. From the start the Soviet Union has opposed the Kissinger-designed step-by-step diplomacy and separate bilateral negotiations in the Middle East, believing they will not work because they will not solve the Palestinian question. The failure to implement the second part of the Camp David accords—dealing with the Palestinians—only confirmed the Soviets in their views. Furthermore, the Soviet Union believes that solutions to the Arab–Israeli conflict should be developed jointly with the United States (as were the cease-fires in 1967 and 1973) and that the U.S.S.R. should participate in peace negotiations.[9] Indeed, it is significant that the Soviet objection to the accords is based in part on their exclusion from the peace process. They were deeply troubled when the October 1977 U.S.–Soviet joint statement on the Middle East and the "legitimate rights of the Palestinian people" was weakened by the subsequent Vance–Dayan statement and then superseded by the Camp David meetings, which effectively excluded them.

The new Soviet initiatives to recapture a role in the peacemaking process in the region are based on five principles, as outlined by the Soviet analyst Evgeni Primakov in 1988:

- The need for a comprehensive settlement of the Arab–Israeli conflict on the basis of a compromise in the interest of all the peoples who have been drawn into the conflict
- The special importance of resolving the Palestinian question by granting the right of self-determination to the Palestinian people through the creation of a national state of their own (the Soviet Union believes that without this state a stable Arab–Israeli settlement is impossible)
- The right of all states in the Middle East to exist
- The need to create arrangements for security and stability for all states in the region—as part of an Arab–Israeli peace settlement
- The importance of keeping the Middle East from becoming a site of U.S.–Soviet confrontation.[10]

These principles have become part of Soviet practice in a number of matters. The very bitter relations with Egypt that followed that country's break with the Soviets have slowly but surely been bettered. The Soviet ambassador returned to Cairo in 1985; Soviet–Egyptian trade increased in 1986, and the Soviets agreed to supply Egypt with badly needed spare parts for its Soviet-built weapons;

in March 1987, Moscow agreed to the fifteen-year-old Egyptian request to reschedule payment of its $3 billion debt. Soviet Foreign Minister Edward Shevardnadze made a highly visible visit in March 1989 to Cairo, where he met not only with President Mubarak but also with Israeli Foreign Minister Moshe Arens and PLO Chairman Yasir Arafat.

Relations between the Soviet Union and Israel have shown cautious but real improvement. Perhaps the most striking move was the speech given by Gorbachev in April 1987 during a visit to Moscow by Syrian President Hafez al-Assad, in which the Soviet leader declared that the absence of diplomatic relations between Israel and the Soviet Union "cannot be considered normal."[11] Some Soviet officials have been quite blunt in stating that the 1967 break in relations with Israel was a mistake. In July 1987, a Soviet consular mission went to Israel ostensibly to inspect Soviet-owned properties and to deal with issues involving Soviet nationals. A Soviet mission has remained in place since then. It took over a year for the reciprocal arrangement to be made, but by late summer 1988 an Israeli consular group was installed in Moscow. In addition, a series of political encounters have taken place, beginning shortly after Gorbachev took office, including meetings in Paris of their ambassadors to France. Arrangements were made shortly after that for the exchange of "interest sections" between Poland and Israel (followed by a similar move in Hungary). Then the Bulgarians invited the Bulgarian-born wife of Yitzhak Shamir, then Foreign Minister, for a visit to Sofia. Meetings have since been held between Prime Minister Shimon Peres and Soviet Foreign Minister Edward Shevardnadze in September 1986 and April 1987. The later meetings included top Soviet Middle East advisers Karen Brutents and Alexander Zotov. Other meetings followed, including Shamir's visit to Budapest in the fall of 1988.[12] While no formal steps toward full diplomatic exchanges were taken by the beginning of 1989, it was quite clear that the Soviets realized that to be able to sit at the peace table they had substantially to ease their relations with Israel.

Reflecting both changing attitudes within the Soviet Union and the importance that Israel and the United States give to the plight of Jews in the Soviet Union, significant steps were taken by Moscow to deal with this problem. In the summer of 1987 a high-level group of Israeli politicians were invited to Moscow and a major item on their agenda was Soviet Jewry. Within a short period almost all the Jews held in Soviet prisons for Jewish activism were released and there was a sharp increase in the number of Jews permitted to emigrate. In early fall 1988 an Israeli team visited the Soviet Union to reestablish Jewish religious education; Hebrew was once again permitted to be taught and a Jewish cultural center established. Small numbers of Russian-born Israelis and Jews from other countries have traveled to the Soviet Union for family visits and tourism.

The Soviets can take some satisfaction from the positive response to the plan they first proposed in September 1982 for an international peace conference to resolve the Arab–Israeli conflict. The Jordanians accepted the plan as a means of legitimizing their own proposed involvement; the Egyptians joined them; and finally, the Israeli political leader Shimon Peres, first in his role as Prime Minister and later as Foreign Minister, accepted the idea if it was the price for Jordanian involvement. Peres at times seemed to put conditions forward for Soviet participation, but the issue was moot since Likud flatly rejected the proposal. Somewhat reluctantly, the United States came to accept a modified version of an international peace conference to be convened by the UN and to involve all the relevant Middle East parties and the five permanent Security Council members. The Americans, although welcoming more Soviet cooperation, still wished to minimize the Soviet role. The PLO accepted the proposal but was caught up in differences over the nature of PLO/Palestinian representation. The Israelis wanted to bar the PLO or at least to have any Palestinians approved by the PLO part of a joint Jordanian–Palestinian delegation. The Soviets, while supporting the principle of direct PLO representation, talked on occasion about a single all-Arab delegation as a means of avoiding bitter conflict over this contentious issue. The Syrians agreed in principle to a conference but advanced so many conditions and cautions as to make clear that they did not expect to see an international conference convened anytime soon.

Syrian–Soviet relations, while extensive and ostensibly close, have not been trouble-free. After the Syrian defeat by Israel in Lebanon in June 1982, the Soviets undertook to bolster Syrian defenses and to rearm their forces. SAM-5 antiaircraft missiles were accompanied by a good number of Soviet advisers and technicians, but the Soviets insisted on restraint in the deployment and use of these and other arms sent to Syria. Gorbachev has warned the Syrians against military adventurism, claiming instead that international conflicts should be resolved politically; in April 1987 he told President Assad that "the reliance on military force has completely lost its credibility as a way of solving Middle East conflict."[13]

Further Soviet–Syrian disagreement concerns the Soviets and the PLO. Soviet support for the PLO has been constant, if at times troubled. Moscow has been generous in arms aid, money, ideas, and diplomatic help. But the Soviets have made it equally clear that their views on how to resolve the Israeli–Palestinian conflict were in numerous respects at odds with the PLO's. They opposed the PLO on its pre-1974 proposal for a "democratic secular state" in all of Palestine. Instead they supported the much more moderate plan for a state limited to the West Bank and Gaza, thus accepting the pre-June 4, 1967, Israeli borders rather than the more limited boundaries given to Israel in the 1947 UN partition plan.[14] That this is what they told the PLO is made clear in documents the Israelis captured during the Lebanon invasion in 1982. One of these, the record of a long conversation between Soviet Foreign Minister Andrei Gromyko and Yasir Arafat (in Moscow on November 13, 1979), stated: "The U.S.S.R. continues its principled policy regarding the Middle East. . . . We are in favor of Israel's withdrawal from the occupied territories and in favor of granting the Palestinians their legitimate rights and the establishment of their independent state, together with the right of all states in the region to be sovereign."[15] Although the Soviets were dissatisfied with the PLO's seeming willingness to become associated with a U.S.-backed plan for negotiations involving Jordan, they refused to accept the Syrian-supported breakaway faction of the PLO. They were actually instrumental in bringing about a reconciliation between two of the more radical PLO factions (PFLP and DFLP), the Palestine Communist Party, and the mainline Fatah/Arafat wing of the PLO at the Algiers meeting of the Palestine National Council in April 1987. This involved some heavy pressure on Syria, but did not succeed in healing the Arafat–Assad rift. It did, however, blunt Syria's bid to gain control of the PLO.[16] The Soviets vigorously supported and probably helped achieve the critical steps toward PLO recognition of Israel and independent statehood alongside Israel implied at the Palestine National Council meeting in Algiers in November 1988 and made explicit by Arafat in Geneva in December 1988.

Elsewhere in the Middle East, the Soviet role has been pragmatic, seeking political, not military solutions, drawing back from open-ended commitments to liberation or revolutionary movements. The Soviets explicitly recognized the interests of other powers—for example, when they recognized legitimate American interests in the Gulf and in the insistence on continued access to Middle East oil. Their role in the Iran–Iraq war was initially cautious and ultimately supportive of the UN mediating role. They have moved to normalize relations with the Gulf states and they have pressed hard to achieve greater cooperation with the United States in the area. In South Yemen, Moscow has tried to sustain a government that was ostracized by the Arab world and that turned to the Soviet Union for support. Two major Soviet naval bases have since been built in South Yemen, matching the U.S. base at the eastern tip of the Arabian peninsula in Oman. The Soviets were not involved in the popular movement that overthrew the Emperor of Ethiopia in 1974 but became involved two and a half years later, after conflict erupted between Ethiopia and Somalia. To this day there continue to be differences between Ethiopia and the Soviet Union on such issues as the right of Eritrea to independence, the forming of political parties, and economic matters. Despite Soviet protestations about ending the hostilities in the Horn of Africa, substantial Soviet military supplies still flow to Ethiopia. Soviet policies in Ethiopia (and Afghanistan) have proved costly. The Soviet Union was spending the equivalent of several million dollars a day to sustain its forces in Afghanistan and has dispatched well over a billion dollars' worth of weapons to Ethiopia with no assurance that Ethiopia will pay for them.[17]

The Gorbachev stamp on Soviet foreign policy is emerging with greater clarity. A new approach is being developed: avoid superpower confrontation; find political rather than military solutions; don't be left out of the conflict-resolving or peacemaking processes; keep options open by extending the range of political and diplomatic relations; give up sole reliance on socialist/radical nations;

increase support for the United Nations and other multilateral agencies in resolving conflicts. The Gorbachev approach, however, faces challenges in dealing with seemingly intractable conflicts in Lebanon and between Israel and the Palestinians. How long can his policies survive without results? To a significant extent, achieving results depends not only on Soviet willingness (and, of course, the nature of the local situation) but also on whether Washington will cooperate or offer further confrontation. As Fred Halliday has noted, the Soviet Union—unlike the United States, which could forget about Vietnam when it withdrew its forces—cannot abandon and turn its back on the Middle East: the region is too close and it is also much too volatile.

11

United States Policy

United States policy in the Middle East has been dominated by three occasionally contradictory goals since the end of World War II:

- Unrestricted access to the region's vast oil reserves
- The strategic location of the region making it a bridge between Europe, Africa, and Asia and therefore a critical place to contain or thwart the Soviet Union
- Support for Israel and its security among hostile neighbors.

This policy has largely ignored the domestic political, social, and human needs of the countries in the region; the growing force of Arab nationalism was consistently underestimated and too often cast in the light of U.S.–Soviet confrontation; internal political challenges to conservative regimes were regularly interpreted as threats to stability; growing militant Islamic movements in many parts of the region were either "demonized" or belittled. These facts have given rise to the distortions and in some cases the negative impact of the U.S. role in the area. A major and continuing thread running through U.S. policy has been the Arab–Israeli conflict.

The eight years of the Reagan administration have distorted the country's Middle East policy; first, in the move to cast the whole of the complex of issues into the framework of the U.S.–Soviet confrontation; second, by designating Israel as a major "strategic asset" in this rivalry and promoting Israel as the only reliable U.S. ally; and finally, by not taking peacemaking processes seriously and thereby missing key opportunities to resolve the Arab–Israeli conflict.

Israel's stunning victory in the June 1967 war did nothing to settle the problems between Israel and its Arab neighbors; indeed, it significantly increased some of them. After the war Israel occupied territories that belonged to Syria, Jordan, and Egypt, and the intensity of the differences between Israel and the Palestinians was sharply increased as more than a million Palestinians came under Israeli occupation.

The 1967 war brought U.S. policy under great strain. Attempts to keep apart the three strands of U.S. interests—especially support for Israel and strategic control over access to Arab oil supplies—failed. This failure reached its climax several years later when the Arab oil-producing states imposed a partial oil embargo in the wake of the October 1973 war. It was against this background that new dimensions of American policy emerged.

Following the war of 1967, the U.S. government became actively involved in efforts to forge a peace settlement in the Arab–Israeli dispute, to achieve regional stability and protect its interests. During the same period Washington was Israel's major arms supplier and became engaged in large-scale arms sales to other parties. The American concept of peace and of the peace process has changed, as the situation and the attitudes of the conflicting parties in the Middle East have evolved. The U.S. role also has shifted between providing good offices and the more difficult task of being an active mediator. During the Reagan years the United States assumed the posture of being Israel's partner. Considerations that compelled this degree of commitment have remained fairly constant through the last six administrations. They may be summarized:

- A commitment to Israel's survival
- A downgrading or ignoring of the Palestinian component of the Arab–Israeli conflict
- An awareness that Arab–Israeli polarization and conflict jeopardize U.S. relations with the Arab countries and put at risk

U.S. relations with strategic allies in much of the Middle East
- A belief that confrontation and conflict in the area provide opportunities for the Soviet Union to increase its influence and a strong commitment is required to minimize any Soviet role in the region
- Concern that active conflict could prompt U.S.–Soviet confrontation, threatening a larger war
- A concern in recent years that U.S., "Western," and Japanese access to Middle East oil is insecure in the absence of a peace settlement and stability
- An important U.S. domestic component: the strong support given to Israel by the active and organized leadership of the Jewish community.

U.S. policy during the years 1967–88 can be divided roughly into four phases.

FIRST PHASE, 1967–73

The United States was one of the key architects of UN Security Council Resolution 242, which established the basis for peace efforts in the wake of the 1967 war. The resolution also was endorsed by the U.S.S.R. It set up a bargain: Israel would withdraw from occupied territories in exchange for assured security for "every State of the region" within its pre-1967 boundaries. To the United States, this bargain required negotiations between the Arabs and Israel, and much of the diplomatic activity in the ensuing years involved searching for an agreement on the terms of the UN resolution. Israel favored direct negotiations, because if the Arab states agreed to negotiate, they would be recognizing the reality of Israel. The Arab states, however, including even those that accepted the UN resolution, refused to bargain for territory they considered rightfully theirs, calling instead for implementation of the resolution's terms—Israeli withdrawal. Washington at first supported the efforts of the UN special representative, Ambassador Gunnar Jarring, to promote agreement on the basis of Resolution 242. When Jarring gave up, the United States became involved more directly, although initially it refrained from offering proposals for peace terms.

In April 1969, the United States joined Britain, France, and the U.S.S.R. in four-way talks under the aegis of the United Nations. In addition, the United States entered bilateral discussions with the Soviets in Washington and Moscow in which they sought a formula that might provide a basis for negotiation among the parties. In the course of these two sets of talks, the United States presented its own proposed guidelines for agreements between Israel and Egypt and Israel and Jordan. In December 1969, Secretary of State William Rogers spelled out the basic elements of these proposals, which became known as the Rogers Plan. Rogers, confirming the necessity of a negotiated settlement, said that "any changes in the pre-existing lines should not reflect the weight of conquest and should be confined to insubstantial alterations required for mutual security. . . . We do not support expansionism." Jerusalem, he said, should be a "unified city" in which both Jordan and Israel would have roles "in the civic, economic, and religious life of the city."[1] Israel objected vigorously, neither the Palestinians nor the Arab states reacted favorably, and the United States did not press its proposals. In fact, the United States, while commenting negatively on Israeli settlement policy in the West Bank and Gaza, continued to give Israel strong general support.

The major U.S. negotiating effort during this phase came to relate less and less to the basic issues of a Middle East settlement and focused instead on frictions between Egypt and Israel in the Sinai. In 1969 the Egyptians, concerned that the highly unfavorable status quo might become generally accepted over time, began artillery bombardment across the Suez Canal. Israel responded with more and more devastating air strikes over Egypt, and a serious exchange developed. History has recorded the fighting as the War of Attrition. The United States proposed a plan for a cease-fire which allowed both sides to find a way out of an increasingly costly conflict; it was accepted by both sides in August 1970. But it left in place continued Israeli occupation of the Sinai and all the other territories seized during the June 1967 war.

SECOND PHASE, 1973–77

No meaningful additional initiatives were undertaken prior to the outbreak of war in October 1973 between Israel and Egypt and Syria.

It was in this war that the conflict between the U.S. policies on oil and on Israel came to a head as conservative and radical Arab oil-producing states jointly imposed a selective oil embargo in retaliation for the massive airlift of American supplies to Israel at a point when Israel appeared threatened. In the wake of the war, circumstances in the Middle East were sufficiently altered—politically and psychologically—so that expanded opportunities for peacemaking seemed available. In particular, the deadlock arising from a general Arab unwillingness to negotiate that had characterized the prewar period ceased to be a factor. UN Security Council Resolution 338 ending the 1973 war called explicitly for negotiations, and the resolution was accepted both by the Arab states that were principally concerned and by Israel.

In turn, U.S. efforts to seek a settlement between Israel and its immediate neighbors were intensified, in part because only the United States seemed able to serve as an intermediary and to "deliver" Israel to the negotiating table. The Soviet Union, having broken relations with Israel in 1967 and having refused to substantially resupply its Arab clients with arms sufficient to match U.S. supplies to Israel, did not have effective influence or credit with either side.

At first the United States collaborated with the Soviet Union in establishing a forum for the negotiations called for in Resolution 338. Under their joint chairmanship, the Geneva Peace Conference was convened on December 21, 1973. Washington, however, while it considered this framework important for the negotiations, doubted that progress could be made at that time by tackling the Arab–Israeli conflict as a whole. It also believed the large formal conference (which Syria, in fact, did not attend) to be an inappropriate forum for serious progress. Several issues lay behind this judgment. The United States, while recognizing the value of Soviet involvement to give legitimacy to the process, did not really consider Moscow a useful or necessary participant in serious negotiations and was in any case not anxious to see the Soviets actively involved in Middle East affairs.

The next U.S. efforts were designed to exclude them. Secretary of State Henry Kissinger undertook an intensive two-year mission to achieve limited agreements between Israel on the one hand and Egypt and Syria on the other. Through what became known as "shuttle diplomacy," Kissinger hoped to win a series of agreements that would ultimately create an atmosphere in which it would be possible to defuse the Palestinian question but not resolve it. The Palestinian component of the Arab–Israel conflict was downplayed in Kissinger's plans. A solution to the issues involving the Palestinians was to be sought through negotiations between Israel and the Arab states. Rather than seek a comprehensive settlement at the outset, Kissinger committed the United States to step-by-step bilateral diplomacy. These efforts led to disengagement agreements between Egypt and Israel and Syria and Israel, culminating in the Sinai II agreement between Israel and Egypt.[2] Israel, in an effort to prevent any effective Palestinian role, secured from Kissinger a "secret" U.S. commitment to have no negotiations with the PLO until it recognized Israel and accepted UN Security Council Resolutions 242 and 338.

In addition, the United States promised to supply Israel with new and sophisticated weapons in order to assure its substantial military superiority in the region. The Kissinger view was that an independent, secure, and strong Israel would be more likely to engage in active negotiations with the Arabs. This judgment proved to be incorrect. The Soviet Union, which had previously been reluctant to export its most sophisticated weaponry, quickly followed suit, significantly upgrading the military strength of Libya, Syria, and Iraq. A new phase of the Middle East arms race was underway and all signs of restraint were lost. The Lebanese civil war, which broke out as the Sinai II agreement was being signed, and the 1976 U.S. election campaign prevented a useful U.S. role that year, and the Democratic election victory brought an end to the step-by-step process.

The Carter administration took office with a commitment to seek a Middle East settlement that was at least as great as that of the Nixon administration. It differed in its approach in three important respects, however: (1) It considered that the step-by-step process of putting together a peace in the area had run its course and that the time had come for a comprehensive settlement. (2) It was far more ready than its predecessor had been to accept the need for a Palestinian entity in the West Bank. Following President Carter's early call for a Palestinian "homeland," the administration had a less reserved attitude toward the Palestinians and the PLO, although it never implemented this greater openness. (3) It believed that in return for withdrawing from the occupied territories Israel should receive from the Arab states a full peace rather than only the nonbelligerency provided for in Resolution 242. Thus, within a few months of his inauguration, President Carter had laid down three key elements of what he conceived to be a just settlement: a homeland for the Palestinians, Israeli withdrawal to borders essentially those of 1967, and a comprehensive peace agreement.

After an unsuccessful attempt to get Arab and Israeli agreement on a more detailed and precise basis for negotiation than proposed in Resolution 242, the United States turned, in the late summer of 1977, to an all-out effort to reconvene the Geneva Conference by the end of the year in order to set in motion the negotiation of a comprehensive settlement. During the early weeks of the fall UN General Assembly meeting, Secretary of State Cyrus Vance carried on separate talks with high-level officials of Israel, Egypt, Syria, and Jordan in an attempt to get agreement on the form of the conference. He was also particularly concerned with how to invite the Palestinians. The major, though not the only, stumbling block was the question of whether all Arab participants would negotiate all aspects of the peace, as it affected all Arabs, or whether each Arab state would negotiate with Israel separately about its direct concerns. Syrian suspicion that Egypt planned a separate peace led Damascus to insist that all Arab states participate in each negotiation. The Syrians wanted negotiations focused not on the specific interests of each state but on elements of a general settlement such as borders and security measures, which interested all the parties. The Egyptians rejected this approach and no agreement was reached. Furthermore, the Israelis strenuously objected to explicit inclusion of the PLO. These issues and the general level of Arab–Israeli distrust frustrated the negotiations and by the end of October the negotiators reached an impasse.

Two other U.S. initiatives during this period deserve mention. Seeing merit in some form of contact with the PLO, the United States sought a formula whereby the PLO could accept Resolution 242 while at the same time reserving its position on the resolution's slighting of the Palestinians. This would allow the United States to overcome the restrictions on U.S.–PLO contacts earlier promised to Israel. During Secretary Vance's trip to the Middle East in the summer of 1977, a formula was submitted to the PLO through several Arab governments. Ultimately, the PLO rejected it and instead substituted a demand for a guaranteed role in the negotiation of an Arab–Israeli peace. It subsequently appeared that inter-Arab rivalries and Syrian reservations about direct U.S.–PLO contacts had as much to do with the rejection as PLO reaction to the merits of the proposal.

Secondly, on September 30, 1977, the United States and the Soviet Union issued a joint communiqué setting out an agreed-upon basis for Middle East peace negotiations. To Washington, the language of the communiqué did not differ importantly from positions it had already taken, and a joint U.S.–Soviet statement at this time was unexceptional in view of the expectation that the two countries, as co-chairs, would shortly reconvene the Geneva Conference. The United States, it turned out, was alone in expecting that its interpretation of the joint statement would be widely accepted. The statement, which had been jointly crafted by U.S. Secretary of State Cyrus Vance and Soviet Foreign Minister Andrei Gromyko, brought interesting reactions. The Israelis were furious, and the Egyptians were upset. The PLO, on the other hand, was gratified and later said it could have accepted the statement as the basis for negotiations. Largely because of Israeli pressure brought during a meeting between Vance and Israeli Foreign Minister Moshe Dayan, the U.S. government promptly issued a second statement that had the effect of negating the Vance–Gromyko communiqué. Hope for a comprehensive settlement collapsed.

THIRD PHASE, 1977–80

Following the failure to reconvene the Geneva Conference by the end of 1977, and with the purpose of again excluding Soviet involvement, President Sadat drastically altered Middle East dynamics by traveling to Jerusalem in November. Sadat clearly caught everyone off balance, including the United States. Washington, convinced that a comprehensive negotiation of all aspects of a settlement was the most viable course and engaged in mounting a new effort in this direction, was initially concerned that Sadat's move would lead inevitably to a bilateral treaty. This was still considered undesirable by the Carter administration. As so often happens in the Middle East, however, forces are set in motion by the local states. Washington had no choice, if it wished to play a role, but to follow Sadat's lead, and it did so. While the United States may have wished to link the bilateral process between Israel and Egypt to a comprehensive peace and a settlement of the Palestinian question, the manner in which negotiations proceeded and the very restrictive Israeli definition of the Palestinian question foreclosed this possibility.

During the months that followed Sadat's trip to Jerusalem, it became increasingly clear that the impetus provided by that extraordinary visit would not suffice to bring about an Israeli–Egyptian peace or a broad Middle East settlement. The negative reaction of other Arab states and the PLO, coupled with Israel's reluctance to reciprocate the spirit of Sadat's step, gradually slowed the momentum and soured the atmosphere. With Egyptian–Israeli relations stalemated and the Arabs far too bitterly divided to permit a return to comprehensive negotiations, there seemed little opportunity to move forward.

In these circumstances, in the summer of 1978, President Carter invited Prime Minister Begin and President Sadat to Camp David to negotiate a peace between them.[3] The President, by extending the invitation, and the Israeli and Egyptian leaders, by accepting it, greatly increased the stakes in reaching a peace agreement. The resulting pressure, in the unique environment of the prolonged and isolated summit negotiation, produced a complex set of agreements later interpreted differently by each participant. The one matter of real agreement was that of a bilateral Egyptian–Israeli peace and the treaty to embody it.

The complexity and subsequent differences lay in the establishment of a process for dealing with the Palestinian question. A reading of the treaty shows the precision and clarity gained on the

Egyptian–Israeli front as compared with the vagueness and indecisiveness of the discussions of Palestinian issues. The three leaders agreed to a process whereby Jordan would be invited to join Israel and Egypt in determining procedures for establishing an elected self-governing authority in the West Bank and the Gaza Strip. The so-called autonomy provision provided that the Israeli military and civilian administrations would be withdrawn from these areas upon the election of a self-governing authority. At the same time, a transitional period of five years was established by the end of which the final status of the West Bank and Gaza would have been negotiated and a final Israeli–Jordanian peace concluded. Elected representatives of the West Bank and Gaza were to participate in both negotiations. As Sadat pointed out in his public remarks following Camp David, it was significant for a broader settlement that the United States was at the heart of the process projected by the agreement.

The other Arab parties, including Jordan, reacted with dismay. They interpreted the accords as an Egyptian sellout, stage-managed by the United States. The Palestinians were concerned about the meaning of autonomy for the West Bank and Gaza and saw these provisions as giving Israel continued control over issues of major importance to them—land use, water rights, and political self-determination—thereby foreclosing the possibility of independence. Prime Minister Begin seemed to confirm this restrictive interpretation when he presented the treaty to the Knesset for ratification and proclaimed that Israel was not bound to give up sovereignty over the West Bank and Gaza and had no intention of doing so. The U.S. negotiators, while aware they would encounter problems in obtaining Arab cooperation for the West Bank–Gaza process, seem to have seriously underestimated them. They apparently also underestimated Israel's reluctance to give the process any substance.

American diplomats turned almost at once to the task of persuading Jordan and the Palestinians that if they committed themselves to the autonomy talks and the subsequent negotiations for the long-term disposition of the West Bank and Gaza, the provisions could be made to work for them. In addition, the United States hoped that Saudi Arabia, among the most pro-Western nations in the region, could be drawn into the process. The Arabs were intensely distrustful of a prolonged open-ended process, over which Israel, with military and political control on the ground, could exercise such a high degree of influence and in which their only guarantor was the United States. Almost at once many Arabs concluded that their suspicions of Israel's intentions were well founded and that Washington's goodwill was not to be credited. In particular, the narrow Israeli interpretation of autonomy that emerged as the Egyptian–Israeli–U.S. talks proceeded was disturbing to the Palestinians. The subsequent and repeated Israeli assertion that Israel would remain sovereign in the West Bank after the transition period convinced the Arabs that the so-called self-governing authority in the West Bank and Gaza was intended by Israel to be nothing more than an agency of Israel's continued occupation. Prime Minister Begin and then Foreign Minister Shamir adopted the view that in giving up the Sinai, Israel had fulfilled its commitment to relinquish territory captured in the 1967 war as required by UN Security Council Resolution 242 and therefore was under no obligation to negotiate the sovereignty of the West Bank and Gaza.

By the end of the Carter administration, the Arab–Israeli positions had hardened and events in the Persian gulf and the overthrow of the Shah of Iran were commanding Washington's attention and priority. U.S. diplomacy faced a problem of several dimensions. Washington sought to preserve the gains it believed had been made at Camp David, regarding both Israeli–Egyptian peace and its relations with Egypt. It also accepted involvement in supporting Sadat's legitimacy and the policy he stood for in Egypt, through completion of the phased peace terms and Israeli withdrawal from Sinai. Israel had made an important gain by removing Egypt and therefore the western front as a threat to its security. A largely demilitarized Sinai was a natural buffer between the two countries. Furthermore, the Sinai had never been claimed as part of Eretz Yisrael since it had no special religious-nationalist significance. The West Bank (renamed Judea and Samaria by Israel) and Gaza were the focus of strident religious-nationalist claims and were potentially a more complex security problem. But the Palestinian question remained unresolved. It was more obvious than ever that dealing successfully with it was vital both to the stability of the Egyptian–Israeli treaty and to a lasting comprehensive settlement. Although President Carter viewed the Israeli interpretation with dismay, he did little to challenge it.

Iran proved to be another site where the contradictions in U.S. Middle East policy became dramatically apparent. While not directly related to the Arab–Israeli conflict, the Iranian revolution and the subsequent Iran–Iraq war strongly influenced the contours of all U.S. Middle East policies for the succeeding decade. By continually emphasizing external threats and ignoring the extent to which crises in domestic Iranian policies could catalyze decisive internal opposition to the rule of the Shah, the United States helped pave the way for his downfall. The Iranian revolution, with its strong Islamic orientation and its pronounced anti-Western values, added a new dimension to the revolutionary politics of the Middle East. It demonstrated as well that a ruler and his policies could be rejected when they were perceived by the people to be largely serving external interests and ignoring serious problems at home. That a regime as militarily strong as the Shah's was believed to be could be so easily overthrown suggested that there might be a real threat to the stability of the other governments in the area closely allied to the United States.

For the United States the loss of the Shah and his armies was a setback to the Nixon doctrine of using surrogates to protect U.S. interests abroad. But it also halted the lucrative flow of U.S. arms to Iran, the world's largest importer of weapons. The Shah's downfall also challenged the conviction that sophisticated arms, rapid Western-style development, and an alliance with the United States would provide a basis for stability. No wonder that Henry Kissinger, architect of America's Iran policy for the Nixon administration, called the overthrow of the Shah the worst setback to U.S. policy since World War II, greater even than the debacle in Indochina. The storming of the U.S. embassy in Teheran and the holding of U.S. staff as hostages for over a year provided not only a final indignity to American influence in Iran but also a focus for deep, often racist anti-Iranian attitudes.

In the wake of the Iranian revolution the United States began to develop a policy that would not necessarily shy away from securing U.S. interests through direct military intervention. The Carter administration, even prior to the Soviet invasion of Afghanistan, began to take the steps—upgrading the Indian Ocean naval base at Diego Garcia, seeking additional bases in and near the Gulf region, expanding the Rapid Deployment Force—that became the basic elements of the Carter Doctrine in January 1980. The Soviet invasion of Afghanistan in December 1979 dramatically punctuated Carter's efforts and refocused U.S. attention on the region.

FOURTH PHASE: THE REAGAN ADMINISTRATION

The Reagan administration took office expecting to downgrade the Arab–Israeli conflict, put aside the Palestinian question, and focus instead on its own Middle East agenda. It placed priority on three concerns:

1. Its perception of a Soviet threat in the Middle East and the problem of protecting the oil-rich Persian Gulf countries from both Soviet interference and internal rebellion.

2. The need to build an anti-Soviet strategic consensus in the region and enlist allies such as Egypt, Israel, and Saudi Arabia who might provide military bases and facilities.

3. The desire to strengthen America's military position in the Persian Gulf–Indian Ocean significantly by acquiring basing rights, rebuilding the Rapid Deployment Force into the much more substantial Central Command, and providing sophisticated arms to Middle East allies.

The Middle East, the Reagan government believed, could best be understood through the lens of worldwide U.S.–U.S.S.R. confrontation. As Reagan was quoted as saying during his 1980 presidential campaign: "Let's not delude ourselves. The Soviet Union underlies all the unrest that is going on. If they weren't engaged in this game of dominoes, there wouldn't be any hot spots in the world."[4] In this new formulation, regional disputes and local problems were secondary to the need to deal with what was seen as a worldwide Soviet military advantage.

The President entered office naming Israel as "a major strategic asset to America." Aid to Israel was not a matter of charity but an investment in U.S. security. Reagan at first expressed his belief that Israel's West Bank–Gaza settlements were legal, although he modified this view somewhat during the course of his administration. He was flatly opposed to an independent Palestinian state, and he consistently objected to including the PLO in any peace negotiations, calling them a "terrorist organization."[5] His attitude toward the Camp David process was lukewarm, and while he seemed to favor a Jordanian solution to the Palestinian question, his overall view initially was to oppose an active U.S. role in the peace process.

But the Middle East did not behave according to Reagan's script. The new administration began to implement its Middle East policy when it gave approval to increase the sale of sophisticated aircraft to Saudi Arabia. Within two months of taking office, the Reagan government found itself in the middle of the predictably volatile Arab–Israeli conflict.

The spring and summer of 1981 quickly saw the United States reimmersed in the Arab–Israeli conflict, and any idea of ignoring it was cut short. As part of building the "strategic consensus" in the Middle East, Washington undertook to provide sophisticated new armaments to "friendly" Arab states. In the first instance, plans were put forward to sell to Saudi Arabia sophisticated advance-warning radar planes—AWACs. With its view so firmly focused on the Soviet danger, the United States underestimated the extent to which Israel would feel threatened by this arms sale to the Saudis. Although the Reagan administration ultimately won its battle in Congress, it was strongly opposed by Israel and its U.S. lobby. Next, the sharp escalation in fighting in Lebanon in March and April, culminating in direct Israeli intervention in central Lebanon on behalf of the Phalangist forces and the Syrian countermove introducing into Lebanon sophisticated Soviet-manufactured surface-to-air missiles, commanded U.S. attention. In addition, there was renewed cross-border warfare in southern Lebanon and the large-scale Israeli air raid in June on the Palestinian section of West Beirut that killed over 300 and wounded 800, primarily civilians. All this meant that the Reagan administration could no longer avoid the central Israeli–Palestinian issue.

The United States responded in each instance since it judged that U.S. interests would be adversely affected by heightened conflict in the region. Further, because U.S.-supplied aircraft and ordnance were used in both the attack on the Iraqui Osirak nuclear reactor and the Beirut raid, perhaps in violation of the terms on which they were supplied, there was call for governmental review of arms sales to Israel. The first clear signs appeared that members of the Reagan administration saw a potential divergence between U.S. Middle East interests and Israeli policies and actions.

The flare-up of fighting in Lebanon during the late spring of 1981 and the escalation of Israeli and Syrian involvement prompted the United States to recall from retirement Philip Habib, a veteran State Department Middle East diplomat. His charge was to help the parties back away from confrontation. To do so, he found it necessary to deal with the heightened tension in Israel caused by Syria's introduction into Lebanon of very accurate surface-to-air missiles and with the smoldering civil war in Lebanon that had pitted the Phalange militias, largely Maronite Christian, against a mix of Lebanese Muslim groups, the PLO, and the Syrian forces. Habib encouraged the Saudi Arabians to join diplomats of other Arab states to seek through diplomacy an end to the renewed fighting, a withdrawal of the Syrian missiles, and a reduction in Israeli military involvement. The United States had a political stake in Habib's success and communicated this to Israel, in the hope of postponing threatened Israeli air attacks on the Syrian missiles.

The Israeli bombing of the Iraqui Osirak nuclear reactor on June 8, 1981, occurred just three weeks before Israeli elections and during the joint U.S.–Arab diplomatic efforts in Lebanon. The attack, carried out with U.S.-supplied aircraft, involved crossing the airspace of Jordan and Saudi Arabia, both friendly to the United States. The raid was successful and demonstrated that Israel maintained military dominance in the region. The political fallout, however, was not positive for Israel in the short run, although adverse reactions faded in time and as other serious crises arose.

The timing of the attack brought the criticism from Prime Minister Begin's opponents within Israel that it was motivated by the forthcoming elections. In the international community, questions were raised about the legitimacy as well as the dangers of bombing a nuclear facility. The Arab countries reacted with anger at the Israeli attack across national borders and frustration at being unable to offer any significant response. The United States reacted by immediately placing under embargo a small shipment of F-16 fighter-bombers destined for Israel while it examined whether Israel had broken the prohibition against use of U.S.-supplied weapons for anything but defensive purposes. The examination led to no firm conclusion and the planes were subsequently shipped. Diplomatically, the United States moved to an unfamiliar position of supporting in the UN Security Council a resolution written by Iraq in consultation with Washington.[6] While it was clear that Israel had embarrassed the United States by the timing of its Iraqi raid, coming as it did in the midst of diplomatic efforts, it seemed unlikely that deeper shifts in U.S. policy toward Israel would follow.

The Israelis argued, in justification of their raid, that the Nonproliferation Treaty and the inspections by the International Atomic Energy Agency were inadequate to detect the diversion of materials from the reactor. They justified their unilateral action by claiming that no one else really cared about Israel's security or was in a position to judge what was essential to guarantee it.

Even as this argument was being pursued, Israel launched a series of preemptive attacks against a strong PLO military buildup in southern Lebanon, culminating in the large-scale raid on West Beirut on July 18. The Israeli attacks were followed immediately by heavy shelling of Israeli border settlements by the PLO. Prime Minister Begin claimed that Israel's intent was to attack PLO headquarters and thus prevent their attacks on northern Israel. Further, he said that Israel would not refrain from bombing civilian sectors if the PLO headquarters were located in them, even though he regretted the loss of civilian lives. It is doubtful that Israel anticipated the level of international condemnation that followed or the degree of anger it met from Washington. The Reagan administration immediately suspended the delivery of an additional shipment of F-16s and again sent Ambassador Habib to seek a ceasefire. With Saudi diplomatic help, the guns were silenced along the Lebanese–Israeli border. The world watched as Israel and the PLO, operating through intermediaries, negotiated the terms of a cease-fire. Yasir Arafat enforced the cease-fire on the Palestinian side by disciplining hard-line Palestinian guerrilla groups. The cease-fire held from July 1981 through May 1982, when it collapsed as Israel prepared to invade Lebanon. But the Americans took little advantage during the cease-fire to extend it or try to reach a more lasting Israeli–Palestinian peace. History will almost certainly regard this as a significant "missed opportunity" by the Reagan administration.[7]

It can be argued that the United States, by giving minimal attention to the cease-fire its representative had negotiated and by not attempting to advance Israeli–Palestinian peace efforts, played into the hands of Israeli leaders like Defense Minister Sharon, who felt militarily more powerful with Egypt taken out of the Arab equation and therefore able to engage in a major military adventure. By undertaking an invasion of Lebanon, Sharon believed he could install a stable, pro-Israeli Christian government in Lebanon, crush the PLO presence in Lebanon, "tame" the Palestinians under occupation, and also seriously damage Syrian forces and drive them from Lebanon, thereby humiliating the Soviets' leading ally in the Middle East. Sharon believed he had been given a "green light" for the action by U.S. Secretary of State Alexander Haig; Haig, in fact, did act to fend off serious condemnation of Israel in the United Nations.[8] The administration's displeasure at Haig's role and distrust of him forced his resignation. He was replaced by George Shultz, a seasoned Cabinet member (former Secretary of Labor and Secretary of the Treasury). Under his guidance special ambassador Habib was deeply involved in bringing the fighting to a close in August 1982 in an effort that saw U.S. forces sent to Lebanon to help oversee the evacuation of the PLO fighters.

In the closing days of August 1982, perhaps stimulated by the seeming success of U.S. diplomacy in Lebanon, the State Department formulated a plan for a diplomatic initiative to resolve the Israeli–Palestinian conflict. The "Reagan Plan," outlined in a speech by the President on September 1, 1982, while having the Camp David accords as its basis, attempted directly to address the issue of the ultimate status of Gaza and the West Bank. A series of "Talking Points" detailing the plan were sent to Prime Minister Begin. It rejected Israeli annexation of the West Bank and Gaza but also opposed the formation of an independent Palestinian state, limiting self-determination to Palestinian involvement in deciding on issues of self-government and participation in discussions of the final status of the territories. The preferred solution "is association of the West Bank and Gaza with Jordan." Syria was left totally out of the plan. Egypt was sidelined, and the focus was placed on Jordan and the Palestinians. Israel's response was an immediate "no" since the plan called for Israeli withdrawal from the occupied territories. The Arabs, while not outrightly rejecting the plan, did not accept it; in their meeting at Fez, Morocco, on September 9,

1982, just a week after the Reagan speech, they adopted an Arab peace plan initially proposed a year earlier by King Fahd of Saudi Arabia. The eight points put forward, while having some overlap with the American initiative–"guarantees for peace for all the states of the region"—also supported Palestinian self-determination interpreted as an independent Palestinian state. While there might have been some room for U.S.–Arab dialogue on the outstanding issues, none ensued.

Instead, U.S. policy, with its tacit acceptance of Sharon's "plans" for Lebanon, faced a major setback with the sequence of events that occurred there: the assassination of the newly chosen Lebanese President, Bashir Gemayel, on September 14, 1982, immediately followed by the Israeli decision to send its troops into Beirut and the subsequent massacres of Palestinians in the refugee areas of Sabra and Shatila; the return of U.S. Marines to Beirut, culminating in the disastrous bombings by Lebanese guerrilla forces of both the American embassy and a U.S. Marine base; the U.S. effort to show military muscle by massing naval forces offshore, which resulted in a confrontation with Syrian forces in which two American planes were shot down—one pilot killed, the other captured; and finally the rejection by Syria and its supporters in Lebanon of the treaty of May 1983 between Israel and Lebanon, which the United States worked very hard to achieve. Syrian and Israeli troops remained in the country; the Lebanese government and society remained fractured; Secretary of State Shultz, who had been reluctant to get too involved in Middle East affairs, went into what one commentator called a "long sulk"; and U.S. Middle East peacemaking efforts were shunted to a slow track. The Reagan Plan, which never had been really vigorously pursued, dropped out of sight by April 1983, when King Hussein of Jordan, unable to reach agreement with the PLO for joint participation in the plan, rejected it.

One other effort which had some potential was the joint Jordanian–PLO attempt to put together a negotiating position. Probably reflecting the PLO's need to rebuild itself politically following the setbacks of 1983 and 1984 and Jordan's recognition that it could not act on its own on behalf of the Palestinians, they announced on February 11, 1985, that Jordan and the PLO would jointly engage in efforts to convene an international peace conference.

They declared a Jordanian–Palestinian confederation as their goal for the occupied territories. Except for some low-level diplomatic efforts the United States showed very little interest and instead tossed the issue back to the parties in the region for direct negotiations. Secretary Shultz's general disillusionment and unwillingness to deal with the PLO probably reinforced American reluctance to get involved.[9]

The concept of an international conference to deal with Middle East peace is not new and has its legitimacy in UN Security Council Resolution 338 of October 1973, which ended the 1973 Arab–Israeli war; this resolution called for negotiations between the parties concerned under appropriate auspices aimed at establishing a just and durable peace in the Middle East. The United States had been consistently reluctant to agree to such negotiations as long as they involved the Soviet Union; much American diplomacy in the past decade and a half has sought to achieve settlements brokered by the United States alone. On the other hand, the Arab states, even the more conservative among them, felt that Soviet participation could be helpful, particularly since the United States had become so closely allied with Israel. Internationalization was also seen as a means of covering or protecting any Arab state from "breaking unity" and making a separate peace. This became more important following the separate peace the Egypt made with Israel at Camp David in 1978. While Egypt, as the largest and most independent of the Arab states, might be able to "pull off" a separate peace, Jordan believed itself to be much more vulnerable—probably an accurate assessment.

Jordan realized that any negotiations with Israel, either direct or through an international conference, would involve compromises. On its own Jordan would be unable to compromise the rights or territories of the Palestinians, whom the King at times tried to represent. Thus a series of agreements for a "joint" or combined Jordanian–PLO delegation emerged over the years. For Israel and the United States the combined delegation represented a means of including a legitimate Palestinian representation while avoiding "direct" involvement of the PLO. All the agreements were marked by fragility.

With the collapse of the Jordanian–PLO agreement on February 14, 1986, just one year after its signing, several factors encouraged Jordan to develop a renewed interest in the concept of an international conference early in 1987. First, Shimon Peres had been pressing King Hussein to breathe life into his "Jordanian option" and without the PLO the King more than ever needed an alternative cover. Second, the Soviets had been urging an international conference as a means of reentering the Middle East peacemeaking process and Jordan saw Soviet participation as helpful for involving Syria and the PLO; Jordan, also stung by the Reagan administration's inability to push a Jordanian arms package past Congress, saw the chance to increase its leverage; it also presented Jordan with an opportunity to improve its relations with Syria, a necessary participant. The United States, which had been urged by both Jordan and Egypt to accept the idea of an international venue, slowly came to adopt the concept when Shimon Peres, first as Prime Minister and then, after rotation, as Foreign Minister, adopted it himself.

A high point of planning for an international conference occurred on April 11, 1987, when King Hussein and Foreign Minister Peres met secretly in London and initialed a document outlining their understandings of the structure and procedure of such a conference. It was a minimalist plan, with the major focus on bilateral negotiations, giving only a limited role to the plenary. Since it was certain that Prime Minister Shamir would reject the proposed conference, it appeared important for the United States to give it full and enthusiastic backing. This, however, was not forthcoming, Secretary Shultz held back, and Shamir's veto effectively killed the plan. In what appears to be an afterthought, Shultz suggested an alternative idea, a joint Hussein–Shamir meeting in Washington at the time of the Gorbachev–Reagan summit. Shamir accepted it, for there was no reason to believe the Soviets would agree and certainly the Syrians, who were asked to the conference at the last minute, would say no; Hussein, in the midst of planning for the November 1987 Arab summit in Amman, was in no position to support the ill-planned initiative. There is no real indication that the United States expected the meeting to occur; it showed no disappointment that it did not materialize. The Reagan administration seemed relieved that it would not have to tackle the thorny Palestinian–Israeli conflict before the November 1988 U.S. elections. The fact that the Amman summit devoted most of its attention to the Iran–Iraq war, all but ignoring the conflict with Israel, was a further indication that the "peace process" was on hold.

On examination it seems apparent that the Reagan administration never was enthusiastic about the idea of an international conference and never gave it vigorous support. The United States put itself in the position of allowing the hard-line wing of the Israeli government to veto the idea and thus substantially undermine what support there was in Israel for a conference through which an exchange of land for peace might emerge. It is fair to say that this U.S. approach was backed tacitly and on occasion explicitly by the leadership of the Jewish community in the United States and the pro-Israel lobby. Abba Eban, the liberal Israeli leader and foreign affairs veteran, on numerous occasions complained about the lack of support given to liberal Israeli positions on peace by influential Israel supporters in the United States.[10]

Just three weeks after the end of the Amman meeting the Palestinian uprising or *intifadah* thoroughly shook the complacency that had set in. After several months of large-scale demonstrations, strikes, boycotts, and other acts of civil disobedience, it became quite clear that the situation had qualitatively changed. The violent nature of Israel's attempts to repress the uprising and the growing dismay among many of Israel's friends, including significant members of the Jewish leadership in the United States, seemed to force the Reagan administration into making one more effort at peace. The "Shultz initiative," as it was popularly called, involved an unusual commitment of time by the Secretary of State, even though it included little that was substantively new. In a pair of letters sent to Prime Minister Shamir and King Hussein, on March 4, 1988, and in a series of press statements, Shultz outlined his plan.[11] It involved speeded-up bilateral negotiations based on Resolutions 242 and 338. There would be an overlap of transition and final status negotiations for the West Bank and Gaza, with the transition timetable shortened and final status achieved in three years. The United States would prepare drafts and play a key role in the direct talks. The bilateral negotiating sessions themselves would be introduced in the context of an international conference of the regional parties involved and the permanent members of the UN Security Council. Acceptance of Resolutions 242 and 338 was the condition of participation, a clause obviously aimed at the PLO.

The Palestinians themselves were to be included in a joint Jordanian–Palestinian delegation.

The Shultz initiative was dismissed by Shamir and accepted by Peres. As Shamir put it, the idea of the exchange of territory for peace was foreign to him.[12] Once again the Palestinians were considered an appendage to Jordan; they were pleased that the United States had begun to respond, but the dynamics of the *intifadah* led them to reject a secondary role for Jordan. The local Palestinians invited by Shultz to meet him in Jerusalem declined the invitation, suggesting instead a team that included two senior, semi-independent figures linked to the PLO. The Secretary refused the meeting and the effort petered out. Although Shultz made several additional visits to the region, including Syria, he withdrew from the scene by late spring. The uprising continued; the Israelis began their election campaign in earnest; the Jordanians on July 31 announced their break with the West Bank; and another opportunity at peacemaking passed with the United States back on the sidelines and the core Palestinian issue not yet given clear recognition by U.S. policy. Nor, for that matter, was there any clear policy designed to bring the Likud-led faction into serious negotiations.

In defining U.S. policy toward the Middle East there is a critically important domestic component that cannot be overlooked. Sometimes referred to as the "Israel lobby" or noted as the Jewish constituency, it has come to wield influence far out of proportion to its size. The lobby has been well organized and highly effective. Its key goal has been to ensure that Israel's interests are well served in American Middle East policy; its success is the envy of many other political interest groups. There is nothing illegitimate in its aims, and if its methods at times seemed "strong-arm" they have been well within the range of acceptable political behavior. The pro-Israel lobby has relied to an exceptional degree on the maintenance of a unified voice where Israel was concerned among the leadership of the Jewish community. Its effectiveness in Congress has derived from its ability to shape the legislative outcome of many government initiatives directly or indirectly affecting Israel—from encouraging economic and military assistance to Israel to blocking arms deals with conservative or moderate Arab states. It has worked tirelessly and often effectively to support elected officials helpful to Israel and to unseat those whose efforts were judged to be detrimental (Senator Charles Percy of Illinois, the Republican chair of the Senate Foreign Relations Committee, who steered the Reagan AWACs package through the Senate in 1981, was defeated for reelection). It has been highly successful in de-legitimizing Palestinian nationalism and the PLO on the American political scene and was instrumental in congressional and administration efforts to close the PLO information office in Washington (successful) and the PLO observer mission at the UN (turned down by the federal courts). It lobbied vigorously and successfully to deny Yasir Arafat a visa and thereby prevent him from addressing the UN General Assembly in New York in December 1988.

But the lobbying effort had to face real problems as the government of Israel turned increasingly conservative following the 1977 elections and its foreign policy reflected a hard line. The American Jewish community has been traditionally liberal on most social and international issues and it became increasingly uneasy with some of Israel's new actions. The growing pace of settlements in the occupied territories reflected an extreme religious nationalism not found in the American Jewish mainstream; the continued occupation of the West Bank and Gaza and the abrogation of human rights were criticized by such respected groups as Amnesty International; the invasion of Lebanon, viewed by many as a non-defensive war, and the massacre by Lebanese Christians of civilians at the Sabra and Shatila refugee camps, then under the control of Israeli forces, aroused substantial opposition in Israel that was joined by many American Jews; the rejection by Prime Minister Shamir of two initiatives supported by both Foreign Minister Peres and Washington—the calling of an international peace conference and the "Shultz initiative" to revitalize negotiations to end the occupation—and the hard-line response to the *intifadah*, the call by Defense Minister Rabin for "force, might, and beatings," and the several hundred Palestinian deaths—worried American Jews. Among Jewish leaders in the United States the consensus was broken and a good number of prominent Jews became openly critical of Israel's actions. Within the Jewish community independent voices were heard in public statements, petitions, and meetings. Arthur Hertzberg, Balfour Brickner, Rita Hauser, Michael Lerner, Bernard Avishai, Irving Howe, Albert Vorspan, and many others voiced their misgivings and criticisms.[13] In Congress twenty-

eight senators, largely friends of Israel, led by Senators Rudy Bos-
chwitz and Carl Levin, on March 8, 1988, wrote a letter of support
to Secretary of State Shultz criticizing Shamir's rejection of the
"Shultz initiative."

One other underlying factor in the attitude of American Jews
toward Israel had been the sharply increased role in Israel's political and social life of the ultra-Orthodox movements. The 1988
Israeli election, which saw a 50 percent rise in voters supporting
Orthodox candidates and gave this group a potentially pivotal role
in shaping the governing coalition, was particularly worrisome to
American Jews, who are largely members of Conservative and
Reform congregations. This does not translate directly into criticism of Israeli government policy but leaves uncertainty about the
nature of a government coalition built upon extreme nationalist
and ultra-Orthodox minorities. There is a sense that Israel has
moved significantly to the right. It should be very clear, however,
that there is still strong support of Israel by the American Jewish
community, but it is not uncritical; nor is it unaware of the deep
divisions which have emerged within Israel. It does, nonetheless,
suggest that there may be a residue of sympathy for American
policies which, while protective of Israel and its security, take into
account the need to resolve the conflict with the Palestinians in a
peaceful and just manner.

Other elements of American attitudes emerge from recent polls.
While general sympathy for Israel has been maintained over the
years, sympathy for the Palestinians has jumped 50 percent (from
14 to 22 percent) in the last year, due to a large extent to the
intifadah and the Israeli response. Among well-informed and more
highly educated Americans, sympathy for the Palestinians is even
higher and, equally important, sympathy for Israel among this
group of "issue leaders" has dropped. By April 1988, 33 percent
of all Americans felt the Palestinians were justified in wanting to
establish a homeland in the occupied territories, with another 8
percent believing the goal was right but their methods wrong. Only
25 percent believed the homeland quest was wrong. Over 50 percent of "issue leaders" supported the Palestinian desire for a homeland in Israeli-occupied territory.[14] On the sensitive issue of foreign
aid, 41 percent of Americans in August of 1988 believed that aid

to Israel ought to be cut, compared with 39 percent wanting it maintained and only 14 percent believing it should be increased. Israel is among the eight highest recipients of aid; conversely, Israel headed the list of nations who Americans believed should receive less aid.[15] These polls, together with many others, suggest that public attitudes toward the Israeli–Palestinian conflict are more evenhanded than those held in Congress and the administration. They indicate that there is a good deal of latitude in terms of public support for innovative policies to resolve the long-standing conflict.

The few positive signs in the region were not really the direct result of American policies or actions, though such actions were welcome enough. The Soviet withdrawal from Afghanistan has to be credited largely to Gorbachev's dramatic policy shifts, and the sudden end of fighting (not yet peace) between Iran and Iraq seems largely to have been a function of the severe costs of continuing the war and internal dynamics of the regime in Teheran.

The Reagan administration did not bring important achievements in the Middle East. The Iran-Contra affair and the disasters of Lebanon still cloud any final assessment of its record. There are, however, some important lessons available for the Bush administration. To ignore Syria will court failure or frustration. Jordan has probably not been a viable "option" for some years as the surrogate in solving the Palestine question; by now it is absolutely clear that Jordan does not offer a separate option at all. Jordan's recognition of the Palestinian declaration of an independent state on November 15, 1988, coupled with its renunciation in July of claims to the occupied territories, means that American policy will finally have to come to terms with Palestinian self-determination and statehood as accepted elements of any solution. The centrality of the Palestinian question, so long shunted aside in U.S. policy, will provide the most direct challenge to the Bush administration. The Soviet Union, by taking major steps to end the Cold War and by recapturing positive diplomatic initiatives in the Middle East, will certainly have to be included, and can be helpful, in the Arab–Israeli peacemaking process.

History and compassion should compel the United States to be more concerned with the needs and interests of the people in the

Middle East, to seek peace because it will serve those who suffer from war and conflict, and to aid political and economic change because it will relieve the burdens of oppression and poverty. Serving these considerations also will serve the true interests of the American people.

12

Conclusions

Our report treats what have often appeared to be intractable problems. As we examine the numerous issues of conflict and the many layers of apparently contradictory interests, we can sympathize with the despair that often overcomes those engaged in the problems of the Middle East. We can understand why emotion runs so strong and why effective discourse can be so hard to achieve.

Our ability to continue without despair to deal with these issues has gained strength from the numerous personal contacts that the AFSC has developed over the years with people in the Middle East who are deeply involved in and committed to one or another issue or side in the conflicts there. We are realistic about the seriousness and depth of the problems in the Middle East but we are still committed to keep trying.

As we neared the completion of writing this report, we shared it with individuals who we know represent deeply held positions in the various Middle East conflicts. We have been impressed by the seriousness and helpfulness of their often critical responses, and we have incorporated many of their perspectives and considerations into this document. More important, these responses supported our view that there does exist within the Middle East a reservoir of will and ability to face squarely and seek resolution of the most difficult problems.

Our criticisms, suggestions, and proposals are spread through the volume in the contexts in which they arose. We bring them together here to show relationships among the problems and among solutions to them. We hope that they can serve as guideposts to new perspectives and new policies.

THE ISRAELI–PALESTINIAN/ARAB CONFLICT

The core of any solution to the Arab–Israeli conflict is the resolution of the Palestinian question. Major initiatives must be taken by the countries and peoples of the Middle East. It is equally certain that there are crucial efforts that can be taken by the United Nations, the United States, the U.S.S.R., and the nations of Europe. The outlines for most of the needed steps can be found in resolutions of the UN Security Council and General Assembly. What is required now is the will to break out of the continuing stalemate.

The uprising by Palestinians in the West Bank and Gaza, coming as it did after more than twenty years of Israeli occupation and lasting more than a year, qualitatively altered the relations between Israel and the Palestinians. Although it did not end the occupation, it demonstrated that the status quo of Israeli occupation is untenable. While military force may keep the uprising in check, only a political solution can resolve the conflict.

We believe that the solution of the Palestinian question will involve compromises of positions currently held by both the Israelis and the Palestinians. The underlying principles of the solution are worth restating: self-determination for both Israelis and Palestinians, mutual recognition, and mutual security. We believe that to conclude a just peace which provides for the security of all nations, the basic provisions of UN Security Council Resolution 242 should be carried out: Israeli withdrawal from occupied territories and the right of all states in the region to live at peace within secure and recognized borders. In addition, we believe that Palestinian self-determination should set the terms for the ultimate decision about the West Bank and the Gaza Strip and that an independent Palestinian state in these territories should be supported. We welcome the declaration of an independent Palestinian state in the occupied West Bank and Gaza on November 15, 1988, and see it as Palestinian acceptance of territorial compromise and the proposal of exchanging "territory for peace." (The United States should grant recognition when a government is established.) Older claims for regaining all of Palestine have been abandoned. In turn, Palestinian recognition of Israel and its right to a secure and peaceful existence within the pre-1967 borders is an essential element. All parties must renounce terrorism, whether carried out by individuals or states. We believe that this solution provides a measure of justice for both parties who have contested the same lands. It will bring a long-awaited peace to both and provide a greater degree of security for Israel than continued occupation and its reliance on military force. Through resolution of a deep political dispute, Israel will remove the enmity that has been at the core of the Arab–Israeli conflict.

To break the impasse, each side must be willing to undertake bold actions. The PLO, through its acceptance of UN Security Council Resolutions 242 and 338 as the bases for negotiations in an international peace conference, its explicit recognition of Israel's right to exist, and its renunciation of terrorism, has taken major steps forward in its political program for securing peace. By making explicit its willingness to recognize Israel as a state and make peace with it in return for Israel's recognition of the right of Palestinian self-determination in the West Bank and the Gaza Strip, it has removed any ambiguities about its intentions. By its willingness to accept criticism from rejectionists for its recognition of Israel, the PLO has already taken on that burden. Recognition by itself is not the final step, but it is an important element to initiate serious peace negotiations. The PLO has now shown its willingness to take political risks for the goal of a separate Palestinian state. Discussion of any future reunification of all of Palestine, the "dream" which some Palestinians talk of, must be completely separated from the terms of a negotiated settlement. To confuse the agreements to be made in real time and place with historical, psychological, or religious "dreams" by either Israelis or Palestinians would be a critical mistake and would potentially undermine the credibility of a negotiated agreement. Even the "dreamers" must renounce the use of force and think in terms of mutually acceptable desires.

For a PLO proposal to have full credibility it must be supported by the Arab states who have made the resolution of the Palestinian question a key element in ending the Arab–Israeli conflict. Serious proposals of the sort advanced at Fez, Morocco, in the Arab Peace Plan of September 9, 1982, can demonstrate Arab intent and strengthen the will to peace among all the parties. But to be successful, proposals must be diplomatically and politically pursued so as to overcome current fears and rigidities. Such proposals should be recognized as the beginning of a process and not necessarily its final outcome. Full Arab support for the compromise proposals advanced by the PLO at Algiers in November 1988 is essential. This underlines the importance of Syria as one of the key parties to a comprehensive settlement. Syria cannot be ignored; nor can it be left in the position of blocking or slowing the peacemaking process. Serious diplomatic and political efforts, by the other Arab parties, by the United States, and by the Soviet Union, will be necessary to ensure full Syrian involvement.

For Israel's commitment to peace to be fully appreciated, Israel must drop its claim to extended sovereignty over the West Bank and Gaza and deal openly and positively with Palestinian desires for self-determination and statehood. Israel should be generous in its interpretation of UN Security Council Resolution 242 and, in return for withdrawal to the pre-1967 borders and recognition of Palestinian nationalism, realize that it is achieving the long-desired goal of Palestinian and Arab recognition of Israel's legitimate right to live peacefully within secure borders. Israel's desire for security and a long-term peace is compromised by its policy of extensive settlement in the West Bank and Gaza and the continued repressive acts taken to maintain the occupation. For Israel, the choice is between peace and occupation. If continued steps to integrate the occupied territories into the political economy of Israel are taken, a future agreement with the Palestinians and Arabs may be all but foreclosed. As part of any negotiated peace, Israel must either withdraw its settlements or negotiate terms for the settlers to live under Palestinian sovereignty. Just as Israel insists on its right to determine its national leadership, realism dictates that Israel will have to negotiate agreements with the leadership whom the Palestinians, the Arab states, and now much of the international community recognize—the PLO. All present evidence indicates that the Israeli government is deeply reluctant to consider proposals of this sort. Therefore, we believe that Israelis, American Jews, and others who care about Israel's democratic traditions, its Jewish character, and its responsible role in the world of nations must undertake vigorous action to bring a change in Israeli government policies concerning the Palestinian question. In response to the positive moves toward compromise exhibited in the new Palestinian initiatives, Israel and its friends must be willing to accept "yes" for an answer.

We believe all parties, Israeli and Palestinian, should stop the cycle of violence and terror that has held the area in its grip and instead rely solely on political, diplomatic, and other nonviolent means to resolve conflict and achieve agreements.

We hope for more than an end to conflict and seek more than a mere coexistence of two states sharing a nervously guarded border. Important as these are, their very achievement should be used to propel Israelis and Palestinians toward a new relationship with each other. These two peoples who have common histories of persecution and dispersion will, we hope, come to respect—and support—each other's quests for self-determination and self-identity.

The United States alone cannot bring peace to the Middle East, but it can aid the process in important ways. As the primary economic supporter of Israel and major supplier of armaments, the United States is in a position to reassure Israel of continued concern for its security within its pre-1967 borders and to encourage strongly the adoption of policies that can effectively resolve the Palestinian question. The United States government must strengthen its opposition to land expropriation, West Bank and Gaza settlements, the seizure of water resources, deportation of civic leaders, and other repressive moves whose purpose is to ensure long-term Israeli control of the West Bank and the Gaza Strip. The United States must use more than words to indicate its belief that the current occupation and settlement policies are harmful to the peace process. In its genuine support for Israel, the United States must not by default support these policies. The U.S. administration and Congress must more closely monitor aid to Israel and hold it accountable for the uses to which that aid is put. The normal restrictions on economic and military aid should be enforced, as is the case with all other U.S. aid recipients. Human rights standards and nuclear nonproliferation rules must be applied to Israel (as they should be applied to other countries) if the Israelis are to take seriously American urgings and warnings. If they do not, specific actions should be taken. For example, U.S. aid might be reduced if Israel continues to use funds to maintain the occupation and to build and maintain settlements in the West Bank and Gaza.

The United States has an additional important role to play in bringing all parties into the peace process. It should, therefore, take very seriously its newly opened substantive dialogue with the PLO. The aim should be vigorously to encourage the PLO's involvement in the political and diplomatic efforts toward establishing peace. Similarly, the United States cannot continue to try to exclude the Soviet Union from meaningful involvement in the peace process. The Soviets are a needed and important element in achieving negotiated agreements in the Middle East. Further, international agencies such as the UN ought to be reintegrated into the peace process. The important UN role in achieving a cease-fire in the Iran–Iraq war suggests the place it can have in resolving the Arab–Israeli conflict.

The U.S. commitment to a just peace should be based both on Israel's right to live at peace and in security and on the right of the Palestinians to create an independent and secure state alongside Israel.

We are aware that the adoption of these policies will require changes in the views of the U.S. administration. We believe that these changes are in the best interests of both the Israeli and Palestinian peoples, and Americans as well, and we urge thoughtful and vigorous support for them.

LEBANON

The survival of Lebanon and the well-being of the Lebanese people depend upon the policies and actions of the nations of the Middle East and the engaged support of the international community. Although the long-term solution is almost certainly tied to a resolution of the Israeli–Palestinian conflict and lifting the pressures it has put upon Lebanon, there are immediate steps that can be taken which will save lives and possibly bring order to Lebanon.

Lebanon should be insulated to the greatest extent possible from the external conflicts in the region. The United States working with Israel and the Soviet Union with Syria should begin a process of serious disengagement from Lebanon and stop the use of their surrogates to fight on Lebanese soil.

The UN Secretary-General, using the new respect that the UN has earned by its successful mediation of the Iran–Iraq war and of the Afghanistan war, should call a meeting of the relevant parties and establish the limited terms necessary to protect Lebanon's independence and integrity as a unified nation.

Steps must be taken to help reestablish an active polity in Lebanon and reverse the trend toward partition into confessional- and political-based cantons.

It is important for all parties—Lebanese, Israeli, Palestinian, and Syrian—to show true compassion for the war-battered civilian population and to refrain from further violence.

THE ARMS RACE

The major supplier nations should declare a moratorium on the shipment of all new weapons and halt all current arms-transfer agreements. Working together, the United States and the Soviet Union, as the largest suppliers, can take a crucial lead in freezing the arms race in the Middle East. During a moratorium they can work with the other supplier nations and the recipients to develop strict long-term agreements on Middle East arms limitations. Every effort must be made to halt the transfer of highly sophisticated new weapons, especially missiles. The increased range and augmented firepower of weapons now entering the Middle East ensures that future wars will be substantially more destructive of civilian as well as military targets; the experiences of the Iran–Iraq war are a sobering reminder. Poison gas has recently been used in the Middle East. We cannot by our silence seem to condone its use. The nations of the world must strongly condemn the use of chemical weapons; the Geneva protocols, the oldest arms-control treaty in effect, must be substantially strengthened, with inspection, controls, and sanctions fully developed. The new Chemical Weapons Convention should be speedily completed and an active international campaign for ratification and adherence undertaken.

The Middle East should be declared a nuclear-weapons-free

zone, and the suppliers and users of nuclear technologies should work quickly to secure full agreement by all states in the region to the Nuclear Nonproliferation Treaty. Its terms must be vigorously enforced. The states that supply nuclear technology should, for example, refuse to supply nuclear fuels or technologies to states not in compliance with the treaty. They should also tighten their bilateral safeguards as part of nuclear export agreements. In order to indicate the seriousness of their commitments to halt nuclear weapons proliferation, the United States and the U.S.S.R. should immediately take steps to control and reduce their own nuclear weapons. For the call of nonproliferation to be taken seriously, more drastic weapons reductions must be effected by the superpowers.

Israel, as the technologically most advanced nation in the region and the one state with nuclear weapons, has the potential either to stop or to encourage a Middle East nuclear arms race. If it takes the crucial steps of signing the Nonproliferation Treaty, dismantling its weapons, and opening its facilities to international inspection, Israel can go far to block the nuclear arms race and make the Middle East free from nuclear weapons.

THE IRAN–IRAQ WAR AND AFGHANISTAN

In both the Iran–Iraq war and the bitter conflict in Afghanistan a revitalized United Nations was able to play an important role as mediator. This was possible only because the superpowers were willing to allow meaningful international efforts. In the long and destructive war between Iran and Iraq determined negotiations brought about a cease-fire. The longer-term peacemaking between these bitter foes will require both the skill of continued mediation and the full commitment of outside powers to bring success.

In Afghanistan the Soviet pullout guaranteed by both the Soviet Union and the United States and overseen by the United Nations must not be followed by a never-ending civil war in which U.S. arms support for the guerrilla groups and Soviet arms support for their allies in Kabul turn the country into a "killing field." The temptation on the part of the United States to take advantage of the Soviet pullout to continue the Cold War by supporting chaos on the Soviet southern frontier would be cynical. The people of

Afghanistan deserve more; they need an end to the fighting, a chance for repatriation of the several million refugees, and an opportunity to rebuild a war-devastated nation. The United States and the Soviet Union must help and must also be held accountable for their actions.

There are real issues that emerge from the conflicts and crises and from the daily lives of people and governments in the Middle East. They are not on the agendas of either the United States or the Soviet Union. They focus instead both on the much more proximate problems—employment, hunger, political liberty, human rights—and on the less tangible questions of national self-identity and political-economic modernization, on Westernization and traditional religious values. It is the United States' ability to understand and to respond to these issues that will govern our real contribution to the Middle East and permit us to render real aid in the amelioration of conflicts in the region. The rush to arms, alliances, and grand strategic designs exacerbates tensions and makes the United States more surely part of the problem rather than the solution.

We believe that peace, security, and justice are possible in the Middle East. The area of the world from which the prophetic religious traditions of Judaism, Christianity, and Islam have come may rediscover the faithfulness of these traditions to justice and peace. If war continues in the area, it will be because the contenders and the rest of us do not truly believe that peace is possible. If peace comes, it will be because one or more of those countries and peoples involved will have believed and, believing, will have acted daringly and faithfully in that belief.

Notes

1. INTRODUCTION

1. American Friends Service Committee, *Search for Peace in the Middle East* (New York: Fawcett Publications, 1970).

2. ISRAEL

1. American Friends Service Committee, op. cit., p. 79.
2. Arie Eliav, *Shalom: Peace in Jewish Tradition* (Israel: Massadah, 1977), p. 1.
3. American Jewish Committee, "Estimated Jewish Population in Muslim Countries of the Middle East and North Africa," and George Gruen, "Jews in Moslem Lands: Living a Precarious Existence," *Na'amat Woman*, November–December 1988.
4. Albert Stern, "A Cautious Visit with Syrian Jews," *Cleveland Jewish News*, January 11, 1980, p. 15. For further information on the treatment of Jews in Arab lands, see Howard M. Sachar, *A History of Israel* (New York: Alfred A. Knopf, 1979), p. 395.
5. For a thorough examination of the Israeli economy, see Ann Crittenden, "Israel's Economic Plight," *Foreign Affairs*, Vol. 57, No. 5 (Summer 1979), pp. 1006–16.
6. Sachar, op. cit., pp. 833–34.
7. Howard M. Sachar, *A History of Israel*, Vol. 2 (New York: Oxford University Press, 1987), p. 233.
8. For the changing Middle East arms balance, see Stockholm International Peace Research Institute, *Yearbook*, 1981, and *The Military Balance* (1981–82), International Institute of Strategic Studies, London.
9. Drew Middleton, "Israel's Might: Are the Arabs Catching Up?" *New York*

Times, October 15, 1981; a more recent Israeli assessment is Yehoshua Raviv, "Arab Israel: Military Balance," *Jerusalem Quarterly*, Vol. 18 (1981), pp. 121–44.

10. See Ze'ev Schiff and Ehud Ya'ari, *Israel's Lebanon War* (New York: Simon & Schuster, 1984).

11. Jacob Talmon, "The Homeland Is in the Diaspora: An Open Letter to Menachim Begin," trans. Arthur Samuelson, *Dissent*, Vol. 27, No. 4 (Fall 1980), pp. 444–45.

12. Ibid., p. 449.

13. For an interesting analysis of the 1981 Israeli election, see Robert Shaplen, "Letter from Israel," *The New Yorker*, July 27, 1981.

14. Mark Heller, "Begin's False Autonomy," *Foreign Policy*, Winter 1979–80, pp. 111–32.

15. "Speech by Prime Minister Begin of Israel to the Knesset on the Occasion of the Visit to Israel of President Sadat of Egypt, Jerusalem, November 20, 1977," *International Documents on Palestine* (Beirut: Institute for Palestine Studies, 1979), pp. 275–79.

16. Sachar, op. cit. (1979), p. 668.

17. Ian Lustick, "Kill the Autonomy Talks," *Foreign Policy*, Winter 1980–81, p. 25, and *Jerusalem Post*, April 6–7, 1981. Other good references on Israeli settlements in the West Bank and Gaza include William W. Harris, *Taking Root: Israeli Settlement in the West Bank, the Golan, and Gaza-Sinai 1967–1981* (Chichester: Research Studies Press, 1980); testimony of Ann Mosely Lesch and Paul Quiring in U.S. Congress, House of Representatives, Committee on International Relations, *Israeli Settlements in the Occupied Territories*, 95th Congress, 1st session (Washington, D.C.: Government Printing Office, 1978), pp. 7–42; Ann Lesch, "Israeli Settlements in the Occupied Territories," *Journal of Palestine Studies*, Issue 25 (Autumn 1977), pp. 26–47, and Vol. 29 (Autumn 1978), pp. 100–19.

18. Bernard Avishai, "The Victory of the New Israel," *New York Review of Books*, August 13, 1981, p. 45.

19. Schiff and Ya'ari, op. cit.

20. See Sachar, op. cit. (1987), pp. 166–232.

21. See the recent study by Ian Lustick, *For the Land and the Lord: Jewish Fundamentalism in Israel* (New York: Council on Foreign Relations, 1988).

22. "Domestic Developments in Israel," in William B. Quandt (ed.), *The Middle East: Ten Years After Camp David* (Washington, D.C.: Brookings Institution, 1988), pp. 157–58.

3. THE OCCUPATION

1. Ann Mosely Lesch, *Political Perceptions of the Palestinians on the West Bank and the Gaza Strip* (Washington, D.C.: The Middle East Institute, 1980), p. 31.

2. William Claiborne and Edward Cody, *The West Bank: Hostage of History*

(Washington, D.C.: Foundation for Middle East Peace, November 1980), p. 3.

3. See his provocative book *Conflicts and Contradictions* (New York: Villard Books, 1986).

4. Raja Shehadeh and Jonathan Kuttab, *The West Bank and the Rule of Law* (Geneva: International Commission of Jurists and Ramallah Law in the Service of Man, 1980), p. 3. For Israel's interpretation of its administrative and legal procedures, see Israel National Section of the International Commission of Jurists, *The Rule of Law in the Areas Administered by Israel* (Tel Aviv: TZATZ, 1981).

5. Geneva Conventions of August 12, 1949, with commentary published under the direction of Jean Pictet (Geneva: International Committee of the Red Cross, 1956), Fourth Convention: Relative to the Protection of Civilians in Times of War.

6. See Raja Shehadeh, *Occupier's Law: Israel and the West Bank* (Washington, D.C.: Institute for Palestine Studies, 1986), p. xiv.

7. Shehadeh and Kuttab, op. cit., pp. 28–29.

8. See Shehadeh, op. cit., pp. 226–27.

9. Israel National Section of the ICJ, op. cit., pp. 28–29, 37–42.

10. Figures on the number of arrests have been provided by AFSC field staff in the Middle East, and Israel National Section of the ICJ, op. cit., pp. 71–73.

11. Shehadeh, op. cit., pp. 228–29.

12. Amnesty International, *Report and Recommendations of an Amnesty International Mission to the State of Israel*, June 3–7, 1979 (London: Amnesty International Publications, 1980).

13. Claiborne and Cody, op. cit., pp. 26–27.

14. Salim Tamari, "The Palestinians in the West Bank and Gaza: Sociology of Dependence," in Khalil Nakhleh and Elia Zurcik (eds.), *Sociology of the Palestinians* (New York: St. Martin's Press, 1980).

15. *Jerusalem Post*, April 7, 1981.

16. From an Israeli report delivered at the United Nations Conference on Desertification, Nairobi, Kenya, August 1977, cited in the Economics Department of Jordan, "The Significance of Some West Bank Resources to Israel," February 1979, p. 6.

17. David K. Shipler, "Israel Plans to Take Over Arab-Run Power Company," *New York Times*, January 1, 1980, p. A2.

18. Yehuda Litani, "Vigilantes in the Wild West (Bank)," *Ha'aretz*, May 11, 1979.

19. See the account in Sachar, op. cit. (1987), pp. 162–63.

20. Shehadeh, op. cit., p. 229.

21. Ann Lesch, "Israeli Deportation of Palestinians from the West Bank and the Gaza Strip, 1967–1978," *Journal of Palestine Studies*, Issue 30 (Winter 1979), pp. 101–31, and Issue 31 (Spring 1979), pp. 81–112, and the *Financial Times*, London, December 4, 1979.

22. Mohammed Milhem, "Autonomy: An Empty Plate," *New Outlook*, January 1981, p. 22, and Mohammed Milhem and Fahd Kawasmeh, *New York Times*, June 1, 1981.

23. *Jerusalem Post*, International Edition, August 20, 1988, p. 3.
24. *Middle East Report*, October 1988, p. 20.
25. Meron Benvenisti, *West Bank Data Base Project, 1987 Report*, p. 1.
26. *Jerusalem Post*, International Edition, August 20, 1988, p. 3.
27. Naseer Aruri, "Repression in Academia: Palestinian Universities vs. the Israeli Military," unpublished paper, February 1981, pp. 13–14.
28. Aruri, op. cit., p. 12.
29. Milton Viorst, "Bir Zeit: The Search for National Identity," *Science*, Vol. 20, No. 5 (December 1980), pp. 1101–2.
30. Excerpt from a paper by Sahar Khalifah delivered at the International Writers' Program, Iowa City, University of Iowa, November 29, 1978.
31. See the suggestive article by Herbert Kelman, "The Palestinianization of the Arab-Israeli Conflict," in Yehuda Lukacs and Abdulla M. Battah (eds.), *The Arab-Israeli Conflict, Two Decades of Change* (Boulder, Colo.: Westview Press, 1988).
32. See Gail Pressberg, "The Uprising: Causes and Consequences," *Journal of Palestine Studies*, Issue 67 (Spring 1988), pp. 38–50.
33. See the report by Joe Stork, "The Significance of the Stones: Notes from the Seventh Month," *Middle East Report*, No. 154 (September–October 1988), pp. 4–11.
34. Quoted from *New York Times*, February 6, 1988, in Pressburg, op. cit.
35. The term is Joe Stork's from *Middle East Report*, No. 154, p. 8.
36. *The New York Times Magazine*, October 16, 1988, p. 35.
37. *Christian Science Monitor*, October 27, 1988, pp. 1 and 18.
38. The text is reprinted in full in *Journal of Palestine Studies*, Issue 67 (Spring 1988), pp. 64–65.
39. Pressburg, op. cit., p. 46.
40. See Stork, *Middle East Report*, No. 154, p. 11.
41. See Mary Curtius, "A Crack in the Wall of Palestinian Unity," *Boston Globe*, August 26, 1988, p. A23.
42. Reported in Stork, *Middle East Report*, No. 154, p. 11.
43. *Jerusalem Post*, International Edition, August 27, 1988, p. 5, and October 22, 1988, p. 2.
44. See *Jerusalem Post*, International Edition, August 27, 1988, p. 2.
45. *Jerusalem Post*, International Edition, October 15, 1988, p. 5.
46. Many of these figures are derived from James Paul, "Israel and the Intifadah, Points of Stress," *Middle East Report*, No. 154 (September–October 1988), pp. 13–16, 48.
47. *Jerusalem Post*, International Edition, September 24, 1988, p. 18.
48. *Jerusalem Post*, International Edition, August 27, 1988, p. 21.
49. *Jerusalem Post*, International Edition, October 1, 1988, p. 5.
50. Paul, op. cit., p. 15.

4. THE PALESTINIANS

1. American Friends Service Committee, *Search for Peace in the Middle East* (New York: Fawcett Publications, 1970), pp. 71–72.
2. See Meron Benvenisti, *West Bank Data Base Project, 1987 Report* (Jerusalem, 1987); an updated estimate of population with significantly higher numbers is Meron Benvenisti and Shlomo Khayat, *The West Bank and Gaza Atlas* (Jerusalem, 1988).
3. See the well-documented British *Minority Rights Group, Report No. 24*: David McDowall, "The Palestinians," rev. October 1987.
4. Frank Epp, *The Palestinians: Portrait of a People in Conflict* (Scottsdale, Pa.: Herald Press, 1976), and John Amos, *Palestinian Resistance: Organization of a Nationalist Movement* (New York: Pergamon Press, 1980), p. 9.
5. Edward Said, *The Question of Palestine* (New York: The New York Times Book Co., 1979), pp. 120–22.
6. For texts of UN Resolutions and 1947 Partition Plan see *The Middle East and North Africa 1980–1981* (London: Europa Publications, 1980); UN 1947 Partition Plan, UN Security Council Resolution 242, November 22, 1967 (see Appendix I); and UN Security Council Resolution 338, October 22, 1973 (see Appendix II).
7. For the text of the Camp David agreements and the Israeli–Egyptian peace treaty, see U.S. Congress, House of Representatives, Committee on Foreign Affairs, Subcommittee on Europe and the Middle East, *The Search for Peace in the Middle East: Documents and Statements 1967–1979*, 96th Congress, 1st session (Washington, D.C.: Government Printing Office, 1979), pp. 20–90.
8. For the text of the 1974 Rabat conference final resolution, see *Middle East and North Africa*, op. cit., p. 73. For the text of the resolutions of the 1978 Baghdad summit, see "Final Statement Issued by Summit Conference 5 Nov.," *Middle East and North Africa Daily FBIS* (Washington, D.C.: Foreign Broadcasting and Information Service, November 6, 1978), p. A14.
9. For full discussion of Fatah, see Amos, op. cit.
10. Abu Iyad, *My Home, My Land: A Narrative of the Palestinian Struggle*, with Eric Rouleau, trans. Linda Butler Koseoglu (New York: Quadrangle/The New York Times Book Co., 1981), p. 106.
11. See the analysis of this question in Emile I. Sahliyeh, *The PLO After the Lebanon War* (Boulder, Colo.: Westview Press, 1986).
12. "Excerpts from Palestine Statement," *New York Times*, November 17, 1988, p. A8.
13. Fouad Ajami, *The Arab Predicament* (Cambridge: Cambridge University Press, 1981), pp. 150–51.
14. Walid Khalidi, "Thinking the Unthinkable: A Sovereign Palestinian State," *Foreign Affairs*, Vol. 56, No. 4 (July 1978), p. 699.
15. *Al-Fajr* (English-language edition), September 12, 1986.
16. Avi Plascov, *A Palestinian State? Examining the Alternatives*, Adelphi Papers, No. 163 (1981), p. 8.
17. Conversations with an AFSC Study Tour, Amman, September 1988.

18. Plascov, op. cit., p. 8.
19. Ibid., p. 9.
20. *Haolam Hazeh*, May 12, 1976.
21. "Statement by the West Bank National Conference Which Met in Beit Hanina, Jerusalem, October 1, 1978," *Journal of Palestine Studies*, Issue 30 (Winter 1979), pp. 194–95.
22. Trudy Rubin, "Exiled West Bank Mayors Hope to Go Home After Israeli Elections," *Christian Science Monitor*, April 30, 1981.
23. Anthony Lewis, "Arafat Says Ambush of Jews in Hebron Was Like U.S. Struggle Against British," *New York Times*, May 8, 1980.
24. Anthony Lewis, "Time Out of Joint," *New York Times*, May 12, 1980, p. A19.
25. See, for example, Khalidi, "Thinking the Unthinkable," loc. cit.
26. Several different translations of the 1968 amended Palestine National Charter exist. We refer you to "The Palestine National Charter Adopted by the Fourth Palestine National Assembly, Cairo, June 17, 1968," *International Documents on Palestine 1968* (Beirut: Institute for Palestine Studies, 1971), pp. 393–94, and Y. Harkabi, *The Palestinian Covenant and Its Meaning* (London: Vallentine, Mitchell, 1979), pp. 119–29.
27. There is a detailed record of these discussions in Sahliyeh, op. cit.
28. Point 7, "Resolutions of the Twelfth Arab League Summit, September 9, 1982. (See Appendix VIII.)
29. Walid Khalidi, "Regiopolitics: Towards a U.S. Policy on the Palestine Problem," *Foreign Affairs*, Vol. 59, No. 5 (Summer 1981), p. 1060.
30. "Political Programme for the PLO Approved by the Palestine National Council, 11th Session, January 6–12, 1973," *International Documents on Palestine 1973* (Beirut: Institute for Palestine Studies, 1976), p. 401.
31. Eric Rouleau, "Les Dirigeants Palestiniens Accepteraient un Compromis," *Le Monde*, November 6, 1973, p. 3. Abu Iyad in *My Home, My Land* (p. 138) notes that as early as 1967 Farouk Qaddoumi, director of foreign affairs for the PLO, advocated a ministate in the West Bank and Gaza.
32. "Political Programme for the Present Stage of the PLO drawn up by the PNC," *Journal of Palestine Studies*, Issue 12 (Summer 1974), p. 224.
33. Said Hammami, *Trouw*, June 28, 1975, quoted in Mordech Nissan, "Palestinian Moderates," *Jerusalem Quarterly*, No. 1 (Fall 1976), p. 73.
34. "Resolutions of the 13th Palestine National Council, Cairo, issued March 21–25, 1977," *Journal of Palestine Studies*, Issue 23 (Spring 1977), p. 189.
35. "Joint Statement issued by the governments of the US and the USSR specifying the necessary steps to be taken to ensure peace in the Middle East," *International Documents on Palestine 1977* (Beirut: Institute for Palestine Studies, 1980), p. 255.
36. "6-Point Programme Agreed to by all Palestinian factions announced by Salah Kalaf, Tripoli, December 4, 1977," *Journal of Palestine Studies*, Issue 27 (Spring 1978), p. 188.
37. Text drafted and supplied to the American Friends Service Committee by Khalid al-Hassan.

38. "Venice Statement on Middle East," June 13, 1980, *Middle East International*, No. 127 (June 20, 1980), p. 13.
39. "What Arafat Really Said," *Israël et Palestine*, April–May 1979, p. 9.
40. The full text is published in William B. Quandt (ed.), *The Middle East: Ten Years After Camp David* (Washington, D.C.: Brookings Institution, 1988), pp. 490–93.
41. Nicholas B. Tatro, "Saudis in Gesture on Israel," *Boston Globe*, August 9, 1981, p. 1.
42. See Sahliyeh, op. cit., pp. 80–82.
43. John Kifner, "Arafat Says Saudi Plan Could Indeed Lead to Lasting Middle East Peace," *New York Times*, August 17, 1981, and John Kifner, "Arafat Welcomes Saudi Proposal for Coexistence with Israelis," *New York Times*, October 31, 1981, p. 6.
44. Ze'ev Schiff and Ehud Ya'ari, *Israel's Lebanon War* (New York: Simon & Schuster, 1984).
45. Daniel Southerland, "Brzezinski: It's Time to Speak to the PLO," *Christian Science Monitor*, August 13, 1981, p. 4.
46. "Why Not Talk with the PLO?" *Christian Science Monitor*, August 7, 1981.
47. "Excerpts from News Conference by Ford and Carter on the Future of Egypt," *New York Times*, October 12, 1981.
48. William Quandt, "U.S. Policy Toward the Arab-Israeli Conflict," in Quandt (ed.), op. cit., p. 384.
49. Khalidi, "Regiopolitics," loc. cit., p. 1063.
50. *Jerusalem Post*, International Edition, October 22, 1988, p. 2.

5. OPTIONS AND PROPOSALS

1. Aharon Yariv, "Strategic Depth," *Jerusalem Quarterly*, No. 17 (Fall 1980), p. 5.
2. Mattityahu Peled, "Dissociating Israeli Security from More Territory," *New York Times*, December 16, 1977.
3. Yariv, op. cit., p. 8.
4. See the thoughtful study of Jewish fundamentalist/extreme nationalism by Ian Lustick, *For the Land and the Lord: Jewish Fundamentalism in Israel* (New York: Council on Foreign Relations, 1988).
5. Ezer Weizman, *The Battle for Peace* (Toronto: Bantam Books, 1981), p. 227.
6. Shai Feldman, "Israel's Security," *Foreign Affairs*, Vol. 59, No. 4 (Spring 1981), p. 762.
7. Shai Feldman, "A Nuclear Middle East," *Survival*, Vol. 23, No. 3 (May–June 1981), and Robert Shaplen, "Letter from Israel," *The New Yorker*, July 27, 1981, p. 67.
8. Avi Plascov, *A Palestinian State? Examining the Alternatives*, Adelphi Papers, No. 163 (1981), p. 51.
9. Meir Pail, *The West Bank and Gaza: A Strategic Analysis for Peace*, New Outlook Discussion Paper, No. 3 (Tel Aviv: New Outlook, 1981), pp. 10–11.

10. Peled, op. cit.
11. Mark Heller, *A Palestinian State, the Implications for Israel* (Cambridge: Harvard University Press, 1983), p. 137.
12. Khalidi, "Thinking the Unthinkable: A Sovereign Palestinian State," *Foreign Affairs*, Vol. 56, No. 4 (July 1978), p. 713.
13. Feldman, "Israel's Security," loc. cit., p. 771.
14. Simha Flapan, "The Maalot Tragedy," *New Outlook*, June 1974, p. 13.
15. See the most recent estimates, Meron Benvenisti and Shlomo Khayat, *The West Bank and Gaza Atlas* (Jerusalem, 1988).
16. Nadav Safran, *Israel, the Embattled Ally* (Cambridge: Harvard University Press, 1978), p. 101.
17. Interview with Moshe Nissim, "Why Autonomy," *Middle East Review*, Winter 1979–80, p. 9.
18. Heller, op. cit., p. 121.
19. "Begin Wins a Close Vote of Confidence," *Boston Globe*, August 6, 1981, p. 5.
20. "Extracts from the Preparatory Committee Recommendations for Political Resolutions Submitted to the 3rd elected Congress of the Israel Labor Party in December 1980," *Middle East International*, June 30, 1981, p. 15.
21. The text of the Shultz initiative, March 4, 1988, is printed in William B. Quandt (ed.), *The Middle East: Ten Years After Camp David* (Washington, D.C.: Brookings Institution, 1988), pp. 488–89.
22. Yigal Allon, "Israel: the Case for Defensible Borders," *Foreign Affairs*, October 1976, pp. 38–53.
23. The Etzion block of settlements, which dates from pre-1948, is located southwest of Bethlehem.
24. See the text in Quandt (ed.), op. cit., pp. 475–76.
25. See Thomas Friedman, "Proposals for Peace," *The New York Times Magazine*, October 30, 1988, p. 62.
26. Ibid., p. 58.
27. Victor Shemtov, "The Sand Is Running Out," *New Outlook*, Vol. 23, No. 4 (May 1980), p. 11.
28. David Richardson, "The Least Dangerous Alternative," *Jerusalem Post Magazine*, June 29–July 1, 1981.
29. Rabbi Arthur Hertzberg, "The West Bank's Future," *New York Times*, June 30, 1981, p. A15.
30. Arthur Hertzberg, "The Turning Point?," *The New York Review of Books*, October 13, 1988, pp. 50–60.
31. For full discussion of rejectionists, see John Amos, *Palestinian Resistance: Organization of a Nationalist Movement* (New York: Pergamon Press, 1980).
32. See Alain Gresh, *The PLO: The Struggle Within* (rev. ed.; London: Zed, 1988), p. 243.
33. See the very suggestive article by Walid Khalidi, "Toward Peace in the Holy Land," *Foreign Affairs*, Spring 1986, p. 788.
34. Daoud Kuttab quotes in "Report from the Occupied Territories: Palestinians Speak," *World Policy Journal*, Vol. 5 (Summer 1988), p. 524.

35. Herbert Kelman, "The Palestinianization of the Arab-Israel Conflict," in Ye-huda Lukacs and Abdalla M. Battah (eds.), *The Arab-Israel Conflict, Two Decades of Changes* (Boulder, Colo.: Westview Press, 1988), p. 343.
36. This presentation of Palestinian views regarding a transition formula draws heavily on an important study: Ann Mosely Lesch, *Political Perceptions of the Palestinians of the West Bank and the Gaza Strip* (Washington, D.C.: Middle East Institute, 1980).
37. Trudy Rubin, "West Bank and Gaza May Produce Few Willing to Participate in Negotiations," *Christian Science Monitor*, March 29, 1979, p. 5.
38. See, for example, Joe Stork, "The Significance of the Stones," *Middle East Report*, No. 154 (September–October 1988); Kuttab, op. cit.
39. Anthony Lewis, "Dissent on the West Bank from Israeli Insider," *New York Times*, May 25, 1980.
40. Yehoshafat Harkabi, *A Policy for the Moment of Truth* (Washington, D.C.: Foundation for the Middle East Peace, 1988).
41. A number of thoughtful proposals have been advanced for the resolution of the complicated question of Jerusalem. One of these is found in a recent article by the current mayor of the city: Teddy Kollek, "Jerusalem: Past and Future," *Foreign Affairs*, Vol. 59, No. 5 (Summer 1981), pp. 1041–49. Other studies of this issue from a variety of perspectives include H. Eugene Bovis, *The Jerusalem Question 1917–1968* (Stanford: Hoover Institution Press, 1971); A. L. Tibawi, *Jerusalem: Its Place in Islam and Arab History* (Beirut: Institute for Palestine Studies, Monograph No. 19, 1969); and Joel Kraemer (ed.), *Jerusalem: Problems and Prospects* (New York: Praeger, 1980).

6. THE TRAGEDY OF LEBANON

1. "Chronology of the Lebanese War," *International IDOC New Series Bulletin*, No. 3–4 (Rome: International Documentation and Center, March–April 1977), p. 17.
2. See Samir Khalaf, "Ideologies of Enmity in Lebanon," *Middle East Insight*, Vol. 6, No. 1–2 (1988), pp. 3–17.
3. A good examination of the economic impact of the Lebanese civil war, particularly in the south, is Elaine Hagopian and Samih Farsoun, *South Lebanon* (Detroit: Association of Arab-American University Graduates, Special Report No. 2, August 1978).
4. For greater detail on the Lebanese civil war, consult John Bullock, *Death of a Country* (London: Weidenfeld & Nicolson, 1977); P. E. Haley and Lewis Snider (eds.), *Lebanon in Crisis* (Syracuse: Syracuse University Press, 1979); Roger Owen (ed.), *Essays on the Crisis in Lebanon* (London: Ithaca Press, 1976); and Walid Khalidi, *Conflict and Violence in Lebanon: Confrontation in the Middle East* (Cambridge: Harvard Studies in International Affairs, 1979).
5. Quoted in James Fine, "The Tragedy of Lebanon," Quaker International Affairs Report (Philadelphia: American Friends Service Committee, March 1981), p. 8.

6. See David McDowall, *Lebanon: A Conflict of Minorities, Minority Rights Group Report*, No. 61 (rev. ed.; London, 1986).
7. Quoted in Fine, "The Tragedy of Lebanon," p. 4.
8. Howard M. Sachar, *A History of Israel*, Vol. 2 (New York: Oxford University Press, 1987), p. 196; further details are given in Ze'ev Schiff and Ehud Ya'ari, *Israel's Lebanon War* (New York: Simon & Schuster, 1984), pp. 250–85.
9. Sachar, op. cit., pp. 196–97.
10. McDowall, op. cit., p. 17.
11. Schiff and Ya'ari, op. cit., p. 42.
12. Ibid., p. 43.
13. See Naomi Chazan, "Domestic Development in Israel," in William B. Quandt (ed.), op. cit., p. 159.
14. Ze'ev Schiff, "Green Light in Lebanon," *Foreign Policy*, Autumn 1983, and Schiff and Ya'ari, op. cit., pp. 73–77.
15. Rashid Khalidi, *Under Siege* (New York: Columbia University Press, 1986), p. 107.
16. See Schiff and Ya'ari, op. cit., pp. 176–82.
17. See Tabitha Petran, *The Struggle Over Lebanon* (New York: Monthly Review, 1987), pp. 329–30.
18. See Itamar Rabinovich, *The War for Lebanon, 1970–1985* (rev. ed.; Ithaca: Cornell University Press, 1985), pp. 186–89.
19. See the report of a conference on Lebanon held at Tufts University, October 1988, *Boston Globe*, p. 3.

7. THE ARMS RACE

1. These are: Libya, Iraq, Saudi Arabia, Israel, Syria, and Egypt.
2. See R. L. Ferrari, R. L. Madrid, and J. Knopf, *U.S. Arms Exports: Policies and Contractors* (Cambridge, Mass.: Ballinger, 1988), pp. 154 ff.
3. See the thoughtful summary by Anthony Cordesman, "The Middle East and the Cost of the Politics of Force," *Middle East Journal*, Vol. 40 (1986), pp. 5–15; see also *SIPRI Yearbook*, 1987, and Jaffee Center for Strategic Studies, *The Middle East Military Balance, 1986* (Jerusalem, 1987).
4. *Middle East Military Balance, 1986*, pp. 167–68.
5. See also Ferrari, Madrid, and Knopf, op. cit., pp. 161–67.
6. *SIPRI Yearbook*, 1987, pp. 186–88, 204–5; also *Middle East Military Balance, 1986*, p. 408.
7. *SIPRI*, pp. 204–5.
8. Ferrari, Madrid, and Knopf, op. cit., p. 160.
9. Stockholm International Peace Research Institute, *World Armaments and Disarmament, SIPRI Yearbook*, 1976 (London: Taylor and Francis, 1976), p. 65.
10. See Leonard S. Spector, *The Undeclared Bomb* (Cambridge, Mass.: Ballinger, 1988), pp. 20, 30–31, 60–61; Aaron Karp, "The Frantic Third World Quest of Ballistic Missiles," *Bulletin of the Atomic Scientists*, June 1988, pp. 14–20.
11. Spector, op. cit., pp. 29, 60–61.
12. Ibid., p. 32.

13. Dore Gold, "Ground-to-Ground Missiles: The Threat Facing Israel," *IDF Journal*, Vol. 4, No. 3 (1987), pp. 31–34, 62–63; *Middle East Military Balance, 1986*, passim.
14. See Karp, op. cit., pp. 14–16.
15. See Spector, op. cit., pp. 20, 180–87, 211–13, 223–24; also *SIPRI Yearbook*, 1987, pp. 104–7, 110–11, 304–5, 384–89.
16. See the update through 1986 in *SIPRI Yearbook*, 1987, p. 169.
17. *SIPRI Yearbook*, 1987, p. 199; see also Naomi Chazan, "Israeli Perspectives on the Israel-South Africa Relationship," *Research Report*, Institute of Jewish Affairs, December 1987, pp. 13–16.
18. *SIPRI Yearbook*, 1987, pp. 198–99; Aaron Siklieman, *Israel's Global Reach: Arms Sales as Diplomacy* (Washington, D.C.: Pergamon-Brassey's, 1985), pp. 23 ff., 56–63, 123–45.
19. For a study of Egypt's relationship with the U.S.S.R., see Alvin Z. Rubinstein, *Red Star on the Nile* (Princeton: Princeton University Press, 1977), and Mohammed Heikal, *The Sphinx and the Commissar* (New York: Harper & Row, 1978).
20. For an examination of the Soviet–PLO relationship, see Rashid Khalidi, "Arab Views of the Soviet Role in the Middle East," *Middle East Journal*, Vol. 39 (Autumn 1985), pp. 716–32.
21. Central Intelligence Agency, *Communist Aid Activities in Non-Communist Less Developed Countries 1979 and 1954–1979* (National Foreign Assessment Center, April 1980).
22. "Tripartite Declaration Regarding Security in the Near East, May 25, 1950," in John Norton Moore (ed.), *The Arab-Israeli Conflict: Readings and Documents* (Princeton: Princeton University Press, 1977), pp. 988–89.
23. See Ferrari, Madrid, and Knopf, op. cit., p. 157.
24. *Middle East Military Balance, 1986*, p. 167.
25. Ferrari, Madrid, and Knopf, op. cit., p. 259.
26. International Institute for Strategic Studies (IISS), *Military Balance, 1987–8* (London, 1988), p. 102.
27. "Treaty on the Nonproliferation of Nuclear Weapons," July 1, 1968, *World Armaments and Disarmaments, SIPRI Yearbook*, 1981 (London: Taylor and Francis, 1981), pp. 415–16.
28. For a study of nuclear weapons in the Middle East, see Shai Feldman, "A Nuclear Middle East," *Survival*, Vol. 23, No. 3 (May–June 1981), pp. 107–15.
29. Spector, op. cit., p. 161; see also Anthony H. Cordesman, *The Arab-Israeli Military Balance and the Art of Operations* (Washington, D.C.: American Enterprise Institute, 1987), p. 109, where the estimate is "at least 100 nuclear weapons."
30. The earliest full discussion is Shai Feldman, *Israeli Nuclear Deterrence* (New York: Columbia University Press, 1982); see also Louis Rene Beres (ed.), *Security or Armageddon: Israel's Nuclear Strategy* (Lexington, Mass.: D. C. Heath, 1986).
31. Avner Cohen and Benjamin Frankel, "Israel's Nuclear Ambiguity," *Bulletin of the Atomic Scientists*, March 1987, pp. 15–19.

32. "Dayan Says Israelis Have the Capacity to Produce A-Bombs," *New York Times*, June 25, 1981, p. 1.
33. Spector, op. cit., pp. 101, 196–206, 207–18, 219–24.
34. Ibid., p. 162.
35. Ibid.
36. Ibid., pp. 163, 310.
37. See ibid., pp. 314–15.
38. *SIPRI Yearbook*, 1987, p. 460.

8. IRAN

1. Good background sources on the modern history and politics of Iran are Richard Cottam, *Nationalism in Iran* (Pittsburgh: University of Pittsburgh Press, 1979), and Nikki R. Keddie, *Roots of Revolution: An Interpretive History of Modern Iran* (New Haven: Yale University Press, 1981).
2. For a firsthand account of these events and the CIA's involvement in them, see Kermit Roosevelt, *Countercoup: The Struggle for the Control of Iran* (New York: McGraw-Hill, 1979).
3. Former SAVAK agents as well as former CIA analyst Jess Leaf (*New York Times*, January 6, 1980) and Irish Nobel Peace Prize recipient Sean McBride (*The Nation*, March 1, 1980) have made specific allegations in this regard.
4. Mohammed Reza Pahlavi, *Mission for My Country* (New York: McGraw-Hill, 1961).
5. The first Prime Minister appointed by Khomeini after his return to Iran in February 1979. Bazargan resigned after Iranian students seized the U.S. embassy hostages.
6. A widely regarded educator who wrote and lectured on the sociology of Islam, Dr. Shariati was arrested and tortured by SAVAK. He died under suspicious circumstances in London in June 1977. For a sampling of his views, see Ali Shariati, *On the Sociology of Islam*, trans. Hamid Algar (Berkeley: Mizan Press, 1979).
7. See "Iran in Revolution," *MERIP Reports*, No. 75–76, 1979, passim; Ervand Abrahamian, "Structural Causes of the Iranian Revolution," *MERIP Reports*, No. 87 (May 1980), pp. 21–26. See also Keddie, op. cit.
8. William J. Butler and Georges Levasseur, *Human Rights and the Legal System in Iran* (Geneva: International Commission of Jurists, 1976).
9. The Qur'an (also spelled Koran) is Islam's holy scripture. Muslims believe the Qur'an contains God's words as revealed to the prophet Muhammad.
10. For a good introduction to Islam, see Kenneth Cragg, *The House of Islam* (Belmont, Calif.: Wadsworth Press, 1975). For the more advanced reader: Fualur Rahman, *Islam* (2nd ed.; Chicago: University of Chicago Press, 1979). For the most comprehensive history to date on Islam, see Marshall Hodgson, *Venture of Islam*, 3 vols. (Chicago: University of Chicago Press, 1974).
11. For a collection of essays sympathetic to the Iranian revolution, consult David Albert (ed.), *Tell the American People: Perspectives on the Iranian Revolution* (Philadelphia: Movement for a New Society, 1980).

12. "The President's News Conference of October 1, 1981," *Weekly Compilation of Presidential Documents*, Vol. 17, No. 40 (October 5, 1981), p. 1070.
13. Stephen D. Goose, "8. Armed Conflicts in 1986, and the Iraq-Iran War," *SIPRI Yearbook*, 1987, pp. 302–3.
14. Ibid; and Anthony Cordesman, *The Iran-Iraq War and Western Security, 1984–87* (London: Jane's, 1987), pp. 46–47.
15. See *The Middle East*, September 1988, p. 11.
16. See the briefing paper prepared for the AFSC by Billie Marchik.
17. *SIPRI Yearbook*, 1987, pp. 302–4.
18. See Glen Balfour-Paul, "The Prospects for Peace," in M. S. El Azhary (ed.), *The Iran-Iraq War* (New York: St. Martin's Press, 1984), pp. 126–39.
19. Gerd Nonneman, *Iraq, the Gulf States and the War* (London: Ithaca Press, 1986), p. 48.
20. Goose, op. cit., pp. 306–7.
21. David Segal, "The Iran-Iraq War: A Military Analysis," *Foreign Affairs*, Summer 1988, p. 496.
22. *New York Times*, July 21, 1988.
23. *New York Times*, July 4, 1988.
24. Cf. Goose, op. cit., pp. 307–8.
25. Fred Halliday, "The Iranian Revolution and Its Implications," *New Left Review*, No. 166 (November–December 1987), pp. 31 ff.

9. AFGHANISTAN

1. For an excellent background source on Afghanistan, see Louis Dupree, *Afghanistan* (Princeton: Princeton University Press, 1980).
2. For a discussion of Amin's rule just prior to the Soviet invasion, see Fred Halliday, "Afghanistan: A Revolution Consumes Itself," *The Nation*, November 17, 1979.
3. Joe Elder, Barbara Bowman, and Susan McCord, "Report of Quaker Visit to India, Pakistan and Afghanistan," AFSC Trip Report, May 20–June 8, 1980, pp. 10–11.
4. Rodney Tasker, "On the Frontiers of Fear," *Far Eastern Economic Review*, week of October 16–22, 1981, p. 42.
5. IISS, *Strategic Survey, 1987–88*, p. 139; cf. *SIPRI Yearbook*, 1987, pp. 311–12.
6. *SIPRI Yearbook*, 1987, p. 311.
7. See the fine interpretive article by Eqbal Ahmad and Richard J. Barnet, "Bloody Games," *The New Yorker*, April 11, 1988, pp. 44–86.
8. IISS, *Strategic Survey, 1985–86*, p. 135.
9. Ibid., p. 135, and Ahmad and Barnet, op. cit., p. 44.
10. Ahmad and Barnet, op. cit., p. 64.
11. *Strategic Survey, 1985–86*, p. 137.
12. President Carter's 1980 State of the Union address, in ibid., p. 164.
13. *Strategic Survey, 1985–86*, p. 138.
14. See Ahmad and Barnet, op. cit., p. 62.

15. See Alvin Z. Rubinstein, "The Soviet Withdrawal from Afghanistan," *Current History*, October 1988, p. 334.
16. Cf. Ahmad and Barnet, op. cit., p. 83.
17. See *Strategic Survey, 1987–88*, pp. 140–41.
18. Cf. ibid., p. 141; Ahmad and Barnet, op. cit., p. 86; Rubinstein, op. cit., p. 340.

10. THE SOVIET UNION

1. Two recent studies provide background: Rajan Menon, *Soviet Power and the Third World* (New Haven: Yale University Press, 1986); and Marshall D. Shulman (ed.), *East-West Tensions in the Third World* (New York: Norton, 1986).
2. Robert O. Freedman (ed.), *The Middle East After the Israeli Invasion of Lebanon* (Syracuse: Syracuse University Press, 1986), p. 4.
3. See Rashid Khalidi, "Arab Views of the Soviet Role in the Middle East," *Middle East Journal*, Vol. 39 (1985), p. 717.
4. Fred Halliday, *Soviet Policy in the Arc of Crisis* (Washington, D.C.: Institute for Policy Studies, 1981), Chap. 2, sec. 2.
5. Fred Halliday, "Gorbachev and the 'Arab Syndrome': Soviet Policy in the Middle East," *World Policy Journal*, Vol. 4 (1987), p. 418.
6. Cf. ibid., pp. 423–24.
7. Cf. ibid., pp. 428–29.
8. Cf. Galia Golan, "Gorbachev's Middle East Strategy," *Foreign Affairs*, Fall 1987, pp. 48–49.
9. Rashid Khalidi, *Soviet Middle East Policy in the Wake of Camp David*, Institute for Palestine Studies, Paper No. 3 (Beirut: IPS, 1979).
10. Evgeni Primakov, "Soviet Policy Toward the Arab-Israeli Conflict," in William B. Quandt (ed.), *The Middle East: Ten Years After Camp David* (Washington, D.C.: Brookings Institution, 1988), p. 388.
11. Golan, op. cit., p. 41.
12. Ibid., p. 43.
13. Ibid., p. 51.
14. Ibid., pp. 45–46.
15. Raphael Israeli (ed.), *PLO in Lebanon, Selected Documents* (London: Weidenfeld & Nicolson, 1983), Document No. 7, p. 46.
16. See also Khalidi, op. cit., pp. 723–26.
17. Halliday, *Soviet Policy*.

11. UNITED STATES POLICY

1. For the text of the Rogers Plan, see U.S. Congress, House of Representatives, Committee on Foreign Affairs, Subcommittee on Europe and the Middle East, *The Search for Peace in the Middle East: Documents and Statements 1967–1979*, 96th Congress, 1st session (Washington, D.C.: Government Printing Office, 1979), p. 296.

2. For a detailed discussion of Kissinger's shuttle diplomacy in the Middle East, see Nadav Safran, *Israel, the Embattled Ally* (Cambridge: Harvard University Press, 1978), pp. 506–60, 588–94.
3. See the detailed account provided by a member of the U.S. team: William B. Quandt, *Camp David, Peace Making and Politics* (Washington, D.C.: Brookings Institution, 1986).
4. Quoted in William B. Quandt, "U.S. Policy Toward the Arab-Israeli Conflict," in William B. Quandt (ed.), *The Middle East: Ten Years After Camp David*, (Washington, D.C.: Brookings Institution, 1988), p. 362.
5. For views of the early Reagan administration, see "U.S. Would Resist a Mideast Shift," *Washington Post*, March 19, 1981, p. 1.
6. "Text of Draft Resolution at UN on Israel's Raid on Iraqi Reactor," *New York Times*, June 19, 1981.
7. See the report prepared for the AFSC by Ronald J. Young, *Missed Opportunities for Peace, U.S. Middle East Policy 1981–1986* (Philadelphia: AFSC, 1987).
8. See the discussion in Chapter 6 above.
9. See Quandt, "U.S. Policy," pp. 371–72.
10. A recent comment can be found in a column, "The Issue That Won't Go Away," *Jerusalem Post*, International Edition, November 19, 1988, p. 7.
11. See letter reproduced in Quandt (ed.), *The Middle East*, pp. 488–89.
12. Cited in Quandt, "U.S. Policy," p. 377.
13. See Arthur Hertzberg, "The Illusion of Jewish Unity," *The New York Review of Books*, June 16, 1988, pp. 6–12.
14. See *A National Survey of American Voters: Attitudes Toward the Middle East*, prepared for the American Jewish Congress by Martilla and Kiley, April 1988, pp. 9–11.
15. See *Americans Talk Security*, a series of Surveys of American Voters' Attitudes Concerning National Security Issues, No. 8, September 1988.

Bibliography

ISRAEL

Arian, Asher, Ilan Talmud, and Tamar Hermann. *National Security and Public Opinion in Israel*. Tel Aviv: Jaffee Center for Strategic Studies, Study No. 9, 1988. *An examination of domestic politics and national security based on polling data.*

Avineri, Shlomo. *The Making of Modern Zionism: The Intellectual Origins of the Jewish State*. New York: Basic Books, 1981. *A thoughtful analysis of Zionism written by a former member of the Israeli Labor government.*

Avishai, Bernard. *The Tragedy of Zionism: Revolution and Democracy in the Land of Israel*. New York: Farrar, Straus & Giroux, 1985. *Zionism's history, transformations, and current implications.*

Benvenisti, Meron. *Conflicts and Contradictions*. New York: Villard Books, 1986. *Reflections on Israel and its current situation by a leading and controversial scholar.*

Flapan, Simha. *The Birth of Israel: Myths and Realities*. New York: Pantheon Books, 1987. *One of Israel's leading "doves" reexamined the history of the founding of the state and provided a revisionist critique in this book finished shortly before his death.*

Hareven, Alouph (ed.). *Every Sixth Israeli: Relations Between the Jewish Majority and the Arab Minority in Israel*. Jerusalem: Van Leer Foundation, 1983.

Harkabi, Yehoshafat. *Israel's Fateful Decisions*, trans. Lenn Schramm. London: Tauris & Co., 1988. *A former chief of Israeli military intelligence and expert on Arab policies provides a controversial and challenging examination of current Israeli policy.*

Lustick, Ian. *Arabs in the Jewish State: Israel's Control of a National Minority*.

Austin: University of Texas Press, 1980. *An important study of the situation of Israel's Arab minority by a professor at Dartmouth College.*

Lustick, Ian S. *For the Land and the Lord: Jewish Fundamentalism in Israel.* New York: Council on Foreign Relations, 1988. *A knowledgeable examination of religious nationalism and its role in Israeli policy.*

Morris, Benny. *The Birth of the Palestinian Refugee Problem, 1947–1949.* Cambridge: Cambridge University Press, 1987. *A detailed and fair-minded reexamination of the Israeli treatment of Palestinians as the state was formed.*

Oz, Amos. *In the Land of Israel,* trans. Maurie Goldberg-Bartura. New York: Harcourt Brace Jovanovich, 1983. *An evocation of Israeli life by one of Israel's most popular authors.*

Sachar, Howard M. *A History of Israel: From the Rise of Zionism to Our Time.* New York: Alfred A. Knopf, Vol. 1, 1979; Oxford University Press, Vol. 2, 1987. *A comprehensive text on the history of Israel.*

Safran, Nadav. *Israel, the Embattled Ally.* Cambridge: Belknap Press, Harvard University Press, 1981. *A penetrating analysis of the recent history of Israel, with a thorough examination of how domestic and international factors influence policy and action.*

Segev, Tom. *1949: The First Israelis.* New York: Free Press, 1986. *A controversial best-seller in Israel that challenged the official view of Israel's handling of the Palestinians in the first year of the new state.*

Shipler, David. *Arab and Jew: Wounded Spirits in a Promised Land.* New York: Times Books, 1986. *A veteran New York Times correspondent takes a deep look at the people behind the headlines of conflict.*

Shlaim, Avi. *Collusion Across the Jordan: King Abdullah, the Zionist Movement, and the Partition of Palestine.* New York: Columbia University Press, 1988. *Reexamination by a leading Oxford scholar of the founding of Israel, its first years, and the arrangements made for partition with King Abdullah.*

PALESTINE

Al-Haq/Law in the Service of Man. *Punishing a Nation: Human Rights Violations During the Palestinian Uprising, December 1987–December 1988.* Ramallah, West Bank: Al-Haq, 1988. *Detailed chronicle by a Palestinian human rights organization of the first year of the intifadah.*

Aronson, Geoffrey. *Creating Facts: Israel, Palestinians and the West Bank.* Washington, D.C.: Institute for Palestine Studies, 1987. *A critical analysis of Israel's West Bank policies and their implications for the Palestinian communities.*

Aruri, Naseer (ed.). *Occupation: Israel Over Palestine.* Belmont, Mass.: Association of Arab-American University Graduates, 1983. *A collection of original studies of Palestinian life under occupation.*

Brand, Laurie A. *Palestinians in the Arab World, Institution Building and the Search for a State.* New York: Columbia University Press, 1988. *The most up-to-date social and political account of Palestinians in the diaspora.*

Cobban, Helena. *The Palestinian Liberation Organisation: People, Power and Pol-*

itics. Cambridge: Cambridge University Press, 1984. *A detailed, historical examination of the PLO.*

Gersh, Alain. *The PLO: The Struggle Within, Towards an Independent Palestinian State*, trans. A. M. Berrett. Rev. ed.; London: Zed Books, 1988. *A history of the PLO and its emerging political thought.*

Grossman, David. *The Yellow Wind*, trans. Haim Watzman. New York: Farrar, Straus & Giroux, 1988. *An Israeli journalist's personal encounter with the Palestinian people, their homes, and their thoughts in the occupied West Bank.*

Hart, Alan. *Arafat: Terrorist or Peacemaker?* London: Sidgwick and Jackson, 1984. *A detailed but authorized biography produced with the help of Arafat and the PLO leadership.*

Heller, Mark A. *A Palestinian State: The Implications for Israel.* Cambridge: Harvard University Press, 1983. *An Israeli analyst's examination of the political, social, and security implications of Palestinian independence.*

Kiernan, Thomas. *Arafat: The Man and the Myth.* New York: Norton, 1976. *An early, somewhat critical portrait of the Palestinian leader.*

Migdal, Joel S. (ed.). *Palestinian Society and Politics.* Princeton: Princeton University Press, 1980.

Peretz, Don. *The West Bank: History, Politics, Society and Economy.* Boulder, Colo.: Westview, 1986. *A reliable and valuable background text.*

Quandt, William B., Fuad Jabber, and Ann Mosely Lesch. *The Politics of Palestinian Nationalism.* Berkeley: University of California Press, 1973. *Perhaps the seminal work on the subject, this text serves as a useful introduction to the development of the Palestinian national movement from 1947 to 1970.*

Sahliyeh, Emile. *In Search of Leadership: West Bank Politics Since 1967.* Washington, D.C.: Brookings Institution, 1988. *A knowledgeable examination of the internal politics of West Bank Palestinians.*

Sahliyeh, Emile. *The PLO After the Lebanon War.* Boulder, Colo.: Westview Press, 1986. *A political analysis of the PLO controversies, reconciliations, politics, 1982–86.*

Said, Edward. *The Question of Palestine.* New York: The New York Times Book Co., 1979. *A sequel volume to Said's* Orientalism, *this book examines how the West has consistently misunderstood the Arab–Israeli conflict. Illuminating analysis by a leading Palestinian intellectual, a professor at Columbia University.*

Shehadeh, Raja. *Occupier's Law: Israel and the West Bank.* Rev. ed.; Washington, D.C.: Institute for Palestine Studies, 1988. *Detailed examination of legal issues in the occupation. Prepared for Al-Haq/Law in the Service of Man, the West Bank affiliate of the International Commission of Jurists.*

Shehadeh, Raja. *The Third Way: A Journal of Life in the West Bank.* London and New York: Quartet Books, 1982. *A leading Palestinian lawyer and intellectual provides a personal response to life under occupation.*

WEST BANK DATA PROJECT

The West Bank and Gaza Atlas, 1988. Meron Benvenisti and Shlomo Khayat.
The West Bank Handbook, A Political Lexicon, 1986. Meron Benvenisti with Ziad Abn-Zayed and Danny Rubinstein.
1987 Report, Demographic, Economic, Legal, Social and Political Developments in the West Bank. Meron Benvenisti.
The Gaza Strip: A Demographic, Economic, Social and Legal Survey, 1986. Sara Roy.
Agriculture and Water Resources in the West Bank and Gaza (1967–1987). David Kahan.
How Expensive Are West Bank Settlements? 1987. Aaron Dehter.

A monograph series prepared under the direction of Meron Benvenisti. Accurate and reliable facts and assessments.

LEBANON

Barakat, Halim (ed.). *Towards a Viable Lebanon.* London: Croom Helm, and Washington, D.C.: Center for Contemporary Arab Studies, Georgetown University, 1988. *A valuable collection of studies of aspects of current Lebanese problems.*
Khalaf, Samir. *Lebanon's Predicament.* New York: Columbia University Press, 1987. *An in-depth analysis of Lebanese society as a background to current struggles.*
Khalidi, Walid. *Conflict and Violence in Lebanon: Confrontation in the Middle East.* Cambridge: Harvard Center for International Affairs, 1979.
Norton, Augustus Richard. *Amal and the Shi'a: Struggle for the Soul of Lebanon.* Austin: University of Texas Press, 1987. *Shia Islam's influence in the recent history of Lebanon.*
Petran, Tabitha. *The Struggle Over Lebanon.* New York: Monthly Review Press, 1987. *A detailed political history and analysis of the crises of modern Lebanon.*
Rabinovich, Itamar. *The War for Lebanon, 1970–1985.* Rev. ed.; Ithaca: Cornell University Press, 1985. *An Israeli scholar's critical history of the Lebanese wars.*
Schiff, Ze'ev, and Ehud Ya'ari. *Israel's Lebanon War*, trans. and ed. Ira Friedman. New York: Simon & Schuster, 1984. *The "inside" account by two veteran Israeli journalists.*

IRAN

Arjomand, Said Amir. *The Turban for the Crown: The Islamic Revolution in Iran.* New York: Oxford University Press, 1988.
Cottam, Richard W. *Iran and the United States: A Cold War Case Study.* Pittsburgh: University of Pittsburgh Press, 1988. *An up-to-date assessment of what went wrong and why.*

Cottam, Richard W. *Nationalism in Iran.* Pittsburgh: University of Pittsburgh Press, 1979. *An early study of the workings of Iranian politics prior to the revolution by one of the leading American scholars on Iran.*

Fischer, Michael M. J. *Iran: From Religious Dispute to Revolution.* Cambridge: Harvard University Press, 1980. *A sociologist's perspective on factors contributing to the Iranian revolution.*

Halliday, Fred. *Iran: Dictatorship and Development.* Middlesex, Eng.: Penguin Books, 1979.

Keddie Nikki, and Eric Hooglund (eds.). *The Iranian Revolution and the Islamic Republic.* Rev. ed.; Syracuse: Syracuse University Press, 1986. *Papers by critical, knowledgeable experts.*

Keddie, Nikki (ed.). *Religion and Politics in Iran: Shi'ism from Quietism to Revolution.* New Haven: Yale University Press, 1983.

Keddie, Nikki R. *Roots of Revolution: An Interpretive History of Modern Iran.* New Haven: Yale University Press, 1981. *A penetrating study of the Iranian revolution and what contributed to it.*

Milani, Mohsen M. *The Making of Iran's Islamic Revolution: From Monarchy to Islamic Republic.* Boulder, Colo.: Westview Press, 1988.

Ramazani, R. K. *Revolutionary Iran: Challenge and Response in the Middle East.* Rev. ed.; Baltimore: Johns Hopkins University Press, 1988. *Implications of the Iranian revolution for the Middle East region.*

Sick, Gary. *All Fall Down: America's Tragic Encounter with Iran.* New York: Viking Penguin, 1985, 1986. *An insider's penetrating analysis by a former staff member of the White House National Security Council.*

AFGHANISTAN

Bradshaw, Henry S. *Afghanistan and the Soviet Union.* Durham, N.C.: Duke University Press, 1983.

Dupree, Louis. *Afghanistan.* Princeton: Princeton University Press, 1980. *A comprehensive resource on Afghanistan, its people, history, and culture. The final section examines the Soviet invasion in December 1979.*

Newell, Nancy Peabody, and Richard S. Newell. *The Struggle for Afghanistan.* Ithaca: Cornell University Press, 1981. *The first years of the Afghani revolution and Soviet invasion.*

U.S. MIDDLE EAST POLICY

Feldman, Shai. *U.S. Middle East Policy: The Domestic Setting.* Tel Aviv: Jaffee Center for Strategic Studies, 1988.

Quandt, William B. *Decade of Decisions: American Policy Toward the Arab-Israeli Conflict 1967–1976.* Berkeley: University of California Press, 1977. *A study of U.S. Middle East policy as it developed in the decade after the Six Day War by a former National Security Council expert on the Middle East.*

Rubenberg, Cheryl A. *Israel and the American National Interest: A Critical Examination.* Urbana: University of Illinois Press, 1986.

Spiegel, Steven L. *The Other Arab-Israeli Conflict: Making America's Middle East Policy from Truman to Reagan.* Chicago: University of Chicago Press, 1985.
Tillman, Seth P. *The United States in the Middle East: Interests and Obstacles.* Bloomington: Indiana University Press, 1982.
Young, Ronald J. *Missed Opportunities for Peace: U.S. Middle East Policy 1981–1986.* Philadelphia: American Friends Service Committee, 1987.
Zureik, Elia, and Fouad Monghrabi (eds.). *Public Opinion and the Palestine Question.* New York: St. Martin's Press, 1987. *Detailed look at American public opinion on Middle East issues.*

SOVIET POLICY IN THE MIDDLE EAST

Halliday, Fred. *Soviet Policy in the Arc of Crisis.* Washington, D.C.: Institute for Policy Studies, 1981.
Klinghoffer, Arthur Jay, with Judith Apter. *Israel and the Soviet Union: Alienation or Reconciliation?* Boulder, Colo.: Westview Press, 1985.
Leitenberg, Milton, and Gabriel Sheffer (eds.). *Great Power Intervention in the Middle East.* New York: Pergamon Press, 1979. *A good selection of essays on superpower involvement in the Middle East.*
Spiegel, Steven L., Mark A. Heller, and Jacob Goldberg (eds.). *The Soviet-American Competition in the Middle East.* Lexington, Mass.: D. C. Heath, 1988. *A joint effort of Israeli and American scholars and analysts.*

ISLAM AND POLITICS

Esposito, John L. *Islam and Politics.* Syracuse: Syracuse University Press, 1984. *Islamic politics in the modern Middle East.*
Hunter, Shireen T. (ed.). *The Politics of Islamic Revivalism: Diversity and Unity.* Bloomington: Indiana University Press, 1988. *A country-by-country assessment of Islam as a factor in national life.*
Mortimer, Edward. *Faith and Power: The Politics of Islam.* New York: Vintage Books, 1982. *A well-written journalist's account.*
Said, Edward. *Covering Islam: How the Media and the Experts Determine How We See the Rest of the World.* New York: Pantheon Books, 1981. *A vigorous critique of press handling of Islam and related issues.*
Stowasser, Barbara Freyer (ed.). *The Islamic Impulse.* London: Croom Helm, and Washington, D.C.: Center for Contemporary Arab Studies, 1987. *A useful collection of studies examining the Islamic influence in various sectors of Middle East society.*
Taylor, Alan R. *The Islamic Question in Middle East Politics.* Boulder, Colo.: Westview Press, 1988. *The interaction between secular nationalism and militant Islam in the Middle East.*
Wright, Robin. *Sacred Rage: The Crusade of Modern Islam.* New York: Simon & Schuster, 1985. *A journalist's assessment of the contemporary role of Islam.*

GENERAL

Day, Arthur R. *East Bank/West Bank: Jordan and the Prospects for Peace.* New York: Council on Foreign Relations, 1986.

Lukacs, Yehuda, and Abdulla M. Battah (eds.). *The Arab-Israeli Conflict: Two Decades of Change.* Boulder, Colo.: Westview Press, 1988.

Polk, William R. *The Arab World.* Cambridge: Harvard University Press, 1980.

Quandt, William B. (ed.). *The Middle East: Ten Years After Camp David.* Washington, D.C.: Brookings Institution, 1988. *A valuable collection of essays representing diverse perspectives, regional and great-power.*

Appendixes

I. General Assembly Resolution 181 (II) Concerning the Future Government of Palestine, November 29, 1947 (Excerpts)

PLAN OF PARTITION WITH ECONOMIC UNION

Part I
Future Constitution and Government of Palestine

A. Termination of Mandate, Partition and Independence

1. The Mandate for Palestine shall terminate as soon as possible, but in any case not later than 1 August 1948.

2. The armed forces of the mandatory Power shall be progressively withdrawn from Palestine, the withdrawal to be completed as soon as possible, but in any case not later than 1 August 1948.

The mandatory Power shall advise the Commission, as far in advance as possible, of its intention to terminate the Mandate and to evacuate each area.

The mandatory Power shall use its best endeavours to ensure that an area situated in the territory of the Jewish State, including a seaport and hinterland adequate to provide facilities for a substantial immigration, shall be evacuated at the earliest possible date and in any event not later than 1 February 1948.

3. Independent Arab and Jewish States and the Special International Regime for the City of Jerusalem, set forth in part III of this plan, shall come into existence in Palestine two months after the evacuation of the armed forces of the mandatory Power has been completed, but in any case not later than 1 October 1948. The boundaries of the Arab State, the Jewish State, and the City of Jerusalem shall be as described in parts II and III below.

4. The period between the adoption by the General Assembly of its recommendation on the question of Palestine and the establishment of the independence of the Arab and Jewish States shall be a transitional period.

B. Steps Preparatory to Independence

1. A Commission shall be set up consisting of one representative of each of five Member States. The Members represented on the Commission shall be elected by the General Assembly on as broad a basis, geographically and otherwise, as possible.

2. The administration of Palestine shall, as the mandatory Power withdraws its armed forces, be progressively turned over to the Commission; which shall act in conformity with the recommendations of the General Assembly, under the guidance of the Security Council. The mandatory Power shall to the fullest possible extent coordinate its plans for withdrawal with the plans of the Commission to take over and administer areas which have been evacuated.

In the discharge of this administrative responsibility the Commission shall have authority to issue necessary regulations and take other measures as required.

The mandatory Power shall not take any action to prevent, obstruct or delay the implementation by the Commission of the measures recommended by the General Assembly.

3. On its arrival in Palestine the Commission shall proceed to carry out measures for the establishment of the frontiers of the Arab and Jewish States and the City of Jerusalem in accordance with the general lines of the recommendations of the General Assembly on the partition of Palestine. Nevertheless, the boundaries as described in part II of this plan are to be modified in such a way that village areas as a rule will not be divided by state boundaries unless pressing reasons make that necessary.

4. The Commission, after consultation with the democratic parties and other public organizations of the Arab and Jewish States, shall select and establish in each State as rapidly as possible a Provisional Council of Government. The activities of both the Arab and Jewish Provisional Councils of Government shall be carried out under the general direction of the Commission.

If by 1 April 1948 a Provisional Council of Government cannot be selected for either of the States, or, if selected, cannot carry out its functions, the Commission shall communicate that fact to the Security Council for such action with respect to that State as the Security Council may deem proper, and to the Secretary-General for communication to the Members of the United Nations.

5. Subject to the provisions of these recommendations, during the transitional period the Provisional Councils of Government, acting under the Commission, shall have full authority in the areas under their control, including authority over matters of immigration and land regulation.

6. The Provisional Council of Government of each State, acting under the Commission, shall progressively receive from the Commission full responsibility for the administration of that State in the period between the termination of the Mandate and the establishment of the State's independence.

7. The Commission shall instruct the Provisional Councils of Government of both the Arab and Jewish States, after their formation, to proceed to the establishment of administrative organs of government, central and local.

8. The Provisional Council of Government of each State shall, within the shortest time possible, recruit an armed militia from the residents of that State, sufficient in number to maintain internal order and to prevent frontier clashes.

This armed militia in each State shall, for operational purposes, be under the command of Jewish or Arab officers resident in that State, but general political and military control, including the choice of the militia's High Command, shall be exercised by the Commission.

9. The Provisional Council of Government of each State shall, not later than two months after the withdrawal of the armed forces of the mandatory Power, hold elections to the Constituent Assembly which shall be conducted on democratic lines.

The election regulations in each State shall be drawn up by the Provisional Council of Government and approved by the Commission. Qualified voters for each State for this election shall be persons over eighteen years of age who are: (a) Palestinian citizens residing in that State and (b) Arabs and Jews residing in the State, although not Palestinian citizens, who, before voting, have signed a notice of intention to become citizens of such State.

Arabs and Jews residing in the City of Jerusalem who have signed a notice of intention to become citizens, the Arabs of the Arab State and the Jews of the Jewish State, shall be entitled to vote in the Arab and Jewish States respectively.

Women may vote and be elected to the Constituent Assemblies.

During the transitional period no Jew shall be permitted to establish residence in the area of the proposed Arab State, and no Arab shall be permitted to establish residence in the area of the proposed Jewish State, except by special leave of the Commission.

10. The Constituent Assembly of each State shall draft a democratic constitution for its State and choose a provisional government to succeed the Provisional Council of Government appointed by the Commission. The constitutions of the States shall embody chapters 1 and 2 of the Declaration provided for in section C below and include *inter alia* provisions for:

(a) Establishing in each State a legislative body elected by universal suffrage and by secret ballot on the basis of proportional representation, and an executive body responsible to the legislature;

(b) Settling all international disputes in which the State may be involved by peaceful means in such a manner that international peace and security, and justice, are not endangered;

(c) Accepting the obligation of the State to refrain in its international relations from the threat or use of force against the territorial integrity or political independence of any State, or in any other manner inconsistent with the purposes of the United Nations;

(d) Guaranteeing to all persons equal and non-discriminatory rights in civil, political, economic and religious matters and the enjoyment of human rights and fundamental freedoms, including freedom of religion, language, speech and publication, education, assembly and association;

(e) Preserving freedom of transit and visit for all residents and citizens of the other State in Palestine and the City of Jerusalem, subject to considerations of national security, provided that each State shall control residence within its borders.

11. The Commission shall appoint a preparatory economic commission of three members to make whatever arrangements are possible for economic cooperation, with a view to establishing, as soon as practicable, the Economic Union and the Joint Economic Board, as provided in section D below.

12. During the period between the adoption of the recommendations on the question of Palestine by the General Assembly and the termination of the Mandate, the mandatory Power in Palestine shall maintain full responsibility for administration in areas from which it has not withdrawn its armed forces. The Commission shall assist the mandatory Power in the carrying out of these functions. Similarly the mandatory Power shall cooperate with the Commission in the execution of its functions.

13. With a view to ensuring that there shall be continuity in the functioning of administrative services and that, on the withdrawal of the armed forces of the mandatory Power, the whole administration shall be in the charge of the Provisional Councils and the Joint Economic Board, respectively, acting under the Commission, there shall be a progressive transfer, from the mandatory Power to the Commission, of responsibility for all the functions of government, including that of maintaining law and order in the areas from which the forces of the mandatory Power have been withdrawn.

14. The Commission shall be guided in its activities by the recommen-

dations of the General Assembly and by such instructions as the Security Council may consider necessary to issue.

The measures taken by the Commission, within the recommendations of the General Assembly, shall become immediately effective unless the Commission has previously received contrary instructions from the Security Council.

The Commission shall render periodic monthly progress reports, or more frequently if desirable, to the Security Council simultaneously.

II. Security Council Resolution 242
Concerning Principles for a Just and Lasting Peace in the Middle East, November 22, 1967

The Security Council

Expressing its continuing concern with the grave situation in the Middle East.

Emphasizing the inadmissibility of the acquisition of territory by war and the need to work for a just and lasting peace in which every State in the area can live in security.

Emphasizing further that all Member States in their acceptance of the Charter of the United Nations have undertaken a commitment to act in accordance with Article 2 of the Charter.

1. Affirms that the fulfilment of Charter principles requires the establishment of a just and lasting peace in the Middle East which should include the application of both the following principles:

(i) Withdrawal of Israel armed forces from territories occupied in the recent conflict;

(ii) Termination of all claims or states of belligerency and respect for and acknowledgement of the sovereignty, territorial integrity and political independence of every State in the area and their right to live in peace within secure and recognized boundaries free from threats or acts of force;

2. Affirms further the necessity

(a) For guaranteeing freedom of navigation through international waterways in the area;

(b) For achieving a just settlement of the refugee problem;

(c) For guaranteeing the territorial inviolability and political independence of every State in the area, through measures including the establishment of demilitarized zones;

3. Requests the Secretary-General to designate a Special Representative to proceed to the Middle East to establish and maintain contacts with the States concerned in order to promote agreement and assist efforts to

achieve a peaceful and accepted settlement in accordance with the provisions and principles in this resolution;

4. Requests the Secretary-General to report to the Security Council on the progress of the efforts of the Special Representative as soon as possible.

III. Security Council Resolution 338 Concerning the October War, October 22, 1973

The Security Council

1. Calls upon all parties to the present fighting to cease all firing and terminate all military activity immediately, no later than 12 hours after the moment of the adoption of this decision, in the positions they now occupy;

2. Calls upon the parties concerned to start immediately after the cease-fire the implementation of Security Council Resolution 242 (1976) in all of its parts;

3. Decides that, immediately and concurrently with the cease-fire, negotiations start between the parties concerned under appropriate auspices aimed at establishing a just and durable peace in the Middle East.

IV. A Framework for Peace in the Middle East Agreed at Camp David* September 17, 1978

Muhammad Anwar al-Sadat, President of the Arab Republic of Egypt, and Menachem Begin, Prime Minister of Israel, met with Jimmy Carter, President of the United States of America, at Camp David from September 5 to September 17, 1978, and have agreed on the following framework for peace in the Middle East. They invite other parties to the Arab-Israeli conflict to adhere to it.

Preamble

The search for peace in the Middle East must be guided by the following:
    The agreed basis for a peaceful settlement of the conflict between Israel

---

* Accompanying letters may be found in *The Camp David Summit, September 1978*, Department of State Publication 8954, Near East and South Asian Series 88 (Washington, D.C.: Government Printing Office, 1978).

and its neighbors is United Nations Security Council Resolution 242, in all its parts.

After four wars during thirty years, despite intensive human efforts, the Middle East, which is the cradle of civilization and the birthplace of three great religions, does not yet enjoy the blessings of peace. The people of the Middle East yearn for peace so that the vast human and natural resources of the region can be turned to the pursuits of peace and so that this area can become a model for coexistence and cooperation among nations.

The historic initiative of President Sadat in visiting Jerusalem and the reception accorded to him by the Parliament, government and people of Israel, and the reciprocal visit of Prime Minister Begin to Ismailia, the peace proposals made by both leaders, as well as the warm reception of these missions by the peoples of both countries, have created an unprecedented opportunity for peace which must not be lost if this generation and future generations are to be spared the tragedies of war.

The provisions of the Charter of the United Nations and the other accepted norms of international law and legitimacy now provide accepted standards for the conduct of relations among all states.

To achieve a relationship of peace, in the spirit of Article 2 of the United Nations Charter, future negotiations between Israel and any neighbor prepared to negotiate peace and security with it, are necessary for the purpose of carrying out all the provisions and principles of Resolutions 242 and 338.

Peace requires respect for the sovereignty, territorial integrity and political independence of every state in the area and their right to live in peace within secure and recognized boundaries free from threats or acts of force. Progress toward that goal can accelerate movement toward a new era of reconciliation in the Middle East marked by cooperation in promoting economic development, in maintaining stability, and in assuring security.

Security is enhanced by a relationship of peace and by cooperation between nations which enjoy normal relations. In addition, under the terms of peace treaties, the parties can, on the basis of reciprocity, agree to special security arrangements such as demilitarized zones, limited armaments areas, early warning stations, the presence of international forces, liaison, agreed measures for monitoring, and other arrangements that they agree are useful.

Framework

Taking these factors into account, the parties are determined to reach a just, comprehensive, and durable settlement of the Middle East conflict through the conclusion of peace treaties based on Security Council Resolutions 242 and 338 in all their parts. Their purpose is to achieve peace and good neighborly relations. They recognize that, for peace to endure, it must involve all those who have been most deeply affected by the conflict. They therefore agree that this framework as appropriate is intended by them to constitute a basis for peace not only between Egypt and Israel, but also between Israel and each of its other neighbors which is prepared to negotiate peace with Israel on this basis. With that objective in mind, they have agreed to proceed as follows:

A. WEST BANK AND GAZA

1. Egypt, Israel, Jordan, and the representatives of the Palestinian people should participate in negotiations on the resolution of the Palestinian problem in all its aspects. To achieve that objective, negotiations relating to the West Bank and Gaza should proceed in three stages:

(a) Egypt and Israel agree that, in order to ensure a peaceful and orderly transfer of authority, and taking into account the security concerns of all the parties, there should be transitional arrangements for the West Bank and Gaza for a period not exceeding five years. In order to provide full autonomy to the inhabitants, under these arrangements the Israeli military government and its civilian administration will be withdrawn as soon as a self-governing authority has been freely elected by the inhabitants of these areas to replace the existing military government. To negotiate the details of a transitional arrangement, the Government of Jordan will be invited to join the negotiations on the basis of this framework. These new arrangements should give due consideration both to the principle of self-government by the inhabitants of these territories and to the legitimate security concerns of the parties involved.

(b) Egypt, Israel, and Jordan will agree on the modalities for establishing the elected self-governing authority in the West Bank and Gaza. The delegations of Egypt and Jordan may include Palestinians from the West Bank and Gaza or other Palestinians as mutually agreed. The parties will negotiate an agreement which will define the powers and responsibilities of the self-governing authority to be exercised in the West Bank and Gaza. A withdrawal of Israeli armed forces will take place and there will be a redeployment of the remaining Israeli forces into specified security locations. The agreement will also include arrangements for assuring internal and external security and public order. A strong local police force will be established, which may include Jordanian citizens. In addition, Israeli and Jordanian forces will participate in joint patrols and in the manning of control posts to assure the security of the borders.

(c) When the self-governing authority (administrative council) in the West Bank and Gaza is established and inaugurated, the transitional period of five years will begin. As soon as possible, but not later than the third year after the beginning of the transitional period, negotiations will take place to determine the final status of the West Bank and Gaza and its relationship with its neighbors, and to conclude a peace treaty between Israel and Jordan by the end of the transitional period. These negotiations will be conducted among Egypt, Israel, Jordan, and the elected representatives of the inhabitants of the West Bank and Gaza. Two separate but related committees will be convened, one committee, consisting of representatives of the four parties which will negotiate and agree on the final status of the West Bank and Gaza, and its relationship with its neighbors, and the second committee, consisting of representatives of the inhabitants of the West Bank and Gaza, to negotiate the peace treaty between Israel and Jordan, taking into account the agreement reached on the final status of the West Bank and Gaza. The negotiations shall be based on all the provisions and principles of UN Security Council Resolution 242. The negotiations will resolve, among other matters, the location of the boundaries and the nature of the security arrangements. The solution from the negotiations must also recognize the legitimate rights of the Palestinian people and their just requirements. In this way, the Palestinians will participate in the determination of their own future through:

1) The negotiations among Egypt, Israel, Jordan and the representatives of the inhabitants of the West Bank and Gaza to agree on the final status of the West Bank and Gaza and other outstanding issues by the end of the transitional period.

2) Submitting their agreement to a vote by the elected representatives of the inhabitants of the West Bank and Gaza.

3) Providing for the elected representatives of the inhabitants of the West Bank and Gaza to decide how they shall govern themselves consistent with the provisions of their agreement.

4) Participating as stated above in the work of the committee negotiating the peace treaty between Israel and Jordan.

2. All necessary measures will be taken and provisions made to assure the security of Israel and its neighbors during the transitional period and beyond. To assist in providing such security, a strong local police force will be constituted by the self-governing authority. It will be composed of inhabitants of the West Bank and Gaza. The police will maintain continuing liaison on internal security matters with the designated Israeli, Jordanian, and Egyptian officers.

3. During the transitional period, representatives of Egypt, Israel, Jordan, and the self-governing authority will constitute a continuing committee to decide by agreement on the modalities of admission of persons displaced from the West Bank and Gaza in 1967, together with necessary measures to prevent disruption and disorder. Other matters of common concern may also be dealt with by this committee.

4. Egypt and Israel will work with each other and with other interested parties to establish agreed procedures for a prompt, just and permanent implementation of the resolution of the refugee problem.

B. Egypt-Israel

1. Egypt and Israel undertake not to resort to the threat or the use of force to settle disputes. Any disputes shall be settled by peaceful means in accordance with the provisions of Article 33 of the Charter of the United Nations.

2. In order to achieve peace between them, the parties agree to negotiate in good faith with a goal of concluding within three months from the signing of this Framework a peace treaty between them, while inviting the other parties to the conflict to proceed simultaneously to negotiate and conclude similar peace treaties with a view to achieving a comprehensive peace in the area. The Framework for the Conclusion of a Peace Treaty between Egypt and Israel will govern the peace negotiations between them. The parties will agree on the modalities and the timetable for the implementation of their obligations under the treaty.

C. Associated Principles

1. Egypt and Israel state that the principles and provisions described below should apply to peace treaties between Israel and each of its neighbors—Egypt, Jordan, Syria, and Lebanon.

2. Signatories shall establish among themselves relationships normal to states at peace with one another. To this end, they should undertake to abide by all the provisions of the Charter of the United Nations. Steps to be taken in this respect include:

    (a) full recognition;

    (b) abolishing economic boycotts;

    (c) guaranteeing that under their jurisdiction the citizens of the other parties shall enjoy the protection of the due process of law.

3. Signatories should explore possibilities for economic development in the context of final peace treaties, with the objective of contributing to the atmosphere of peace, cooperation and friendship which is their common goal.

4. Claims Commissions may be established for the mutual settlement of all financial claims.

5. The United States shall be invited to participate in the talks on matters related to the modalities of the implementation of the agreements and working out the timetable for the carrying out of the obligations of the parties.

6. The United Nations Security Council shall be requested to endorse the peace treaties and ensure that their provisions shall not be violated. The permanent members of the Security Council shall be requested to underwrite the peace treaties and ensure respect for their provisions. They shall also be requested to conform their policies and actions with the undertakings contained in this Framework.

FRAMEWORK FOR THE CONCLUSION OF A
PEACE TREATY BETWEEN EGYPT AND ISRAEL

In order to achieve peace between them, Israel and Egypt agree to negotiate in good faith with a goal of concluding within three months of the signing of this framework a peace treaty between them.

It is agreed that:

The site of the negotiations will be under a United Nations flag at a location or locations to be mutually agreed.

All of the principles of U.N. Resolution 242 will apply in this resolution of the dispute between Israel and Egypt.

Unless otherwise mutually agreed, terms of the peace treaty will be implemented between two and three years after the peace treaty is signed.

The following matters are agreed between the parties:

(a) the full exercise of Egyptian sovereignty up to the internationally recognized border between Egypt and mandated Palestine;

(b) the withdrawal of Israeli armed forces from the Sinai;

(c) the use of airfields left by the Israelis near El Arish, Rafah, Ras en Naqb, and Sharm el Sheikh for civilian purposes only, including possible commercial use by all nations;

(d) the right of free passage by ships of Israel through the Gulf of Suez and the Suez Canal on the basis of the Constantinople Convention of 1888 applying to all nations; the Strait of Tiran and the Gulf of Aqaba are international waterways to be open to all nations for unimpeded and nonsuspendable freedom of navigation and overflight;

(e) the construction of a highway between the Sinai and Jordan near Elat with guaranteed free and peaceful passage by Egypt and Jordan; and

(f) the stationing of military forces listed below.

Stationing of Forces

A. No more than one division (mechanized or infantry) of Egyptian armed forces will be stationed within an area lying approximately 50 kilometers (km) east of the Gulf of Suez and the Suez Canal.

B. Only United Nations forces and civil police equipped with light weapons to perform normal police functions will be stationed within an area lying west of the international border and the Gulf of Aqaba, varying in width from 20 km to 40 km.

C. In the area within 3 km of the international border there will be Israeli limited military forces not to exceed four infantry battalions and United Nations observers.

D. Border patrol units, not to exceed three battalions, will supplement the civil police in maintaining order in the area not included above.

The exact demarcation of the above areas will be as decided during the peace negotiations.

Early warning stations may exist to insure compliance with the terms of the agreement.

United Nations forces will be stationed: (a) in part of the area in the Sinai lying within about 20 km of the Mediterranean Sea and adjacent to the international border, and (b) in the Sharm el Sheikh area to ensure freedom of passage through the Strait of Tiran; and these forces will not be removed unless such removal is approved by the Security Council of the United Nations with a unanimous vote of the five permanent members.

After a peace treaty is signed, and after the interim withdrawal is complete, normal relations will be established between Egypt and Israel, including: full recognition, including diplomatic, economic and cultural relations; termination of economic boycotts and barriers to the free movement of goods and people; and mutual protection of citizens by the due process of law.

Interim Withdrawal

Between the three months and nine months after the signing of the peace treaty, all Israeli forces will withdraw east of a line extending from a point east of El Arish to Ras Muhammad, the exact location of this time to be determined by mutual agreement.

V. The Egyptian-Israeli Peace Treaty

TREATY OF PEACE BETWEEN THE ARAB REPUBLIC OF EGPYT AND THE STATE OF ISRAEL* MARCH 26, 1979

The Government of the Arab Republic of Egypt and the Government of the State of Israel:

Preamble

Convinced of the urgent necessity of the establishment of a just, comprehensive and lasting peace in the Middle East in accordance with Security Council Resolutions 242 and 338;

* The additional Treaty Protocols may be found in *The Egyptian-Israeli Peace Treaty, March 26, 1979*, Department of State Publication 8976, Near Eastern and South Asian Series 91, Selected Documents no. 11 (Washington, D.C.: Government Printing Office, 1979).

Reaffirming their adherence to the "Framework for Peace in the Middle East Agreed at Camp David," dated September 17, 1978;

Noting that the aforementioned Framework as appropriate is intended to constitute a basis for peace not only between Egypt and Israel but also between Israel and each of its other Arab neighbors which is prepared to negotiate peace with it on this basis;

Desiring to bring to an end the state of war between them and to establish a peace in which every state in the area can live in security;

Convinced that the conclusion of a Treaty of Peace between Egypt and Israel is an important step in the search for comprehensive peace in the area and for the attainment of the settlement of the Arab-Israeli conflict in all its aspects;

Inviting the other Arab parties to this dispute to join the peace process with Israel guided by and based on the principles of the aforementioned Framework;

Desiring as well to develop friendly relations and cooperation between themselves in accordance with the United Nations Charter and the principles of international law governing international relations in times of peace;

Agree to the following provisions in the free exercise of their sovereignty, in order to implement the "Framework for the Conclusion of a Peace Treaty Between Egypt and Israel":

Article I

1. The state of war between the Parties will be terminated and peace will be established between them upon the exchange of instruments of ratification of this Treaty.

2. Israel will withdraw all its armed forces and civilians from the Sinai behind the international boundary between Egypt and mandated Palestine, as provided in the annexed protocol (Annex I), and Egypt will resume the exercise of its full sovereignty over the Sinai.

3. Upon completion of the interim withdrawal provided for in Annex I, the Parties will establish normal and friendly relations, in accordance with Article III (3).

Article II

The permanent boundary between Egypt and Israel is the recognized international boundary between Egypt and the former mandated territory of Palestine, as shown on the map at Annex II, without prejudice to the issue of the status of the Gaza Strip. The Parties recognize this boundary as inviolable. Each will respect the territorial integrity of the other, including their territorial waters and airspace.

Article III

1. The Parties will apply between them the provisions of the Charter of the United Nations and the principles of international law governing relations among states in times of peace. In particular:

a. They recognize and will respect each other's sovereignty, territorial integrity and political independence;

b. They recognize and will respect each other's right to live in peace within their secure and recognized boundaries;

c. They will refrain from the threat or use of force, directly or indirectly, against each other and will settle all disputes between them by peaceful means.

2. Each Party undertakes to ensure that acts or threats of belligerency, hostility, or violence do not originate from and are not committed from within its territory, or by any forces subject to its control or by any other forces stationed on its territory, against the population, citizens or property of the other Party. Each Party also undertakes to refrain from organizing, instigating, inciting, assisting or participating in acts or threats of belligerency, hostility, subversion or violence against the other Party, anywhere, and undertakes to ensure that perpetrators of such acts are brought to justice.

3. The Parties agree that the normal relationship established between them will include full recognition, diplomatic, economic and cultural relations, termination of economic boycotts and discriminatory barriers to the free movement of people and goods, and will guarantee the mutual enjoyment by citizens of the due process of law. The process by which they undertake to achieve such a relationship parallel to the implementation of other provisions of this Treaty is set out in the annexed protocol (Annex III).

Article IV

1. In order to provide maximum security for both Parties on the basis of reciprocity, agreed security arrangements will be established including limited force zones in Egyptian and Israeli territory, and United Nations forces and observers, described in detail as to nature and timing in Annex I, and other security arrangements the Parties may agree upon.

2. The Parties agree to the stationing of United Nations personnel in areas described in Annex I. The Parties agree not to request withdrawal of the United Nations personnel and that these personnel will not be removed unless such removal is approved by the Security Council of the United Nations, with the affirmative vote of the five Permanent Members, unless the Parties otherwise agree.

3. A Joint Commission will be established to facilitate the implementation of the Treaty, as provided for in Annex I.

4. The security arrangements provided for in paragraphs 1 and 2 of this

Article may at the request of either party be reviewed and amended by mutual agreement of the Parties.

Article V

1. Ships of Israel, and cargoes destined for or coming from Israel, shall enjoy the right of free passage through the Suez Canal and its approaches through the Gulf of Suez and the Mediterranean Sea on the basis of the Constantinople Convention of 1888, applying to all nations. Israeli nationals, vessels and cargoes, as well as persons, vessels and cargoes destined for or coming from Israel, shall be accorded non-discriminatory treatment in all matters connected with usage of the canal.

2. The Parties consider the Strait of Tiran and the Gulf of Aqaba to be international waterways open to all nations for unimpeded and non-suspendable freedom of navigation and overflight. The Parties will respect each other's right to navigation and overflight for access to either country through the Strait of Tiran and the Gulf of Aqaba.

Article VI

1. The Treaty does not affect and shall not be interpreted as affecting in any way the rights and obligations of the Parties under the Charter of the United Nations.

2. The Parties undertake to fulfill in good faith their obligations under this Treaty, without regard to action or inaction of any other party and independently of any instrument external to this Treaty.

3. They further undertake to take all the necessary measures for the application in their relations of the provisions of the multilateral conventions to which they are parties, including the submission of appropriate notification to the Secretary-General of the United Nations and other depositaries of such conventions.

4. The Parties undertake not to enter into any obligation in conflict with this Treaty.

5. Subject to Article 103 of the United Nations Charter, in the event of a conflict between the obligations of the Parties under the present Treaty and any of their other obligations, the obligations under this Treaty will be binding and implemented.

Article VII

1. Disputes arising out of the application or interpretation of this Treaty shall be resolved by negotiations.

2. Any such disputes which cannot be settled by negotiations shall be resolved by conciliation or submitted to arbitration.

Article VIII

The Parties agree to establish a claims commission for the mutual settlement of all financial claims.

Article IX

1. This Treaty shall enter into force upon exchange of instruments of ratification.
2. This Treaty supersedes the Agreement between Egypt and Israel of September, 1975.
3. All protocols, annexes, and maps attached to this Treaty shall be regarded as an integral part hereof.
4. The Treaty shall be communicated to the Secretary-General of the United Nations for registration in accordance with the provisions of Article 102 of the Charter of the United Nations.

VI. The European Declaration

Following is the text of the declaration on the Middle East by the European Economic Community issued at the conclusion of a two-day summit in Venice, June 13, 1980.

1. The heads of state and government and the ministers of foreign affairs held a comprehensive exchange of views on all aspects of the present situation in the Middle East, including the state of negotiations resulting from the agreements signed between Egypt and Israel in March 1979. They agreed that growing tensions affecting this region constitute a serious danger and render a comprehensive solution to the Israeli-Arab conflict more necessary and pressing than ever.
2. The nine member states of the European Community consider that the traditional ties and common interests which link Europe to the Middle East oblige them to play a special role and now require them to work in a more concrete way toward peace.
3. In this regard the nine countries of the Community base on Security Council Resolutions 242 and 338 and the positions which they have expressed on several occasions, notably in their declarations of 29 June 1977, 19 September 1978, 26 March and 18 June 1979, as well as the speech made on their behalf on 25 September 1979 by the Irish Minister of Foreign Affairs at the 34th United Nations General Assembly.
4. On the bases thus set out, the time has come to promote the recognition and implementation of the two principles universally accepted

by the international community: the right to existence and to security of all the states in the region, including Israel, and justice for all the peoples, which implies the recognition of the legitimate rights of the Palestinian people.

5. All of the countries in the area are entitled to live in peace within secure, recognized and guaranteed borders. The necessary guarantees for a peace settlement should be provided by the United Nations by a decision of the Security Council and, if necessary, on the basis of other mutually agreed procedures. The Nine declare that they are prepared to participate within the framework of a comprehensive settlement in a system of concrete and binding international guarantees, including guarantees on the ground.

6. A just solution must finally be found to the Palestinian problem, which is not simply one of refugees. The Palestinian people, which is conscious of existing as such, must be placed in a position, by an appropriate process defined within the framework for the comprehensive peace settlement, to exercise fully its right to self-determination.

7. The achievement of these objectives requires the involvement and support of all the parties concerned in the peace settlement which the Nine are endeavoring to promote in keeping with the principles formulated in the declaration referred to above. These principles apply to all the parties concerned, and thus the Palestinian people, and to the Palestine Liberation Organization, which will have to be associated with the negotiations.

8. The Nine recognize the special importance of the role played by the question of Jerusalem for all the parties concerned. The Nine stress that they will not accept any unilateral initiative designed to change the status of Jerusalem and that any agreement on the city's status should guarantee freedom of access of everyone to the holy places.

9. The Nine stress the need for Israel to put an end to the territorial occupation which it has maintained since the conflict of 1967, as it has done for part of Sinai. They are deeply convinced that the Israeli settlements constitute a serious obstacle to the peace process in the Middle East. The Nine consider that these settlements, as well as modifications in population and property in the occupied Arab territories, are illegal under international law.

10. Concerned as they are to put an end to violence, the Nine consider that only the renunciation of force or the threatened use of force by all the parties can create a climate of confidence in the area, and constitute a basic element for a comprehensive settlement of the conflict in the Middle East.

11. The Nine have decided to make the necessary contacts with all the parties concerned. The objective of these contacts would be to ascertain the position of the various parties with respect to the principles set out in this declaration and in the light of the results of this consultation process to determine the form which such an initiative on their part could take.

VII. President Ronald Reagan's Speech and Talking Points, September 1, 1982 (Excerpts)

RESOLVING THE ROOT CAUSES OF CONFLICT

But the opportunities for peace in the Middle East do not begin and end in Lebanon. As we help Lebanon rebuild, we must also move to resolve the root causes of conflict between Arabs and Israelis. The War in Lebanon has demonstrated many things, but two consequences are key to the peace process:

First, the military losses of the PLO have not diminished the yearning of the Palestinian people for a just solution of their claims.

Second, while Israel's military successes in Lebanon have demonstrated that its armed forces are second to none in the region, they alone cannot bring just and lasting peace to Israel and her neighbors.

The question now is how to reconcile Israel's legitimate security concerns with the legitimate rights of the Palestinians. And that answer can only come at the negotiating table. Each party must recognize that the outcome must be acceptable to all and that true peace will require compromises by all.

So, tonight I'm calling for a fresh start. This is the moment for all those directly concerned to get involved—or lend their support—to a workable basis for peace. The Camp David agreement remains the foundation of our policy. Its language provides all parties with the leeway they need for successful negotiations.

I call on Israel to make clear that the security for which she yearns can only be achieved through genuine peace, a peace requiring magnanimity, vision and courage.

I call on the Palestinian people to recognize that their own political aspirations are inextricably bound to recognition of Israel's right to a secure future.

And I call on the Arab states to accept the reality of Israel, and the reality that peace and justice are to gained only through hard, fair, direct negotiation.

In making these calls upon others, I recognize that the United States has a special responsibility. No other nation is in a position to deal with the key parties to the conflict on the basis of trust and reliability.

The time has come for a new realism on the part of all the peoples of the Middle East. The State of Israel is an accomplished fact; it deserves unchallenged legitimacy within the community of nations. But Israel's legitimacy has thus far been recognized by too few countries, and has been denied by every Arab state except Egypt. Israel exists. It has a right to exist in peace, behind secure and defensible borders, and it has a right to demand of its neighbors that they recognize those facts.

I have personally followed and supported Israel's heroic struggle for survival ever since the founding of the State of Israel 34 years ago. In the pre-1967 borders, Israel was barely 10 miles wide as its narrowest point. The bulk of Israel's population lived within artillery range of hostile Arab armies. I am not about to ask Israel to live that way again.

The war in Lebanon has demonstrated another reality in the region. The departure of the Palestinians from Beirut dramatizes more than ever the homelessness of the Palestinian people. Palestinians feel strongly that their cause is more than a question of refugees. I agree. The Camp David agreement recognized that fact when it spoke of the legitimate rights of the Palestinian people and their just requirements. For peace to endure, it must involve all those who have been more deeply affected by the conflict. Only through broader participation in the peace process, most immediately by Jordan and by the Palestinians, will Israel be able to rest confident in the knowledge that its security and integrity will be respected by its neighbors. Only through the process of negotiation can all the nations of the Middle East achieve a secure peace.

New Proposals

These then are our general goals. What are the specific new American positions, and why are we taking them?

In the Camp David talks thus far, both Israel and Egypt have felt free to express openly their views as to what the outcome should be. Understandably, their views have differed on many points.

The United States has thus far sought to play the role of mediator. We have avoided public comment on the key issues. We have always recognized, and continue to recognize, that only the voluntary agreement of those parties most directly involved in the conflict can provide an enduring solution. But it has become evident to me that some clearer sense of America's position on the key issues is necessary to encourage wider support for the peace process.

First, as outlined in the Camp David accords, there must be a period of time during which the Palestinian inhabitants of the West Bank and Gaza will have full autonomy over their own affairs. Due consideration must be given to the principle of self-government by the inhabitants of the territories and to the legitimate security concerns of the parties involved.

The purpose of the five-year period of transition which would begin after free elections for a self-governing Palestinian authority is to prove to the Palestinians that they can run their own affairs, and that such Palestinian autonomy poses no threat to Israel's security.

The United States will not support the use of any additional land for the purpose of settlements during the transitional period. Indeed, the immediate adoption of a settlement freeze by Israel, more than any other action, could create the confidence needed for wider participation in these talks. Further settlement activity is in no way necessary for the security of Israel and only diminishes the confidence of the Arabs that a final outcome can be freely and fairly negotiated.

I want to make the American position well understood: the purpose of this transition period is the peaceful and orderly transfer of authority from Israel to the Palestinian inhabitants of the West Bank and Gaza. At the same time, such a transfer must not interfere with Israel's security requirements.

Beyond the transition period, as we look to the future of the West Bank and Gaza, it is clear to me that peace cannot be achieved by the formation of an independent Palestinian state in those territories. Nor is it achievable on the basis of Israeli sovereignty or permanent control over the West Bank and Gaza.

So the United States will not support the establishment of an independent Palestinian state in the West Bank and Gaza, and we will not support annexation or permanent control by Israel.

There is, however, another way to peace. The final status of these lands must, of course, be reached through the give-and-take of negotiations. But it is the firm view of the United States that self-government by the Palestinians of the West Bank and Gaza in association with Jordan offers the best chance for a durable, just and lasting peace.

We base our approach squarely on the principle that the Arab-Israeli conflict should be resolved through negotiations involving an exchange of territory for peace. This exchange is enshrined in United Nations Security Council Resolution 242, which is, in turn, incorporated in all its parts in the Camp David agreements. U.N. Resolution 242 remains wholly valid as the foundation stone of America's Middle East peace effort.

It is the United States' position that—in return for peace—the withdrawal provision of Resolution 242 applies to all fronts, including the West Bank and Gaza.

When the border is negotiated between Jordan and Israel, our view on the extent to which Israel should be asked to give up territory will be heavily affected by the extent of true peace and normalization and the security arrangements offered in return.

Finally, we remain convinced that Jerusalem must remain undivided, but its final status should be decided through negotiations.

In the course of the negotiations to come, the United States will support positions that seem to us fair and reasonable compromises, and likely to promote a sound agreement. We will also put forward our own detailed proposals when we believe they can be helpful. And, make no mistake, the United States will oppose any proposal—from any party and at any point in the negotiating process—that threatens the security of Israel. America's commitment to the security of Israel is ironclad and, I might add, so is mine.

Text of Talking Points Sent to Prime Minister
Begin by President Reagan

General Principles

A. We will maintain our commitment to Camp David.

B. We will maintain our commitment to the conditions we require for recognition of and negotiation with the PLO.

C. We can offer guarantees on the position we will adopt in negotiations. We will not be able, however, to guarantee in advance the results of these negotiations.

Transitional Measures

A. Our position is that the objective of the transitional period is the peaceful and orderly transfer of authority from Israel to the Palestinian inhabitants.

B. We will support:

The decision of full autonomy as giving the Palestinian inhabitants real authority over themselves, the land and its resources, subject to fair safeguards on water.

Economic, commercial, social and cultural ties between the West Bank, Gaza and Jordan.

Participation by the Palestinian inhabitants of East Jerusalem in the election of the West Bank–Gaza authority.

Real settlement freeze.

Progressive Palestinian responsibility for internal security based on capability and performance.

C. We will oppose:

Dismantlement of the existing settlements.

Provisions which represent a legitimate threat to Israel's security, reasonably defined.

Isolation of the West Bank and Gaza from Israel.

Measures which accord either the Palestinians or the Israelis generally recognized sovereign rights with the exception of external security, which must remain in Israel's hands during the transitional period.

Final Status Issues

A. U.N.S.C. Resolution 242

It is our position that Resolution 242 applies to the West Bank and Gaza and requires Israeli withdrawal in return for peace. Negotiations must determine the borders. The U.S. position in these negotiations on the extent of the withdrawal will be significantly influenced by the extent and nature of the peace and security arrangements offered in return.

B. Israeli Sovereignty

It is our belief that the Palestinian problem cannot be resolved [through] Israeli sovereignty or control over the West Bank and Gaza. Accordingly, we will not support such a solution.

C. Palestinian State

The Preference we will pursue in the final status negotiation is association of the West Bank and Gaza with Jordan. We will not support the formation of a Palestinian state in those negotiations. There is no foundation of political support in Israel or the United States for such a solution. The outcome, however, must be determined by negotiations.

D. Self-Determination

In the Middle East context the term self-determination has been identified exclusively with the formation of a Palestinian state. We will not support this definition of self-determination. We believe that the Palestinians must take the leading role in determining their own future and fully support the provision in Camp David providing for the elected representatives of the inhabitants of the West Bank and Gaza to decide how they shall govern themselves consistent with the provision of their agreement in the final status negotiations.

E. Jerusalem

We will fully support the position that the status of Jerusalem must be determined through negotiations.

F. Settlements.

The status of Israeli settlements must be determined in the course of the final status negotiations. We will not support their continuation as extraterritorial outposts.

Additional Talking Points

1. Approach to Hussein

The President has approached Hussein to determine the extent to which he may be interested in participating.

King Hussein has received the same U.S. positions as you.

Hussein considers our proposals serious and gives them serious attention.

Hussein understands that Camp David is the only base that we will accept for negotiations.

We are also discussing these proposals with the Saudis.

2. Public Commitment

Whatever the support from these or other Arab States, this is what the President has concluded must be done.

The President is convinced his positions are fair and balanced and fully protective of Israel's security. Beyond that they offer the practical opportunity of eventually achieving the peace treaties Israel must have with its neighbors.

He will be making a speech announcing these positions, probably within a week.

3. Next Procedural Steps

Should the response to the President's proposal be positive, the U.S. would take immediate steps to relaunch the autonomy negotiations with the broadest possible participation as envisaged under the Camp David agreements.

We also contemplate an early visit by Secretary Shultz in the area.

Should there not be a positive response, the President, as he has said in his letter to you, will nonetheless stand by his position with proper dedication.

VIII. Resolutions of the Twelfth Arab League Summit, Fez, Morocco, September 9, 1982

The twelfth Arab summit conference convened at Fez on November 25, 1981. The conference adjourned its meetings and later resumed them on September 6, 1982, under the chairmanship of King Hassan II of Morocco.

All Arab countries with the exception of the Socialist People's Libyan Arab Jamahiriyah participated in the conference.

In view of the grave conditions through which the Arab nation is passing and out of a sense of historical and pan-Arab responsibility, their majesties and excellencies and highnesses the kings, presidents and emirs of the Arab nation discussed the important issues submitted to their conference and adopted the following resolution in regard to them:

The conference greeted the steadfastness of the Palestine revolutionary forces, the Lebanese and Palestinian peoples and the Syrian Arab Armed Forces and declared its support for the Palestinian people in their struggle for the retrieval of their established national rights.

Out of the conference's belief in the ability of the Arab nation to achieve its legitimate objectives and eliminate the aggression, and out of the principles and basis laid down by the Arab summit conferences, and out of the Arab countries' determination to continue to work by all means for the establishment of peace based on justice in the Middle East and using the plan of President Habib Bourguiba, which is based on international legitimacy, as the foundation for solving the Palestinian question and the plan of His Majesty King Fahd ibn Abd al-Aziz, which deals with peace in the Middle East, and in the light of the discussions and notes made by their majesties, excellencies and highnesses the kings, presidents and emirs, the conference has decided to adopt the following principles:

1. Israel's withdrawal from all Arab territories occupied in 1967, including Arab Jerusalem.

2. The removal of settlements set up by Israel in the Arab territories after 1967.

3. Guarantees of the freedom of worship and the performance of religious rites for all religions at the holy places.

4. Confirmation of the right of the Palestinian people to self-determination and to exercise their firm and inalienable national rights, under the leaderhip of the PLO, its sole legitimate representative, and compensation for those who do not wish to return.

5. The placing of the West Bank and Gaza Strip under UN supervision for a transitional period, not longer than several months.

6. The creation of an independent Palestinian state with Jerusalem as its capital.

7. The drawing up by the Security Council of guarantees for peace for all the states of the region, including the independent Palestinian state.

8. Security Council guarantees for the implementation of these principles.

IX. Statement by Palestinian Institutions from the West Bank and Gaza, January 14, 1988

During the past few weeks the occupied territories have witnessed a popular uprising against Israel's occupation and its oppressive measures. This uprising has so far resulted in the martyrdom of tens of our people, the wounding of hundreds more, and the imprisonment of thousands of unarmed civilians.

This uprising has come to further affirm our people's unbreakable commitment to its national aspirations. These aspirations include our people's firm national rights of self-determination and of the establishment of an independent state on our national soil under the leadership of the PLO, as our sole legitimate representative. The uprising also comes as further proof of our indefatigable spirit and our rejection of the sense of despair which has begun to creep to the minds of some who claim that the uprising is the result of despair.

The conclusion to be drawn from this uprising is that the present state of affairs in the Palestinian occupied territories is unnatural and that Israeli occupation cannot continue forever. Real peace cannot be achieved except through the recognition of the Palestinian national rights, including the right of self-determination and the establishment of an independent Palestinian state on Palestinian national soil. Should these rights not be recognized, then the continuation of Israeli occupation will lead to further violence and bloodshed and the further deepening of hatred. The opportunity for achieving peace will also move further away.

The only way to extricate ourselves from this scenario is through the convening of an international conference with the participation of all concerned parties, including the PLO, the sole legitimate representative of the Palestinian people, as an equal partner, as well as the five permanent members of the Security Council, under the supervision of the two Superpowers.

On this basis we call upon the Israeli authorities to comply with the following list of demands as a means to prepare the atmosphere for the convening of the suggested international peace conference which will achieve a just and lasting settlement of the Palestinian problem in all its aspects, bringing about the realization of the inalienable national rights of the Palestinian people, peace and stability for the peoples of the region and an end to violence and bloodshed:

1. To abide by the Fourth Geneva Convention and all other international agreements pertaining to the protection of civilians, their properties and rights under a state of military occupation; to declare the Emergency Regulations of the British Mandate null and void, and to stop applying the iron fist policy.

2. The immediate compliance with Security Council Resolutions 605 and 607, which call upon Israel to abide by the Geneva Convention of 1949 and the Declaration of Human Rights; and which further call for the achievement of a just and lasting settlement of the Arab-Israeli conflict.

3. The release of all prisoners who were arrested during the recent uprising, and foremost among them our children. Also the rescinding of all proceedings and indictments against them.

4. The cancellation of the policy of expulsion and allowing all exiled Palestinians, including the four expelled to Lebanon on January 13, 1988, to return to their homes and families. Also the release of all administrative detainees and the cancellation of the hundreds of house arrest orders. In this connection, special mention must be made of the hundreds of applications for family reunions which we call upon the authorities to accept forthwith.

5. The immediate lifting of the siege of all Palestinian refugee camps in the West Bank and Gaza, and the withdrawal of the Israeli army from all population centers.

6. Carrying out a formal inquiry into the behavior of soldiers and settlers in the West Bank and Gaza, as well as inside jails and detention camps, and taking due punitive measures against all those convicted of having unduly caused death or bodily harm to unarmed civilians.

7. A cessation of all settlement activity and land confiscation and the release of lands already confiscated, especially in the Gaza strip. Also putting an end to the harassments and provocations of the Arab population by settlers in the West Bank and Gaza as well as in the Old City of Jerusalem. In particular, the curtailment of the provocative activities in the Old City of Jerusalem by Ariel Sharon and the ultrareligious settlers of Shuvu Banim and Ateret Kohanim.

8. Refraining from any act which might impinge on the Muslim and Christian holy sites or which might introduce changes to the status quo in the City of Jerusalem.

9. The cancellation of the Value Added Tax (V.A.T.) and all other

direct Israeli taxes which are imposed on Palestinian residents in Jerusalem, the rest of the West Bank, and in Gaza; and putting an end to the harassment caused to Palestinian business and tradesmen.

10. The cancellation of all restrictions on political freedoms including restrictions on freedom of assembly and association; also making provisions for free municipal elections under the supervision of a neutral authority.

11. The immediate release of all funds deducted from the wages of laborers from the territories who worked and still work inside the Green Line, which amount to several hundreds of millions of dollars. These accumulated deductions, with interest, must be returned to their rightful owners through the agency of the nationalist institutions headed by the Workers' Unions.

12. The removal of all restrictions on building permits and licenses for industrial projects and artesian water wells as well as agricultural development programs in the occupied territories. Also rescinding all measures taken to deprive the territories of their water resources.

13. Terminating the policy of discrimination being practiced against industrial and agricultural produce from the occupied territories either by removing the restrictions on the transfer of goods to within the Green Line, or by placing comparable trade restrictions on the transfer of Israeli goods into the territories.

14. Removing the restrictions on political contacts between inhabitants of the occupied territories and the PLO, in such a way as to allow for the participation of Palestinians from the territories in the proceedings of the Palestine National Council, in order to ensure a direct input into the decision-making processes of the Palestinian nation by the Palestinians under occupation.

> *Palestinian nationalist institutions and*
> *personalities from the West Bank and Gaza*

X. The Shultz Initiative, March 4, 1988

I set forth below the statement of understandings which I am convinced is necessary to achieve the prompt opening of negotiations on a comprehensive peace. This statement of understandings emerges from discussions held with you and other regional leaders. I look forward to the letter of reply of the Government of Israel in confirmation of this statement.

The agreed objective is a comprehensive peace providing for the security of all the states in the region and for the legitimate rights of the Palestinian people.

Negotiations will start on an early date between Israel and the Jordanian-Palestinian delegation, negotiations will begin on arrangements for a transitional period, with the objective of completing them within six months. Seven months after transitional negotiations begin, final status negotiations will begin, with the objective of completing them within one year. These negotiations will be based on all the provisions and principles of United Nations Security Council Resolution 242. Finally status talks will start before the transitional period begins. The transitional period will begin three months after the conclusion of the transitional agreement and will last for three years. The United States will participate in both negotiations and will promote their rapid conclusion. In particular, the United States will submit a draft agreement for the parties' consideration at the outset of the negotiations on transitional arrangements.

Two weeks before the opening of negotiations, an international conference will be held. The Secretary-General of the United Nations will be asked to issue invitations to the parties involved in the Arab-Israel conflict and the five permanent members of the United Nations Security Council. All participants in the conference must accept United Nations Security Council Resolutions 242 and 338, and renounce violence and terrorism. The parties to each bilateral negotiation may refer reports on the status of their negotiations to the conference, in a manner to be agreed. The conference will not be able to impose solutions or veto agreements reached.

Palestinian representation will be within the Jordanian-Palestinian delegation. The Palestinian issue will be addressed in the negotiations between the Jordanian-Palestinian and Israeli delegations. Negotiations between the Israeli delegation and the Jordanian-Palestinian delegation will proceed independently of any other negotiations.

This statement of understandings is an integral whole. The United States understands that your acceptance is dependent on the implementation of each element in good faith.

Sincerely yours,
George P. Shultz

Text of the letter that Secretary of State George P. Shultz wrote to Prime Minister Yitzhak Shamir of Israel outlining the American peace proposal. A similar letter was sent to King Hussein of Jordan. See *The New York Times*, March 10, 1988.

XI. Security Council Resolution 598 (1987) of July 20, 1987 (Iran-Iraq War)

The Security Council.
Reaffirming its Resolution 582 (1986).

Deeply concerned that, despite its calls for a cease-fire, the conflict between the Islamic Republic of Iran and Iraq continues unabated, with further heavy loss of human life and material destruction.

Deploring the initiation and continuation of the conflict.

Deploring also the bombing of purely civilian population centres, attacks on neutral shipping or civilian aricraft, and, in particular, the use of chemical weapons contrary to obligations under the 1925 Geneva Protocol.

Deeply concerned that further escalation and widening of the conflict may take place.

Determined to bring to an end all military actions between Iran and Iraq.

Convinced that a comprehensive, just, honorable and durable settlement should be achieved between Iran and Iraq.

Recalling the provisions of the Charter of the United Nations, and in particular the obligation of all Member States to settle their international disputes by peaceful means in such a manner that international peace and security and justice are not endangered.

Determining that there exists a breach of the peace as regards the conflict between Iran and Iraq.

Acting under Articles 39 and 40 of the Charter.

1. *Demands* that, as a first step towards a negotiated settlement, the Islamic Republic of Iran and Iraq observe an immediate cease-fire, discontinue all military actions on land, at sea and in the air, and withdraw all forces to the internationally recognized boundaries without delay:

2. *Requests* the Secretary-General to dispatch a team of United Nations observers to verify, confirm and supervise the cease-fire and withdrawal and further requests the Secretary-General to make the necessary arrangements in consultation with the Parties and to submit a report thereon to the Security Council:

3. *Urges* that prisoners-of-war be released and repatriated without delay after the cessation of active hostilities in accordance with the Third Geneva Convention of 12 August 1949:

4. *Calls upon* Iran and Iraq to cooperate with the Secretary-General in implementing this resolution and in mediation efforts to achieve a comprehensive, just and honorable settlement, acceptable to both sides, of all outstanding issues, in accordance with the principles contained in the Charter of the United Nations:

5. *Calls upon* all other States to exercise the utmost restraint and to refrain from any act which may lead to further escalation and widening of the conflict, and thus to facilitate the implementation of the present resolution:

6. *Requests* the Secretary-General to explore, in consultation with Iran and Iraq, the question of entrusting an impartial body with inquiring into responsibility for the conflict and to report to the Council as soon as possible:

7. *Recognizes* the magnitude of the damage inflicted during the conflict

and the need for reconstruction efforts, with appropriate international assistance, once the conflict is ended, and, in this regard, requests the Secretary-General to assign a team of experts to study the question of reconstruction and to report to the Council:

8. *Further requests* the Secretary-General to examine, in consultation with Iran and Iraq and with other States of the region, measures to enhance the security and stability of the region:

9. *Requests* the Secretary-General to keep the Council informed on the implementation of this resolution:

10. *Decides* to meet again as necessary to consider further steps to ensure compliance with this resolution.

XII. Political Resolution Adopted by the Palestine National Council, November 15, 1988 (Excerpts)

2. In the political field:

. . . the Palestine National Council—in accordance with its responsibility towards the Palestinian people, its national rights and its desire for peace, on the basis of the Declaration of Independence issued on November 15, 1988, and as an expression of the humanitarian desire to strive for the reinforcement of international détente, nuclear disarmament and the settlement of regional disputes by peaceful means—affirms the determination of the Palestine Liberation Organization to reach a comprehensive political settlement of the Arab-Israeli conflict and of its essence, the question of Palestine, within the framework of the Charter of the United Nations, the principles and provisions of international legitimacy, the rules of international law, the resolutions of the United Nations—the most recent being Security Council Resolutions 605 (1987), 607 (1988) and 608 (1988)—and the resolutions of the Arab summit conferences, in a manner that ensures the right of the Palestinian Arab people to return, to exercise self-determination and to establish its independent national State on its national soil, while also making arrangements for the security and peace of every State in the region.

With a view to putting this affirmation into practice, the Palestine National Council insists on the following:

(a) The need to convene an effective international conference on the subject of the Middle East problem and its essence, the question of Palestine, under the auspices of the United Nations and with the participation of the permanent members of the Security Council and all parties to the conflict in the region, including the Palestine Liberation Organization, the sole legitimate representative of the Palestinian people, on an equal footing, with the provision that the said international conference shall be convened on the basis of Security Council Resolutions 242 (1967) and 338 (1973) and shall guarantee the legitimate national rights of the Palestinian people, first and foremost among which is the right to self-determination, in accordance with the principles and provisions of the Charter of the United Nations concerning the right to self-determination of peoples, the inadmissibility of seizure of land belonging to others by means of force or military invasion, and in accordance with United Nations resolutions concerning the question of Palestine;

(b) Israel's withdrawal from all the Palestinian and Arab territories which it has occupied since 1967, including Arab Jerusalem;

(c) Cancellation of all measures of attachment and annexation and removal of the settlements established by Israel in the Palestinian and Arab territories since the year 1967;

(d) An endeavour to place the occupied Palestinian territories, including Arab Jerusalem, under United Nations supervision for a limited period, in order to protect our people and to provide an atmosphere conducive to a successful outcome for the international conference, the attainment of a comprehensive political settlement and the establishment of security and peace for all through mutual acceptance and satisfaction, and in order to enable the Palestinian State to exercise its effective authority over those territories;

(e) Solution of the Palestine refugee problem in accordance with United Nations resolutions on that subject;

(f) Assurance of freedom of worship and the practice of religious rites of the holy places in Palestine for adherents of all religions;

(g) The Security Council's establishment and assurance of arrangements for security and peace among all the concerned States in the region, including the Palestinian State.

The Palestine National Council confirms its previous resolutions with regard to the privileged relationship between the two fraternal peoples of Jordan and Palestine, together with the fact that the future relationship between the States of Jordan and Palestine will be established on the basis of a confederacy and of free and voluntary choice by the two fraternal peoples, in corroboration of the historical ties and vital common interests which link them.

The Palestine National Council renews its commitment to United Nations resolutions affirming the right of people to resist foreign occupation, colonialism and racial discrimination, and their right to struggle for their independence. It once again states its rejection of terrorism in all its forms, including State terrorism, and affirms its commitment to its previous resolutions in that regard, to the resolution of the Arab Summit Conference at Algiers in 1988, to General Assembly Resolutions 42/159 of 1987 and 40/61 of 1985, and to the relevant passage in the Cairo Declaration issued on 7 November 1985.

XIII. Declaration of Independence of the State of Palestine, November 15, 1988 (Excerpts)

By virtue of the natural, historical and legal right of the Palestinian Arab people to its homeland, Palestine, and of the sacrifices of its succeeding generations in defence of the freedom and independence of that homeland.

Pursuant to the resolutions of the Arab Summit Conferences and on the basis of the international legitimacy embodied in the resolutions of the United Nations since 1947, and

Through the exercise by the Palestinian Arab people of its right to self-determination, political independence and sovereignty over its territory:

The Palestine National Council hereby declares, in the Name of God and on behalf of the Palestinian Arab people, the establishment of the State of Palestine in the land of Palestine with its capital at Jerusalem.

The State of Palestine shall be for Palestinians, wherever they may be, therein to develop their national and cultural identity and therein to enjoy full equality of rights. Their religious and political beliefs and human dignity shall therein be safeguarded under a democratic parliamentary system based on freedom of opinion and the freedom to form parties, on the heed of the majority for minority rights and the respect of minorities for majority decisions, on social justice and equality, and on non-discrimination in civil rights on grounds of race, religion or colour or as between men and women, under a Constitution ensuring the rule of law and an independent judiciary and on the basis of true fidelity to the age-old spiritual and cultural heritage of Palestine with respect to mutual tolerance, coexistence and magnanimity among religions.

The State of Palestine shall be an Arab state and shall be an integral part of the Arab nation, of its heritage and civilization and of its present endeavour for the achievement of the goals of liberation, development, democracy and unity. In affirming its commitment to the Pact of the League of Arab States and its concern for the strengthening of joint Arab action, the State of Palestine calls upon the members of the Arab nation for their assistance in achieving its de facto emergence by mobilizing their capacities and intensifying the efforts made to bring the Israeli occupation to an end.

The State of Palestine declares its commitment to the purposes and principles of the United Nations, to the Universal Declaration of Human Rights and to the policy and principles of non-alignment.

The State of Palestine, in declaring that it is a peace-loving State committed to the principles of peaceful coexistence, shall strive, together with all other States and peoples, for the achievement of a lasting peace based on justice and respect for rights, under which the human potential for constructive activity may flourish, mutual competition may centre on life-sustaining innovation and there is no fear for the future, since the future bears only assurance for those who have acted justly or made amends to justice.

In the context of its struggle to bring peace to a land of peace and love, the State of Palestine calls upon the United Nations, which bears a special responsibility towards the Palestinian Arab people and its homeland, and upon the peace-loving States and peoples of the world and those that cherish freedom to assist it in achieving its goals, in bringing the plight of its people to an end. In ensuring the safety and security of that people and in endeavouring to end the Israeli occupation of Palestinian territory.

The State of Palestine further declares, in that connection, that it believes in the solution of international and regional problems by peaceful means in accordance with the Charter of the United Nations and the resolutions adopted by it, and that, without prejudice to its natural right to defend itself, it rejects the threat or use of force, violence and intimidation against its territorial integrity and political independence or those of any other State.

On this momentous day, the fifteenth day of November 1988, as we stand on the threshold of a new era, we bow our heads in deference and humility to the departed souls of our martyrs and the martyrs of the Arab nation who, by virtue of the pure blood shed by them, have lit the glimmer of this auspicious dawn and who have died so that the homeland might live. We lift up our hearts so that they may be filled with light from the radiance of the hallowed uprising, of the epic resistance of those in the camps, in the dispersion and in exile, and of those who have borne the banner of freedom: our children, our elders and our youth; our prisoners, detainees and wounded based on the hallowed soil and in every camp, village and city; the valiant Palestinian women, the guardians of our life and our survival and keepers of our eternal flame. To the spirits of our righteous martyrs, to the masses of our Palestinian Arab people and our Arab nation and to all free and honourable men, we give our solemn pledge to continue the struggle for an end to the occupation and the establishment of sovereignty and independence. We call upon our great people to rally to the Palestinian flag, to take pride in it and defend it so that it shall remain forever a symbol of our freedom and dignity in a homeland that shall be forever free and the abode of a people of free men.

In the name of God, the Merciful, the Compassionate
"Say: 'O God, Master of the Kingdom, Thou givest the Kingdom to whom Thou wilt, and seizest the Kingdom from whom Thou wilt, Thou exaltest whom Thou wilt, and Thou abasest whom Thou wilt; in Thy hand is the good; Thou art powerful over everything . . .' "
Almighty God has spoken the truth.

Index